Alexander the Great

IAN WORTHINGTON

Alexander the Great

Man and God

PEARSON
Longman

Harlow, England • London • New York • Boston • San Francisco • Toronto
Sydney • Tokyo • Singapore • Hong Kong • Seoul • Taipei • New Delhi
Cape Town • Madrid • Mexico City • Amsterdam • Munich • Paris • Milan

PEARSON EDUCATION LIMITED

Edinburgh Gate
Harlow CM20 2JE
Tel: +44 (0)1279 623623
Fax: +44 (0)1279 431059
Website: pearsoneduc.com
www.history-minds.com

First edition published in Great Britain in 2004

ISBN 0 582 77224 9

British Library Cataloguing in Publication Data
A CIP catalogue record for this book can be obtained from the British Library

Library of Congress Cataloging in Publication Data
A CIP catalog record for this book can be obtained from the Library of Congress

10 9 8 7 6 5 4 3 2 1

Set by Fakenham Photosetting Limited, Fakenham, Norfolk
Printed and bound in Great Britain by Biddles Ltd, Guildford & King's Lynn

The Publishers' policy is to use paper manufactured from sustainable forests.

Contents

List of Plates

List of Figures

List of Maps

Preface

Of all the figures from antiquity Alexander the Great of Macedonia is arguably the best known, and the one who most excites the imagination. Reared on the heroic idealism of Homer, Alexander waged war as a Homeric hero and tried to live as one. He conquered territories on a superhuman scale. He extended the empire of Macedonia, created by his father Philip II, from Greece in the west to Asia Minor, the Levant, Egypt and Central Asia to what the Greeks called India (Pakistan and Kashmir today) in the east. Some of his subjects even worshipped him while he was still alive. But Alexander was more than a conqueror. He was an intellectual, taught by Aristotle, who spread Greek culture in the areas through which he travelled.

Alexander was king for only 13 years (336–323 BC), and he was not quite 33 years old when he died. His achievements are even more astonishing given his short reign and age. He was at the height of his power when he died in June 323, and he had already put into action his next major project, the invasion of Arabia. Only death stopped him.

Yet, every coin has two sides. Alexander combined ruthlessness with heroism to a degree that today would cause concern. He fought battles that showed his genius as a general, and he was prepared to sacrifice his own men as well as himself but not always for the greater good. As his reign continued, he thought himself a god on earth, the son of Zeus. His belief did not sit well with his men, but disagreement was often fatal. He engineered the executions or murders of even his close friends and generals whom he suspected of conspiring against him or who simply criticised him. Copious drinking fuelled his violent outbursts when reason gave way to emotion. Those at his court lived in an atmosphere of fear. When he died, the Macedonian empire died with him. His generals carved it up, and for several decades after his death they and their families battled for supremacy. The Macedonian throne became no more than a pawn in their power struggles.

It is easy to see why Alexander was called 'Great' by posterity, given his phenomenal military successes. He was the type of man of whom legends are made, and therein lies the problem. Much of Alexander's image today was the product of later generations, and one of the thorniest problems is separating the historical Alexander from the legendary. I deal with this problem in Chapter 1.

Alexander was not just a general though. He was a king, and a Macedonian king was a warrior king, a general, a leader, a diplomat and a statesman. The bulk of the book is a narrative of Alexander's reign that treats him as the 'package' that is a king. In the process a different Alexander from the one of legend arises. Worsening relations between Alexander and his father made him desperate to outstrip Philip at all costs. Military conquest was not enough, but deification was a different matter. As Alexander's reign progressed, he came to believe that he was a god on earth. My approach to Alexander is that his pretension to personal divinity is the key to the motives and actions of his reign.

This book is a serious and authoritative one that is accessible also to a non-specialist readership. My publisher does not want notes that are monographic in style or go into detailed discussion and points of interpretation. Hence, my notes are deliberately kept to a minimum, and are meant to provide references to ancient sources, and where necessary further specific reading. When I quote a source my preference is to give a contemporary account rather than a later one (see Chapter 1). The bibliographic essay at the rear of the book discusses the ancient sources and some of the important modern works on Alexander. There are many biographies of Alexander, and I hope that mine is less pompous in style than some, and less dry than others. By far the best in terms of attention to detail, discussion and citation of ancient sources and modern scholars' works is A.B. Bosworth, *Conquest and Empire. The Reign of Alexander the Great* (Cambridge, 1988). My reliance on Bosworth's writings will be obvious.

Having said all that, my book is also meant to contribute to Alexander scholarship. Where there is room to expand or discuss a particular problem or controversy in a new light I have done so. Not everyone will agree with what I say, or with my Alexander, and there are bound to be many who will take comfort in disputing the content of nearly every page. However, let me say at the outset that I intend to be provocative and to challenge traditional approaches to Alexander, for that is the only way to do a figure such as him justice.

All dates are BC except where indicated.

I have many people to thank. First, Heather McCallum at Pearson, who invited me to write this book. I have been working on Alexander and on fourth-century Greek history for many years, but I never thought of writing a biography of Alexander until she asked me. She is the editor par excellence: always willing to act as a sounding board, diplomatic in her comments, supportive and only cruel to be kind in order to ensure the timely delivery of the manuscript.

Second, Melanie Carter and Helen Marsden at Pearson, and Penelope Allport of Penelope Allport Editorial Services for their amazing patience and hard work.

Third, a group of colleagues from my own department whom I am happy to call friends for their company on our regular Friday evening get-togethers, and for putting up with my talk about Alexander.

Fourth, the students I have taught over the years, especially the ones at Missouri who were inflicted with more Alexander than usual as I worked on this book.

Fifth, the scholars and friends who, over many years, have put up with me, talked Alexander with me and from whom I have learnt so much: Ernst Badian, Liz Baynham, the late Peter Bicknell, Brian Bosworth, Craig Cooper, Bob Dise, Jack Ellis, Ernst Fredricksmeyer, the late Nicholas Hammond, Phillip Harding, Waldemar Heckel, Mark Golden, Stanley Ireland, Robin Lane Fox, Marianne McDonald, Bob Milns, Peter Rhodes, Joseph Roisman, Tim Ryder (who introduced me formally to Alexander when I was an undergraduate at the University of Hull), Richard Stoneman, Carol Thomas, Peter Toohey and Pat Wheatley.

Last, but by no means least, my wife Tracy and son Oliver. When I finished the book there was the loudest sigh of relief I have ever heard from them that I could return to being a father and to doing household chores. The final six weeks or so as I worked on the book were especially intensive, and they had to endure my constant disappearances into my office and my whinging. They bore all of it with goodwill (most of the time), and for their support, I am, as ever, more grateful than mere words can say.

Ian Worthington
University of Missouri-Columbia
September 2003

Acknowledgements

The author and publishers wish to thank the following for permission to use copyright material:

The Bridgeman Art Library and the Bibliotheque Nationale de Belgique for 'Alexander the Great being lowered to the sea-bed in a glass "cage" where the fish crowd round him and pay homage';

AAA Collection Ltd for 'Mount Olympus'; and 'Alexander Mosaic';

John Heseltine/CORBIS for 'Cobbled floor and ruins at Pella';

Akg-images for 'Gold medallion with head of Philip II of Macedonia';

'A Macedonian phalanx formation carrying sarissas'; 'Battle of Issus"'; 'Battle of Guagamela'; 'Battle of the Hydaspes River'; from N.G.L. Hammond, "The Genius of Alexander the Great", Gerald Duckworth & Sons Ltd (1997);

Bettmann/CORBIS for 'Marble statue of Demosthenes, the Athenian orator and politician';

Bridgeman Art Library and Louvre, Paris for 'Bust of Alexander the Great (marble) attributed to Lysippus (fl.370–310 BC)';

Bridgeman Art Library and Archaeological Museum, Thessaloniki for 'Two classical figures fighting a lion, early hellenistic period (mosaic)' and 'Gold larnax from the casket of Philip II of Macedonia at Vergina, decorated with the star emblem of the Macedonian dynasty, 4th century BC (gold)';

Hellenic Ministry of Culture and Exhibition of the Royal Tombs at Vergina for 'Ivory group of Pan-Dionysus-Ariadne', and 'Ivory head of Alexander';

ACKNOWLEDGEMENTS

Gianni Dagli Orti/CORBIS for *'Head of Philip II of Macedonia'*;

National Gallery of Athens for H. Daumier: *'Alexander and Diogenes'*;

Photo Scala, Florence and Louvre, Paris for L. Domeniquin*: 'Timocleia before Alexander'*;

National Gallery, Prague for Fontebasso*: 'Alexander Sacrificing at the Tomb of Achilles'*;

Duckworth Publishers for *'Battle of Granicus: Persian and Macedonian battle lines'*, from N.G.L. Hammond "Alexander the Great: King and Statesman", Bristol Press (1989);

David Wallace and Maya Vision International for *'Temple ruins at Didyma'*;

Réunion des Musées Nationaux and Art Resource, NY for *'Illuminated manuscript showing the attack on the city of Tyre'*;

Michael Wood and Maya Vision International for *'Siwah Oasis'* and *'Iranian tale-teller'*;

Giraudon and Art Resource, NY for *'General view of Apadana, 6th–5th* BC, *Persepolis, Iran'*;

Museum of Fine Arts, Boston for *'Silver coin of Lysimachus showing head of Alexander the Great wearing the horn of Ammon'* and *'Silver coin of Ptolemy showing Alexander wearing an elephant's cap and ram's horn'*;

Map 1 redrawn from map in *Alexander the Great*, published and reprinted by permission of Routledge (Stoneman, R. 1997); Maps 2, 3, 4, 5, 6, 7, 8, 9, 10 and 11 redrawn from Maps 1, 2, 3, 4, 5, 6, 7, 8, 9 and 10 in *Conquest and Empire: The Reign of Alexander the Great*, © Cambridge University Press 1988, reproduced with permission (Bosworth, A.B. 1988).

Every effort has been made to trace the copyright holders but if any have been inadvertently overlooked the publishers will be pleased to make the necessary arrangement at the first opportunity.

Alexander's Reign: The Main Events

336   Assassination of Philip II; Alexander succeeds to the throne of Macedonia as Alexander III; revolt of the Greeks ended by Alexander

335   Alexander campaigns in the north; revolt of Thebes, razed to the ground by Aléxander

334   Alexander invades Asia; Battle of the Granicus River

333   Alexander conquers coastal Asia Minor; goes to Gordium; Battle of Issus

332   Sieges of Tyre and Gaza; conquest of the Levant; Alexander enters Egypt, which surrenders to him

331   Alexander founds Alexandria and visits the oracle of Zeus Ammon at Siwah; Agis III of Sparta's war against Macedonia begins in Greece; Battle of Gaugamela

330   Alexander burns Persepolis; death of Darius III; executions of Philotas and Parmenion; defeat of Agis III by Antipater

329   Crossing of the Hindu Kush; capture of Bessus; revolt of Bactria and Sogdiana starts

328   Alexander in Bactria and Sogdiana; the murder of Cleitus

327   End of the Bactrian campaign; the attempt to introduce *proskynesis* at Bactra; the Pages' Conspiracy; Alexander marries Roxane; Alexander marches to India

326   Alexander's army crosses the Indus; Battle of the Hydaspes River; the mutiny at the Hyphasis river; start of voyage down the Indus

325   Alexander campaigns against the Malli; end of voyage down the Indus; the march through the Gedrosian Desert; voyage of Nearchus

324   Mass marriage at Susa; the issuing of the Exiles Decree; the mutiny at Opis; the banquet of reconciliation; death of Hephaestion at Ecbatana

323   Alexander goes to Babylon; debate in Greece over Alexander's divinity; 10 June: death of Alexander the Great; Lamian War in Greece (ends 322); start of the wars of Alexander's successors (end 301)

Macedonia and Greece
Redrawn from Stoneman, R. (1997) *Alexander the Great,* published and
reprinted by permission of Routledge.

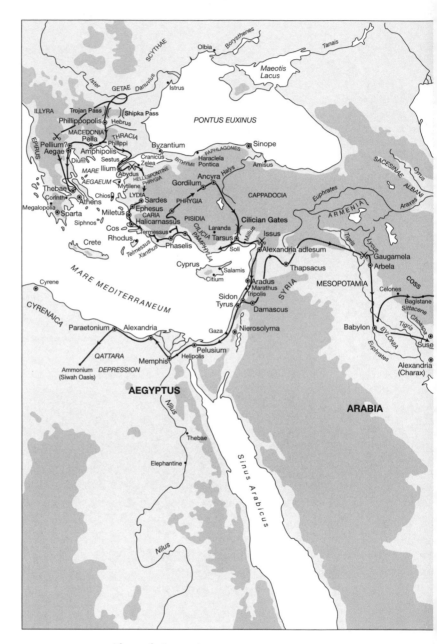

Alexander's empire

Redrawn from Bosworth, A.B. (1988) *Conquest and Empire: The Reign of Alexander the Great* (pub Cambridge University Press), Map 1. © Cambridge University Press 1988, reproduced with permission.

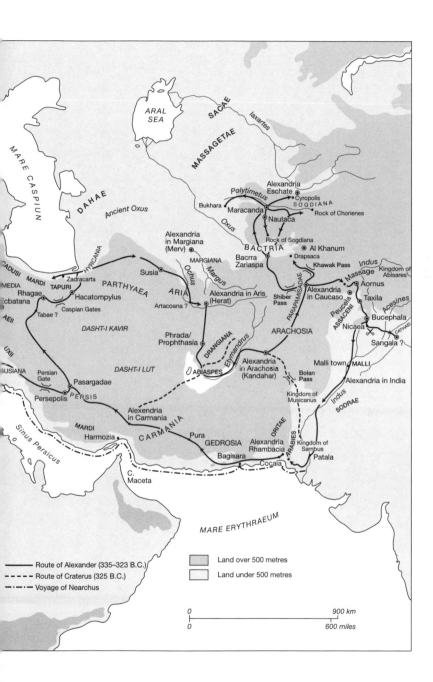

ARAL
SEA

S A C A E

MASSAGETAE

Iaxartes

MARE CASPIUN

DAHAE

Ancient Oxus

Alexandria
Eschate
Polytimetus   Cyropolis
Bukhara   S O G D I A N A
Maracanda   Rock of Chorienes
Nautaca

HYRCANIA

Oxus

Rock of Sogdiana

Alexandria
in Margiana   B A C T R I A   Al Khanum
(Merv)   Bacrra   Drapsaca
MARGIANA   Zariaspa   Khawak Pass

CADUSI   MARDI   Zadracarta   Susia   Ochus   Margus   Indus
MEDIA   PARTHYAEA   ARIA   Massage   Kingdom of
Rhagae   Alexandria in Aris   PARAPAMISADAE   Ablsares
Ecbatana   Hacatompylus   (Herat)   Shiber   Alexandria   Aornus
Caspian Gates   Artacoana ?   Pass   in Caucaso   Taxila
AEII   Tabae ?   Peucela   Acesines
ASSACENI   Bucephala
DASHT-I KAVIR   ARACHOSIA   Nicaea
UXII   Phrada/   Prophthasia   Sangala ?
SUSIANA   Persian   DASHT-I LUT   DRANGIANA   Etymandrus
Gate   Pasargadae   ABIASPES   Alexandria   Malli town   MALLI
Persepolis   P E R S I S   in Arachosia   Bolan   Alexandria in India
(Kandahar)   Pass
Alexendria   Kingdom of   Indus
in Carmania   Musicanus   SODRAE
MARDI   C A R M A N I A   Pura   ORITAE
Harmozia   GEDROSIA   Alexandria   Kingdom of
Sinus Persicus   Bagisara   Rhambacia   Sambus   Patala
Cocala
C.
Maceta

MARE ERYTHRAEUM

—— Route of Alexander (335–323 B.C.)
- - - Route of Craterus (325 B.C.)
-·-·- Voyage of Nearchus

▨ Land over 500 metres
☐ Land under 500 metres

0   900 km
0   600 miles

xix

I

Introduction: Uncovering the Legend

"'How can a man become a god?' was a question that Alexander once put to several Indian philosophers. They answered, "By doing something a man cannot do."'[1]

Alexander III of Macedonia became king in 336 at the age of 20. What he did for posterity to call him 'Great' seems clear enough. By the time he died in 323 in his 33rd year, he had expanded the Macedonian empire from Greece in the west to India in the east. He conquered native peoples on an astonishing scale and in great battles and sieges. He brought down the Persian empire and subdued Egypt, promoted Greek education and culture in his new empire, and was even worshipped as a god by some of his subjects. He took scientists with him who recorded all sorts of information about the areas through which he marched, from flora and fauna to climate. He opened up a world that was much larger than Greece or even the entire Mediterranean. In the process, he introduced to the Greeks a sense of belonging to that larger world, and during the Hellenistic period that followed his death they took to that legacy eagerly. Moreover, he died young, at the height of his power, but he had not planned to return home after his conquests in Asia. When he died his next venture, the invasion of Arabia, was already in motion. His plan to conquer the western Mediterranean after Arabia was already hatched. Only death stopped him.

Alexander is arguably the most famous and most controversial figure from antiquity. Although other kings and generals won many battles and forged many empires, Alexander produced an empire that was, albeit briefly, without parallel. He was a legend in his own lifetime, and he remains one today. Appearance though is not always reality. Therein lies the problem: trying to separate the real or historical Alexander from the legendary.

Was he really the great general, whose genius lay on the battlefield? Was he the philosophical idealist, who integrated foreigners into his administration and army, seemingly as a way of uniting mankind? Was he really the bringer of Greek civilisation to so-called barbarian lands? Was he really a dashing, heroic king who ruled a great empire that led to the physical and cultural formation of the Hellenistic kingdoms? Or was he a paranoid, alcoholic, megalomaniac who thought he was a god, was guilty of murder and genocide, who today would be tried for crimes against humanity, and who destroyed the Macedonian empire? Should he still be called Alexander the Great or, as the modern Persians call him, Alexander the Accursed?

Much of the Alexander that we admire, that we think is great, is the product of later writers and societies that attributed deeds, motives and feelings to him that were unhistorical. Here we reach the core problem with Alexander: the nature of our source material. All of Alexander's most infamous actions added together are less controversial than the problems associated with the sources for him.

I deal with the following in more detail in the Bibliographic Essay at the rear of this book.

It would be natural to suppose that with a figure like Alexander we would have a vast array of source material from his reign, and so have no problem in putting together a picture of it. Not so. It is not until centuries after his death that we start to get a connected narrative of the reign. The most important of these later sources are Diodorus Siculus (first century BC), Quintus Curtius Rufus (first century AD), Arrian (second century AD), Justin, who epitomised an earlier work (third century AD) and Plutarch's biography of Alexander (second century AD). These are the 'big five'.

We also have information on aspects of Alexander's reign, though not in any connected narrative, in other sources. The most important are Strabo (first century BC) and Athenaeus (second/early third century AD). Athenaeus' work was set at a banquet at which guests discussed various intellectual and artistic matters. Accordingly he is less interested in facts and more in anecdotes about people and places.

In a collection called the *Moralia*, which encompasses a vast expanse of topics, by Plutarch, we have numerous references to Alexander. In particular there is a treatise called *On The Fortune or The Virtue of Alexander*. It has had an undue influence on the historical Alexander (see below).

There were accounts of the reign written in Alexander's time and in the generation or so after him, but they have not survived in their entirety. We know of around two dozen authors, including Callisthenes of Olynthus (the court historian), Alexander's general Ptolemy, and Nearchus of Crete who sailed the Indian Ocean. To these we can add other contemporary sources, such as the *Ephemerides*, the *Royal Diaries*, supposedly a daily journal of the king's activities. This probably did not cover the entire length of the reign but just the last few days since it recorded mostly Alexander's drinking habits and how he died. However what remains of all these early works (the 'fragments') are quoted only in the much later narrative histories.

Since we do not have the contemporary works in full, the problem starts to be obvious. Did each one deal with the reign in full or concentrate on only aspects of it, and how accurate are they? For example, the authenticity of the *Ephemerides* is suspect. It was probably written by the royal secretary, Eumenes of Cardia, after Alexander died. How much importance can we therefore attach to it? Another example: How can we be sure that Ptolemy, for example, who was an eyewitness to Alexander's actions, does not get something wrong or (even more likely) that he slants his account in his own favour? These earlier sources' shortcomings are vividly summed up in the Preface to Arrian's narrative: 'Different authors have given different accounts of Alexander's actions, and there is no one about whom more have written, or more at variance with each other.'

Then we encounter the problem of the later narrative sources (the 'big five') that must have been affected by the differences among the contemporary writers. We know, for example, that Nearchus's account of his voyage along the Makran Coast was used extensively by Arrian, as was Ptolemy's essentially military account of the reign, and Cleitarchus was the principal source for Diodorus, Curtius and Plutarch. Often the later writers simply plagiarised from the earlier ones. However, how accurately did they reconcile conflicting earlier information? How and why did they decide that one account was to be preferred over another? To what extent did they impose their own moral judgements and backgrounds on their subject matter? These questions we cannot always answer.

The later legends and stories about Alexander affect the historical king. His larger than life persona lent itself to manipulation and embellishment in his own time and throughout the ages. In the third century, the *Alexander Romance* was begun. This is a stirring account of Alexander's reign that is mostly fictitious. It was rewritten and added to many times over the centuries, and had a massive influence on many cultures. For example, in Hebrew literature, Alexander was a preacher and prophet, and in Persian literature he is Sikandar, sent to punish the impure peoples. Since the *Alexander Romance* was expanded over the years, deeds were attributed to Alexander that are unhistorical. The stories attached to Alexander became fodder for the illuminated manuscripts of the mediaeval period. For example, there is Alexander's voyage to the bottom of the sea in a glass bathysphere along with a cock, a cat and a dog, in a version copied in Flanders in 1340 (see Plate 1).

In the dark depths of the ocean, the cock's crowing would tell Alexander when it was morning, the pure breath of the cat would provide clean air, and if he got into difficulties he could kill the dog and float to the surface. These sorts of stories and images, like Alexander's encounter with the tribe of headless men, we can dismiss, but what about all of them?

In the second century AD we have a treatise supposedly by Plutarch called *On The Fortune or The Virtue of Alexander*. Influenced by his own intellectual and political background, Alexander is depicted in this work as an action man and a philosopher-king, whose mission was to impose Greek civilisation on the 'barbarian' Persians. The work is rhetorical, but that aspect of it came to be disregarded as time continued. Late antiquity and the mediaeval era welcomed the warrior-king who combined military success with wisdom and unification. In the Middle Ages' world of chivalry, warriors and great battles, the historical Alexander faded faster into the invincible general. Artists over the centuries kept his military side, but at the same time he became a symbol for piety, for virtue, for excellence, for unity. It is no accident that his bust is on the modern Greek 100 drachma coin.

The ancient sources portray a variety of Alexanders for a number of reasons. So also do modern scholars, who are equally affected by the source problem, and especially by their own political and cultural backgrounds.

For example, Alexander was a unifier of the world with divine sanction (Droysen, in 1877), an immoral imperialist out to found a new World Order akin to the Nazis (Schachermeyr, in 1949), a ruthless imperialist who found out that absolute power was lonely (Badian, in 1958), a philosophical idealist, who strove to establish a brotherhood of man (Tarn, in 1948), a Homeric hero type (Lane Fox, in 1973), a successful king for the most part, but who had many downsides (Bosworth, in 1988) and, simply, a genius (Hammond, in 1997).

The problem of separating the legendary Alexander from the historical affects our evaluation and appreciation of him. In this book I present my Alexander. He was a genius when it came to strategy and tactics. He was a fierce and unrelenting fighter, an inspiration so often to his men, a conqueror of enormous territories and an intellectual. However, he was not just a general. He was a king, a statesman, a political leader. Everything was concentrated into his hands, and so he needs to be treated as this 'package'. He was also a man who had his demons. He had many influences playing on him, from his ethnic background, to his mother's complaints about his father, to his father himself. His motives for what he did in his reign show its downside, and his downside as a person.

The bulk of my book is a factual, narrative account of Alexander's reign and his exploits, in which I have followed the accounts of ancient authors that today are accepted as generally reliable. Where there is room to expand or discuss a particular problem or controversy within the narrative in a new light I have done so. Two thematic chapters follow. I believe that worsening relations between Alexander and his father, Philip II, made him desperate to outstrip Philip. Deification afforded him the means to do this. However, as his reign progressed, he came to believe that he was a god on earth. How his belief affected him and his reign is examined in Chapter 14. I consider Alexander the 'package', his positives and negatives, in Chapter 15. As reason gave way to delusion, his paranoia, murders and belief that he was a god on earth would prove disastrous for himself, his throne, his empire and everything that Philip II had worked to build. Given this downside, should we still call him Great? The final chapter (16) is a general conclusion.

As I said in my Preface, not everyone will agree with my approach and what I say. My aim is to be provocative, to challenge some of the traditional approaches to Alexander, and in so doing to present a less 'heroic' (in the modern sense) Alexander than is the norm.

Note

In the following chapters, I have decided to quote from the surviving fragments of the otherwise lost, contemporary sources rather than the later, narrative ones. I realise that my approach has its limitations, given the nature of the fragmentary evidence. However, I want to show what ancient writers in and around the time of Alexander actually said, for it is truly from them that Alexander comes alive. For a full narrative of the reign it is essential to read the 'big five'.

All of the contemporary sources (over 400 of them) are collected together in a volume of a multi-volume work by F. Jacoby, *Die Fragmente der grieschischen Historiker* (*The Fragments of the Greek Historians*), commonly abbreviated as *FGrH*. This has a Greek text of the fragments with a commentary in German on them. The fragments of the Alexander historians are in Volume IIB, nos 117–53 (Berlin, 1927) and the German commentary on them is in IID (Berlin, 1927), pp. 403–542. A few extra of dubious worth are in Volume IIIB nos 742–3 (Berlin, 1930). The Alexander historians are translated in C.A. Robinson, *The History of Alexander the Great* 1 (Providence RI, 1953), and about a third are reprinted in my *Alexander the Great: A Reader* (London and New York, 2003).

In Jacoby, each ancient author has his own number (thus, Onesicritus is Number 134), and each fragment of that author is numbered from one. My notes give the references to the sources as in Jacoby followed by the later writer that quotes them for readers who wish to follow them up. Thus, for example, a reference in a note to 'Onesicritus, *FGrH* 134 F 38 = Plutarch, *Alexander* 8.2' would be to the Onesicritus, whose number in Jacoby's *FGrH* is 134, and to Fragment Number 38 of Onesicritus's works. What Onesicritus says there is quoted by Plutarch in his biography of Alexander at Chapter 8, Section 2.

See the Bibliographic Essay for details of the other ancient sources who are cited in the notes.

2

Alexander's Inheritance

Alexander's homeland, and especially his father as a man and his exploits as a king, influenced him to a far greater degree than is often seen.[1] These need to be set in context at the outset in any attempt to understand Alexander as king and why he did what he did with his father's brilliant legacy.

Macedonia, Alexander's home state, was situated north of Mount Olympus (see Plate 2), the home of the gods, which served as the frontier in antiquity between it and the Greeks to the south.

As well as a geographical line of division between those who lived south of Mount Olympus and those who lived to its north, there was an apparent racial one. The Greeks to the south called the Macedonians 'barbarians', a word that was used as late as the last quarter of the fourth century. This does not mean that the Macedonians were uncivilised in our definition of the word, but that the Greeks did not see them as Greek. The word 'barbarian' comes from bar-bar, the noise of a sheep. That was how anyone who did not speak Greek sounded to the Greeks, hence such people were not Greek.

But were the Macedonians really not Greek, and if so, what were they? The ethnicity issue has been much discussed.[2] There is still no consensus, and there probably never will be. The Greeks south of Mount Olympus did not think the Macedonians were Greek, but then they were their enemies so perhaps their attitude does not mean much. What are perhaps the most telling indicators are things like the proper name for the Macedonians, which was 'Makedones' or 'highlanders'. The name is Greek. Moreover, the gods whom the Makedones worshipped, the names of their months, the names of the people and the names of their towns were all Greek. Royal (and perhaps wealthy noble) Macedonians participated in the Olympic Games. For that, a competitor had to be Greek.

It would seem that the case is closed. However, this last argument (participation at the Olympic Games) is tenuous. It is anchored on the tradition that at some time a new dynasty of the Macedonian royal house came from Argos in Greece, the Temenids. The first king was Perdiccas, and because of this link Alexander I competed at Olympia some time before his death in 452. He was allowed to run in the foot race.[3] Even if we discount the Olympic Games argument, there is still more than enough evidence and reasoned theory to suggest that the Macedonians were racially Greek. They spoke Greek; after all, Euripides wrote in Greek, and Socrates spoke it, and it was pointless for Archelaus to invite both men if no one, or only the educated nobility, would understand them (see below).

We know that the people also had a local, Macedonian dialect. Alexander spoke it, one time, when he murdered Cleitus (see Chapter 10), and he referred to it in the trial of Philotas (see Chapter 9). This dialect is hardly a surprise, and was probably generated by the numerous tribes living on Macedonia's border who were in contact with the people. That had to have an influence on language, and Macedonian may even have had in it a number of loan words from those living on the borders. The Greeks to the south of Mount Olympus, then, simply looked down their noses at their counterparts to its north.

To avoid confusion in this book, when I refer to 'Greeks' I mean the people who lived south of Mount Olympus, and when I refer to 'Macedonians' I mean those living to its north. I do not mean to suggest any difference from this designation other than the geographical one.

Unlike Greece, Macedonia was ruled by a monarchy and was rich in natural resources, such as silver, gold, copper and iron, and especially timber, but these were not fully exploited until Alexander's father, Philip II, became king.[4] The Macedonians preferred to barter than use coinage. They worked the lands themselves or were pastoralists rather than making use of slave labour, as was the case south of Mount Olympus. Their practices were viewed contemptuously by their southern counterparts, who also thought those who lived under a monarchy were too stupid to govern themselves. This attitude had to have influenced both Philip and Alexander.

Before Philip Macedonia was split into two parts, Upper and Lower. Upper Macedonia, separated by the Pindus mountain range, consisted mostly of tribes that the Macedonian kings had fought and to some extent conquered. Most prominent were the peoples of Paeonia (around Skopje) in the north and Lyncestis to the west. Those living in Upper Macedonia practised transhumance, moving their flocks of sheep, goats and cattle to different pastures for food. Lower Macedonia, by contrast, had very fertile soil, and the people grew grain and vegetables. Its warmer climate also allowed those in the upper region to move their flocks south during the harsh winters.

The topography of Macedonia was rugged, making travel and communication difficult. The royal capital (originally at Aegae, then after 399 at Pella) was situated in Lower Macedonia, but the tribes of Upper Macedonia had their own kings who maintained their independence of the Macedonian king at the capital. This led to tension and even warfare. To make matters worse, the Macedonian throne was subject to dynastic upheaval on the death of virtually every king.

Macedonia was prone to foraging invasions from neighbouring tribes to the north such as the Illyrians, as well as from incursions by the Greeks south of Mount Olympus. To the east, there were guarded relations with the kings of Thrace, the Greek cities of the Chalcidice region, and, to Macedonia's west, the kingdom of Epirus. The Macedonian army was largely a conscript one of citizen farmers, who had little formal training. For the most part the army fought for survival against invading foes, not for expansion. Thus, for much of its earlier history Macedonia was weak, economically backward and lacked unity.

In 413 Archelaus became king, and set out to promote the power of the monarchy over both regions. He did so by introducing economic and military reforms, and moving the capital from Aegae (modern Vergina) to Pella (a little over an hour's drive west of the modern city of Thessaloniki) in 399. The new capital was to be a cultural one too. The tragic playwright Euripides was invited there, and wrote the *Bacchae* and *Archelaus* (which is lost) during his stay. Socrates too was invited, but chose to stay in Athens. Philip would extend the size of Pella (see Plate 3), and state patronage of artists and writers increased during his and Alexander's reigns.

Art and artwork were exquisite and of the highest standard. Archelaus's palace was decorated with frescoes by Zeuxis from Italy, the leading fresco painter of his day. He established a School whose designs influenced painters in the Hellenistic and Roman periods. Silver drinking vessels and containers have been found all over Macedonia, along with gold artifacts and jewellery. Bronze and iron arms and armour are of the highest calibre, and in Philip's tomb (see below) were found miniature ivory heads that the Greeks could not even make. The magnificent mosaics from the early Hellenistic period that were discovered at Pella are also testimony to the quality of the Macedonian artists (see Chapter 3). There is no question that the Macedonians were genuine lovers of art in all of its forms.

Archelaus's good work was undone in the reign of Amyntas III (393–369), thanks to serious threats from the Illyrians, the Chalcidian League and the Athenians. The same is true of his two sons, Alexander II (369–368) and Perdiccas III (365–360).[5] When Perdiccas and 4,000

Macedonian soldiers died in battle against the Illyrians in 360, the heir to the throne, Amyntas, was only a minor. Then, like vultures hovering over a corpse, some of the northern tribes, the Thracians and the Athenians, prepared to invade.

The vultures were chased away by the new king, Philip II (see Plate 4). Given the desperate situation facing Macedonia, it was decided to bypass the legitimate heir, Amyntas, because of his age, and elect his uncle as king. The people could not have made a better choice, as history would prove.

In 360 when he became king, Philip faced a grim situation.[6] The neighbouring tribes of the Illyrians and the Paeonians were preparing to invade. The king of Thrace was supporting a pretender, Pausanias, to the throne. Finally, the Athenians also were backing a pretender, Argaeus, who had landed at Methone on the Thermaic Gulf with 3,000 men. The Athenians had created a League in 378, and by 360 it had become a powerful empire with the strongest fleet in the Aegean. Philip would have to act fast.

Although the details are unknown, he must have concluded a treaty with the Illyrians, for he married an Illyrian wife, Audata (the first of seven wives), and Illyria stayed clear of Macedonia. He ended the threats from the Paeonians and the Thracians simply by buying them off. To counter the Athenian threat he offered to withdraw the Macedonian garrison from Amphipolis. This was an Athenian colony, taken by Sparta in 424, which the Athenians were desperate to recover. Sparta had abandoned it in 421, but Amphipolis had refused to rejoin Athens's empire. Now, the Athenians believed that Philip's move meant that he was returning their colony to them, and so they withdrew their support of Argaeus. He attempted to seize the throne by himself, but the Macedonian king defeated him.

Within a year, Philip had countered the very real threats to Macedonia. He did so by a diplomacy that included deceit, bribery and political marriage, and speed, a pattern that characterised the rest of his reign.[7] It was time to turn to other things, the consolidation of his power and border security.

A Macedonian king wielded immense power in the state.[8] He was one half of the Macedonian government and perhaps even enjoyed semi-divine power. His person was protected at all times, and to ensure this he was always accompanied by a royal bodyguard of seven trusted men. Among his duties were conducting domestic and foreign policy, making wars, performing state sacrifices, leading processions, organising festivals and acting as final judge in cases of appeal. He was the commander of the army, and expected to lead it in battle.

The king had an advisory council of Companions, but he did not have to follow its counsel. Nor was he bound to follow the decisions of the other half of the government, the Assembly. This was composed of male Macedonian citizens, predominantly the soldiers. Although there is some controversy as to what the Assembly's powers were, it seems to have met to discuss policy and to hear the king on matters of importance. It also acclaimed a new king and may even have had the power to judge treason cases (although the king's presence probably ensured a vote his way). It was convened by the king or, if he was overseas or a minor, by his representative. The Assembly had bypassed Amyntas in favour of acclaiming Philip in 360. Clearly, it was a powerful organ, but it was the king who had the final say in all matters. Alexander would avail himself of this prerogative all the time, even when it came to committing murder.

However, the king was not king of *all* Macedonia because of the division of the Upper and Lower regions. The tribes of Upper Macedonia had their own kings, and cared little about the king in Pella. This was always a weakness in regal power and in state unity. Philip recognised this. Once he was undisputed king, he set out to establish unity in his state, a centralised monarchy and a feeling of nationalistic pride.

He achieved this by creating and exploiting a new army, establishing a dynasty, stimulating the economy, and forging an empire that was the most powerful in the Greek world on his death. Not only had it conquered Greece, but also it was set to invade Asia. He did all of this in a little over two decades. His legacy was brilliant, and it enabled Alexander to have the successes he did, especially in the military field.

It was to the army that Philip turned first.[9] The peasant levies were untrained and poorly equipped, and could not effectively repel invasions by outside powers. It was also necessary to increase manpower as 4,000 men had died with Perdiccas in battle against the Illyrians in 360. Philip intended to create a new and larger army and, more significantly, one that was not merely defensive but offensive. He was spectacularly successful. When first he became king, the army numbered about 10,000 infantry and 600 cavalry; in 334, as Alexander prepared to invade Persia, the Macedonian contingent in his army was 12,000 infantry and 1,800 cavalry. He also left behind with Antipater 12,000 infantry and about 1,500 cavalry in Greece.

In his early teens (from about 13 to 15), Philip had been a hostage in Thebes, the principal city of Boeotia. The Thebans had defeated his brother Alexander II, and part of their terms was the surrender of a hostage. They were also at that time masters of Greece thanks to their brilliant generals Pelopidas and Epaminondas. Philip experienced at first hand what military prowess can do for a state no matter its size and the power of its opponents.[10] This clearly encouraged his dream of establishing a Macedonian empire. He also learned much about military strategy from Epaminondas. When he became king, he put what he had learnt into practice, concentrating on tactics, speed and new weaponry.

First, he decided to introduce tactics that were radically different from standard Greek practice. He switched the main attacking arm of the army from the infantry to the cavalry. Thus, contrary to Greek military practice, the infantry now supported the cavalry. Philip would also feign a retreat in battle so that the enemy would come after him in some disarray. He would then wheel for a counterattack before the enemy realised it had been deceived. This strategy outfoxed the Greeks at the Battle of Chaeronea in 338. He also incorporated specialist and other troops into his army. These included archers, javelinmen and slingers, from conquered areas such as Thrace, together with more cavalry from Thessaly.

It was important to dispense with a conscript army of poorly trained peasants. Instead, Philip created full-time regular soldiers, who would also receive regular pay (for the first time). He trained his men to carry their own arms, equipment and food, and he forbade wagons and women to accompany the army. This self-sufficiency meant that his men could march quickly and easily, especially through narrow mountain passes and over rugged terrain. The oxen or mules that normally pulled the wagons could stay in Macedonia and work the land, contributing to economic prosperity.

The depth of the phalanx infantry formation was often increased to meet a particular situation, and ranged from 8 to 32 ranks. Each man carried a new weapon, the sarissa. This was a 16-foot pike with a pointed iron head. When marching, the men carried these weapons in an upright position, but when charging the first five ranks of the phalanx lowered their sarissas to a horizontal position (pointing forward). The phalanx, with its massive array of deadly weapons protruding in front of the soldiers, must have been a terrifying sight to see (Fig. 1).

Even if Greek hoplite soldiers did manage to kill Macedonian soldiers in the first line, they were likely to be impaled by the sarissas of the other lines. Philip's men must have gone through repeated drilling in order to ensure that they could march and run as and when needed with these long, heavy weapons at the ready. It would have taken only one man to stumble and throw the entire phalanx into a deadly disarray.

For most of his campaigning Philip did not use his entire army but mixed up infantry and cavalry and made sallies rather than large-scale invasions. As expected of a Macedonian warrior king, he led the attack and was always in the thick of fighting to set the right example to his men. Alexander would do likewise, often at his own peril.

Philip kept the army constantly on campaign because through challenge and victory would come unity and pride. That is what happened. The king

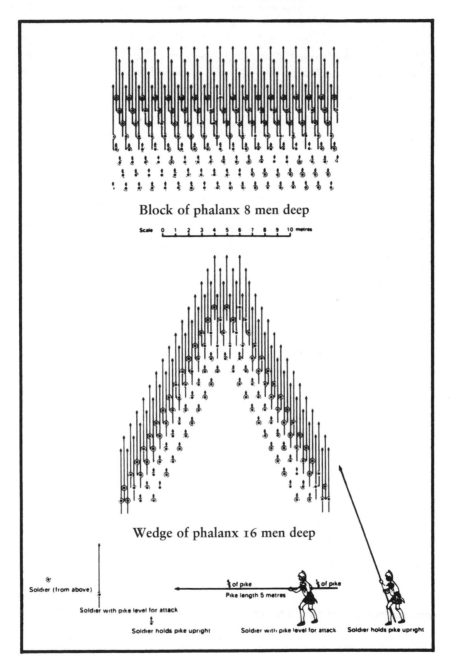

Block of phalanx 8 men deep

Scale 0 1 2 3 4 5 6 7 8 9 10 metres

Wedge of phalanx 16 men deep

Soldier (from above)

Soldier with pike level for attack

Soldier holds pike upright

⅓ of pike   ⅔ of pike
Pike length 5 metres

Soldier with pike level for attack

Soldier holds pike upright

Figure 1. A Macedonian phalanx formation carrying sarissas.
From N.G.L. Hammond, *The Genius of Alexander the Great* (1997), p. 14

was able to unite Lower and Upper Macedonia and to centralise the monarchy. Through the extension of Macedonia's power in the Greek world an empire was created. At the heart of everything was the army. He never forgot this, nor did Alexander – at first. As his reign progressed and he lost touch with the rank and file, Alexander would find out how powerful the army was, to his detriment.

Within a year or so of coming to the throne Philip's new army was ready for battle. It was now time to protect his borders, and he turned first to his northern and eastern. His earlier deals with the Illyrians and Paeonians had bought him the time he needed. Now, in spring 358, he invaded their lands and defeated them. The Illyrians lost 7,000 men in a massive battle. An Upper Macedonia freed from Illyrian influence, and a second marriage alliance, this time to the Illyrian princess Phila, consolidated Macedonian influence in Illyria. Upper and Lower Macedonia were then united as never before.

Philip now set his sights on his southern border, which brought him into contact with Thessaly. This was one of the few fertile areas in Greece and was famous for its fine horses, which he would use for his cavalry. Still in the same year, Philip made a pact with Larissa (the principal city of the Thessalian League) which was then involved in a dispute with another Thessalian town, Pherae. The pact was cemented by his marriage to a Larissan woman called Philinna. His moves in Thessaly meant that he had not merely secured his southern border but also extended it into Greece.

The following year Philip concluded an alliance with Arybbas, king of Epirus, to Macedonia's west. Again, there was a marriage, this time to the king's niece, Olympias – Alexander's mother. The two had apparently met, some years before, when at the Sanctuary of the Great Gods (Cabiri) of Samothrace during a religious festival.

Thus, in 357 Philip's northern, western, eastern and southern borders were now secure (for the present), his position as king was now unchallenged and his army had more than proved itself.

He also had four wives by now, for he was polygamous and did not divorce one wife to marry another. Philip would marry seven times during his reign and, apart from the seventh, all the marriages were political. We know very little about Philip's wives, apart from Olympias.[11] She was the mother of the heir to the throne, who was born in 356. For that reason she may have enjoyed a more privileged position at the court. The others seem to have stayed in the royal palace and performed their wifely duties, which included cooking and keeping house. Olympias was certainly the most outspoken of the wives, and the one who meddled the most in political affairs. She seems to have practised a mystery religion that involved snake handling. This may have been the basis of the later story that a snake had impregnated her with Alexander (see Chapter 3).

When Philip first came to power he had bought off the Athenian threat by promising to withdraw the Macedonian garrison from Amphipolis. Now, in 357, the Athenians discovered how well he combined deceit with diplomacy because, despite their protests, he kept Amphipolis. They declared war on him, a reaction Philip must have known they would make. The scene was thus set for his involvement in affairs in Greece.

The following years saw the power of the Greeks diminish as Philip steadily pushed into central and then southern Greece. The war with Athens did not involve any lengthy campaigns or hard-fought battles because most of the states of central Greece and then Macedonia became embroiled in a Sacred War that broke out in 355 and lasted until 346. It was waged against the small state of Phocis by the Amphicytonic League, an organisation of Greek states charged with the upkeep of the oracle of Apollo at Delphi. Although it was an essentially religious body it wielded great political power in Greek affairs. Phocis had seized Delphi and used the temple treasuries to hire mercenaries in 356. This action was in protest against the Thebans, who had brought up the matter of a fine imposed on the Phocians by the Amphticyonic League that was still unpaid. Their sacrilegious action caused the League to declare war on them on behalf of the god, hence Sacred War.

Despite losing many of its commanders and suffering several reversals in battle, the Phocians fought hard against the armies of the various states. In 352 Thessaly called on its ally Philip for support, and to everyone's surprise the Phocian commander Onomarchus defeated the Macedonian army. Philip was forced to withdraw north. However, he was back within a matter of weeks, probably this time with all his army for it was essential to regain confidence after the earlier defeats, and to maintain the confidence of Thessaly. He defeated the Phocians and killed Onomarchus at the Battle of the Crocus Field.

An expansion east followed. By late 349 Philip began a campaign against the Chalcidice, the last independent Greek state on his seaboard. A year later, when its chief city Olynthus fell to him, the entire Chalcidice was his. He was eager to become involved in the Sacred War again because that would give him the chance to intervene actively in Greek affairs and to be known as the Saviour of Delphi. His opportunity came in 346, when a financially exhausted Thebes appealed for help. For the past few years the events of the Sacred War had centred on clashes between Phocis and Boeotia, and by 346 Thebes had had enough. The timing could not have been better for Philip, who was also working to bring the war with Athens to an end.

The Phocians' position was desperate once the Macedonian army joined the Amphictyonic League. They appealed for help to Sparta and to Philip's enemy Athens, and both states agreed to send help. However, when it arrived the Phocian commander, Phalaecus, dismissed it. His action can only be explained by some tacit agreement reached with Philip, perhaps to moderate the penalty that would be inflicted on Phocis for seizing Delphi (being thrown from the top of Mount Parnassus). When Philip reached Phalaecus, he and his army were allowed to leave untouched. The state of Phocis surrendered to Philip, and the Sacred War was over.

So too would be the war between Philip and Athens. After various diplomatic exchanges between Philip and the Athenians, the war ended with the Peace of Philocrates in 346. This was bilateral peace agreement between the two powers, with each side swearing on behalf of its allies. Despite Philip's power, the Athenians did not suffer unduly. Perhaps this was because of their fleet, and the desirability of having the most powerful city in Greece as an ally rather than as an enemy. At least for now.

The Phocians may well have been prepared to throw in their lot with Philip and end the war in return for his support. If this scenario is true, Philip lived up to his word. At a later Amphictyonic League meeting called to discuss the Phocians' fate, Philip was able to persuade the League to impose a series of punishments on them, including a massive fine and confiscation of their arms. But there was no mass execution.

The power of the Macedonian king in Greece was now shown. He had ended the Sacred War, he was the Saviour of Delphi and he was elected President of the Pythian Games, to be held in September at Delphi. Even more significantly, he was granted a seat on the powerful Amphictyonic League, one of Greece's most hallowed institutions. The Macedonian empire was growing fast. Alexander was now ten years old.

The Peace of Philocrates did not last long. It was in trouble by 344, and in 343 the architect of the Peace, Philocrates, was impeached in Athens, fled into exile before his trial, and was condemned to death *in absentia*. This was also the period when the influence of Philip's greatest opponent in Athens, Demosthenes, was at its highest.[12] This orator and politician constantly urged warfare against Philip and exhorted the Athenians not to be apathetic but to put together a standing army that could be deployed at a moment's notice. Unfortunately, the people did not listen to him until it was too late.

Demosthenes (see Plate 5) has been seen as the ultimate patriot who saw in Philip the end of Greek freedom and preached resistance to him at all costs. He has also been seen as a cynical opportunist who exploited the threat from Philip for his own political career. Whichever of these is true, Athenian policy after the mid-340s was Demosthenes's policy. When the

Athenians refused to attend the Pythian Games in 346 because Philip was President, the king sent an angry letter to Athens. It was Demosthenes who, in his speech, *On The Peace*, persuaded them to go. The Peace might be a bad one, he said, but the Athenians needed to adhere to it or face Philip's wrath. When Philip proposed changes to the Peace in 344, it was Demosthenes, in *Philippic 2*, who successfully opposed them. In 341 Philip complained of Athenian activity in the Thracian Chersonese, and again it was Demosthenes who blasted him in *Philippic 3* and *On The Chersonese*, probably his two finest and most fiery political speeches. Even after Philip's death, Demosthenes remained influential in Athenian political life, though his resistance to Alexander was far less overt.

With the Peace of Philocrates in tatters by 342, Philip moved east and campaigned in Thrace. This represented a direct threat to Athenian interests in that area. Moreover, the Greek cities of Byzantium, Selymbria and Perinthus were worried in case he came after them as well. They were right to be worried, for in spring 340 he besieged Perinthus. For once Philip was unsuccessful because of defences of Perinthus and its support from Persia. He turned to Byzantium, and the Athenians mobilised help. Byzantium was one of the key strategic towns on the Hellespont, through which the Athenian fleet bringing corn from the Black Sea sailed every summer. The Athenians were dependent on imported corn for their survival, and the massive fleet was protected by a flotilla of war vessels. If the Hellespont were blocked to it, then the Athenians would be in dire straits. It was therefore imperative for them to make sure that Byzantium (originally an ally and now independent) did not fall into Philip's hands.

The Macedonian king was well aware of Athenian concerns and how they would react. By now, summer 340, he was looking for a pretext to deal with the Athenians once and for all. When Athens agreed to support Byzantium against him, Philip seized the corn fleet in retaliation. Demosthenes had no trouble in persuading the Athenians to declare war on him. Alexander was now 16 years old. He was about to become regent while Philip campaigned further in the east, and during this time the young Alexander would successfully put down a revolt and found a city (see Chapter 3).

The new war with Athens lasted two years and it would end in Macedonian victory. Philip did have two setbacks in 339. On his way back to Macedonia the Triballi, a Thracian tribe, defeated him, a loss that must have given the Greeks some cause for hope. Then Demosthenes scored a major diplomatic success when he engineered an alliance with Athens's longstanding foe, Thebes. This combination, which was supported by Achaea, Megara, Corinth and several islands, posed no small threat to Philip, and both he and the Greeks staked all on one last-ditch battle. This would be the Battle of Chaeronea (in Boeotia), fought on 1 September 338. If Philip won, Greece was his. If he lost, he lost everything.

He did not lose. The Athenians alone had 1,000 killed and 2,000 taken as prisoners. The heir Alexander proved his battle prowess by commanding the left flank of the Macedonian line and annihilating the 300-strong Sacred Band of Thebes. The Sacred Band fought to the last man, and a tribute to the Sacred Band's bravery, a statue of a lion, was erected over the spot where they allegedly fell. It can still be seen today.

The Macedonian king was now master of Greece, for Greek autonomy ended at Chaeronea. It was therefore one of the world's decisive battles. Alexander was now 18 years old.

Philip treated the majority of his Greek opponents harshly. For example, he imposed a Macedonian-backed oligarchy and garrison in Thebes. The Athenians expected the worst. Demosthenes prudently left the city on the pretext of securing corn in case Philip besieged Athens. Yet Philip did not besiege Athens. The Athenian empire was dissolved, but he did not order the surrender of any opponents (like Demosthenes) nor did he impose an oligarchy or garrison in the city. In fact, he returned the Athenian prisoners from Chaeronea unransomed. Moreover, Alexander, the heir apparent, and Antipater, Philip's key general, brought back the ashes of those who died in the battle.

The Athenians awarded citizenship to Philip and Alexander. This was a token gesture, for Demosthenes was chosen to give the funeral oration to honour those who died at Chaeronea, and some Theban refugees who fled to Athens in the wake of Philip's purge were also made citizens.

That winter, Philip summoned embassies from the Greek states to meet him at Corinth. Only Sparta declined because it refused to acknowledge Macedonian power. At this meeting the Greeks found out how Philip intended to treat them. He announced a Common Peace, in which each state made an individual treaty with Macedon.[13] Under this arrangement, no state could go to war against another or cause trouble for another. If this happened, all the other states combined to retaliate against it. This was a brilliant plan, and showed how well Philip knew the Greeks. The animosity that the various states felt for each other meant that they would relish the chance to attack (legally) a state that jeopardised the peace and security of the Common Peace. This was the deterrent to ensure peace and stability. The League would be under the leadership of a *hegemon* (the Macedonian king), and the Greeks swore an oath of loyalty to Philip and, significantly, his descendants.

The Macedonian hegemony of Greece was formalised in what is called the League of Corinth.[14] Moreover, the oath of loyalty to the king and his descendants showed not only that Philip had established a dynasty but also that it was here to stay. He had come a long way in the 23 years since becoming king.

Soon after, probably late winter or spring 337, Philip called a second meeting at Corinth. Here he presented his plan to invade Persia. One source says that Philip had set his eyes on Persia at the time of the Peace of Philocrates in 346.[15] However, he may not have considered invading Persia until as late as 341 or so, perhaps when Persia assisted Perinthus against him.

Why Persia? Philip's motives are varied.[16] There is the thirst for more personal glory, the need to keep the army on campaign, punishment for helping Perinthus against him and the need to increase state revenue. These were all Macedonian reasons, and had nothing to do with the Greeks. Since he needed the Greeks to ensure the success of the proposed invasion, how could he persuade them to accept the plan and fight with him? The answer is that he made the war against Persia a Greek one. This was to be a war of liberation and revenge. The Greek cities of Asia Minor were to be freed from Persian influence and the Persians were to be punished for their sacrilegious acts in Greece during the Persian War of 480–479.

The Persian empire (which the Greeks called the Empire of the Medes) was vast. It stretched from the eastern Mediterranean and the Levant to Egypt in the south, through Iraq and Iran all the way to Afghanistan in the east, and as far north in Central Asia as the Oxus river. It was founded by Cyrus the Great, the King of Persis (in southern Iran) in 559 when he invaded and annexed Media (which lay in north-west Iran). A decade later he gained control of Asia Minor, including the Greek cities there. His son Cambyses went on to capture Egypt and add it to the empire.

The mainland Greeks had some trading contacts with the Persian empire, and in 499 Athens and Eretria (on the island of Euboea) supported a revolt of the Greeks of Asia Minor. The revolt ended in failure in 494, and Darius, the Persian king, went to punish the two mainland states in 490. The Athenians defeated Persia at the Battle of Marathon in 490, a battle that marked Athens' coming of age as a military power.

Ten years later, Darius's son Xerxes invaded Greece with a huge army, intent on revenge and on adding Greece to his empire. This marked the period of the Persian Wars proper. Though he had some successes, the Persians were defeated at sea and on land. By 479, it was all over, and they had left Greece. During this time, however, the Persian army had invaded Attica. Athens was practically deserted, for the Greeks en masse had collected at the nearby island of Salamis to resist the Persians at sea. The Persians ransacked the city, stole various works of art and burned the

Acropolis. The Greeks (especially the Athenians) never forgave them and they sympathised with those Greeks living in Asia Minor who were subject to Persian rule. One hundred and fifty years later, Philip played on this hatred for Persia to get the response he needed from the Greeks.

The real motive for the war against Persia may have been economic. Philip exploited the natural resources of Macedonia to a far greater extent than any other king.[17] He stimulated agriculture and trade, he exploited the gold and silver mines and his coinage became the strongest in Europe. His annual income from the mines in the Mount Pangaeum region alone was 1,000 talents per annum.[18] On top of that was income from the areas he conquered, as well as from the imposition of dues and property taxes.

Yet, his sources of revenue were not infinite. Throughout his reign, he spent vast sums of money on pay for the men in his army, on providing arms and armour and in maintaining his cultured court at Pella. There were also bribes to influential politicians in the Greek states, so many that it was said that Philip enlarged his kingdom more through bribery than warfare.[19] If the Mount Pangaeum mines were starting to run dry, then Philip needed more revenue. It was said that when Alexander was set to invade Persia in 334, 'he had not more than seventy talents. Duris speaks of supplies for only thirty days, and Onesicritus says he also owed two hundred talents.'[20] However, even if Philip did not have much in the way of real assets, his legacy was still a strong and stable economy, on which was anchored future expansion. Persia, with its vast wealth, was the obvious place to go.

This was the plan (and debt) that Alexander, now 20, would inherit and which the League of Corinth had to endorse. In spring 336, an advance force under the command of Parmenion, Philip's most trusted general, crossed the Hellespont.

Philip himself never invaded Persia. In summer 336 his daughter by Olympias, Cleopatra, married the King of Epirus, in the theatre of Aegae. Olympias had now left the court and Philip may well have arranged the marriage as a move against her (see Chapter 3). However, it was a joyous occasion, for the League of Corinth was now in place and the invasion of Asia had begun. The day after the wedding, games and plays were to be held in the theatre in celebration. A procession entered the theatre carrying statues of the gods, followed by Alexander as heir and the King of Epirus. They took their seats and then the main event appeared. Philip walked in wearing a white cloak and surrounded by his royal bodyguards. When they reached the middle of the *orchestra* (the performance area) of the theatre, they stepped back and away from him, so that he could bask in the cheers of the audience.

It was the last thing he would do or know. One of his royal bodyguards, Pausanias of Orestis, suddenly rushed from his post and stabbed the king. Philip died, within minutes if not instantaneously. He was about 46 years old. Pausanias tried to escape, but he slipped and was speared to death where he fell by three of the other bodyguards.

The motives for the assassination are varied, and we shall probably never know the real story.[21] Pausanias and the king had been involved in a love affair that the king had ended. Unable to handle the rejection, Pausanias killed him in an emotional rage. However, the assassination could have been political, a conspiracy that even involved Alexander and Olympias (see Chapter 3). They could have used Pausanias as a pawn. For one thing, after Pausanias murdered Philip he began to run to waiting horses to make his escape. If he had acted alone he would have needed only one horse.

Philip deserved a better fate. The only positive aspect of the manner in which he died was that the last thing he heard was the crowd roaring his name and acknowledging his greatness. He had made Macedonia a super-power. His military reforms more than revolutionised the army, they revolutionised the state. The continued success of the army and the subsequent expansion of Macedonian power created a feeling of national unity that had never been felt before. He left Alexander the best army in the Greek world, an empire, a centralised monarchy and economic prosperity. 'Philip made himself the greatest of the kings in Europe, and because of the extent of his kingdom he considered himself enthroned with the twelve gods,' says Diodorus at the end of his narrative of Philip's reign.[22] He was right.

Philip might have died, but he did not disappear from Alexander's life, however. Like the ghost of Julius Caesar in Shakespeare's play, Philip remained a constant in Alexander's life and decisions long after his death.

The question now is what the 20-year-old Alexander would do with Philip's legacy.

3

Alexander's Boyhood

Alexander was born on 20 July 356. He was the son of Philip's fourth wife, the Princess Olympias, from Epirus, to Macedonia's west. He may not have been the eldest son for he had a brother, Arrhidaeus. His mother Philinna of Larissa (in Thessaly) had married Philip a year or more before Olympias.[1] Arrhidaeus, though, appears to have been mentally deficient and that incapacitation meant that Alexander was the heir to the throne. From the outset, Alexander was destined for greatness. On the day he was born:

'the Temple of Artemis at Ephesus burned down. It was in connection with it that Hegesias of Magnesia said something cold enough to put out that great fire. He said, namely, that it was no surprise that the Temple of Artemis burnt down as the goddess was busy delivering Alexander into the world. But all the Magi who were then at Ephesus saw the temple's fate as a sign of yet more disaster. They ran around slapping their faces and crying out that that day was born destruction and great disaster for Asia. To Philip, however, who had just taken Potidaea, there came three simultaneous messages. The first was that Parmenion had defeated the Illyrians in a great battle, the second was that his horse had won victory at the Olympic Games, and the third announced Alexander's birth. These things, as might be expected, delighted him. Then the seers raised his spirits even higher by announcing that the son whose birth coincided with three victories would always be victorious.'[2]

The stories did not stop there.[3] Apparently the night before Olympias and Philip married, she dreamed that there was a terrific thunderstorm, during which a thunderbolt smashed down from the sky and landed in her womb. A blinding flash of lightning followed what must have been an uncomfortable experience for her. Philip also had a dream that he took a wax seal and sealed up his wife's womb. When he had done this, he saw the figure of a lion on the seal. A seer then prophesied that Olympias was pregnant and would give birth to a lion of a man as far as bravery and power went.

Another story has it that one night Philip saw a huge snake lying next to his sleeping wife in their bed. This turned out to be the god Zeus Ammon in disguise. Soon after Olympias was pronounced pregnant. It is hardly surprising, as Plutarch notes, that the snake incident 'weakened Philip's passion and cooled his affection for her'. These stories are obviously false as thunderbolts or snakes tend not to impregnate women. It is also part of the course for history's famous figures to have sensational stories attached to them. Alexander may well be the one who started these stories about his birth after he became king because a divine father was something that he would later exploit to dangerous extremes.

Alexander was not a tall man, and he was not a movie star as far as looks went. His neck inclined to the left so his face appeared lop-sided and he had watery eyes (which the *Alexander Romance* says were two different colours, one light blue and the other brown). He also had a round chin, a long, thin nose and his forehead bulged above the eyes. The lop-sided angle of his head might be the result of damage during a difficult birth. Patches of red would later mar his face and chest, perhaps due to his excessive consumption of alcohol. He also had a fierce expression and a loud, harsh voice, both of which were intimidating. But his breath and body had a pleasant odour to them, the result, apparently, of the warmth of his blood.

Some of his features were later softened in court portraiture, but the bust by Lysippus is said to be the best likeness (see Plate 6).[4] One common feature of all busts is the blond hair in ringlets with a central parting. His personality also left a lot to be desired since he was prone to emotional outbursts. His mood would change from self-controlled discussion to uncontrollable passion, often leading to violence. Ephippus ascribes the violence to his being melancholic,[5] which he put down to a preponderance of black bile in Alexander's system. His emotional nature, fuelled by his paranoia, would be, literally, the death of people. However, he was the heir to the Macedonian throne, and so looks and personality did not really matter.

Even as a boy Alexander was very tough and in top physical shape thanks to the training of Leonidas, one of his mother's relatives. This man taught him to fight, to ride and to endure long marches, training that would pay dividends during the long forced marches that Alexander would later impose on his men. A Macedonian youth hunted boar, foxes, lion and birds, and Alexander was no exception. He even enjoyed hunting when on campaign. There is a magnificent mosaic from Pella, to be dated shortly after Alexander's reign, which depicts Alexander on the left and Craterus on the right during a lion hunt. Alexander is trapped by the lion, which has him by its large paw. Craterus, brandishing his sword, is coming to save the king (see Plate 7).

Bucephalus ('Ox-head') is a good example of how as a boy Alexander was without fear and very astute. Bucephalus was a large horse from Thessaly, to Macedonia's south, and a breeding ground of fine horses. Philonicus the Thessalian brought the horse to Philip, asking 13 talents for him. This was a large sum of money, which showed the pedigree and value of Thessalian horses. Philip refused, however, because Bucephalus refused to let anyone ride him, could not follow directions and reared up to kick people.

The young Alexander badgered his father to let him try to ride the horse. The exact date is not known, and hence neither is Alexander's age, but he was probably no more than 10 or 11 at the time. He had noticed that the horse was startled by his own shadow in front of him, and so he turned him to face the sun. This had a calming effect, and after a period of gentle cajoling the young boy mounted the horse and rode him. The adult males, including Philip, who were watching the event in great consternation were taken aback at the scene. A tearful Philip bought the horse for his son and prophesied great things, not least that Macedonia was not big enough to hold him. How true that would be. Bucephalus served Alexander well, dying shortly after the Battle of the Hydaspes against the Indian prince Porus in 326 (see Chapter 11).

Given the man and king that he was, we know surprisingly little about Alexander's boyhood until his 15th year. During this time, he made friends with other noble youths whom he would reward with key positions in his army and administration when he was king. Not all repaid his generosity and loyalty in like manner. He would have been educated at home, as was the custom in Macedonia, and he would have grown used to seeing (and then participating in) the drinking contests that were part of Macedonian court life.

More importantly, he was growing up when his father was fighting in Greece almost every year and working to establish a Macedonian empire. That must have created in him an interest in military affairs and fighting. There is a story that Alexander asked a barrage of questions of some Persian ambassadors who had come to the Macedonian court. He was only seven at the time, but he asked them detailed questions about the size of the Persian army and communications routes within the Persian empire. The story is probably another later creation. However, at its core can be seen the influence that Philip as the warrior king and strategist would have had on his son.

Leonidas, as was said, handled Alexander's physical education, Lysimachus of Acarnania and Aristotle his intellectual. Alexander was naturally intelligent and eager to learn. Lysimachus probably taught him to read and write as well as awakened in him a love for music. Alexander learned to play the lyre – and to play it well. At the age of ten, he played the lyre after a banquet for a visiting Athenian embassy to the Macedonian court. Then when he turned 14 in 342, his father hired Aristotle to be his tutor. Lysimachus had instructed Alexander well, and the famous philosopher had much to work with. Homer was Alexander's bible, and he took Aristotle's edition with him to Asia. This he kept in a casket under his pillow, along with a dagger. The casket had belonged to the Great King, and was said to be his most valuable possession.

Alexander also read much Greek tragedy (especially Euripides), and enjoyed the company of poets and actors. Thessalus, a tragic actor and soon to be one of the leading performers of the day, was one of his friends. Later, in 331, Thessalus would be prominent at a festival held by Alexander at Tyre in Phoenicia, together with many other household names. The Macedonian court at Pella had long been a cultural one, but Alexander made the one that travelled with him a cultural centre too. At his court, and so accompanying him on his expeditions, were two prominent philosophers, Anaxarchus of Abdera and Callisthenes of Olynthus. Callisthenes, Aristotle's nephew, was also the court historian.

When Aristotle arrived at the court in 342, Philip decided that he should not teach Alexander at Pella. Whether this decision was because of the king's Thracian campaign, growing tension with Athens or the influence of Olympias on her son (or all three) is unknown. Aristotle therefore taught Alexander in his own Academy, the Precinct of the Nymphs at Mieza. This was part of the Gardens of Midas, with its abundance of orchards and vineyards, on the slopes of Mount Vermion. There is no evidence that Aristotle formally taught other noble youths, such as Alexander's friends Hephaestion, Ptolemy or Cassander (son of Antipater) along with Alexander while he was in Philip's employ. However, given Aristotle's status and reputation, they may well have listened to his lectures and discussions from time to time in an informal manner.

In the Gardens of Midas Aristotle and Alexander would wander down the pathways or sit on stone benches and discuss topical affairs, ethics, literature and other disciplines. Alexander's love of literature did not abate, for 'when he could find no other books in the middle of Asia, he ordered Harpalus to send him some'.[6] Harpalus, one of Alexander's boyhood friends, was the imperial treasurer based at Babylon. Aristotle built on Alexander's literary accomplishments by probably introducing him to philosophy, rhetoric, zoology, medicine, rhetoric and geometry.[7] During his campaigns Alexander was always intent on finding out everything he could about the areas through which he passed. He took with him an entourage of scientists to record and analyse this information, from botany, biology, zoology and meteorology, to topography. His desire to

learn, and to have information recorded as scientifically as possible, probably stemmed from Aristotle's teachings and enthusiasm. Probably in 330,
Alexander sent Aristotle 800 talents. This allowed Aristotle to set up in
Athens a library of literary texts and to prepare a large range of specimens
for the serious study of zoology.

Whether Aristotle's own views about Greeks ruling barbarians had any
real effect on Alexander is unknown. Aristotle believed that all non-
Greeks ('barbarians') were slaves by nature, and that Greeks should rule
them. He was not alone in this idea, for Plato and Isocrates thought the
same. Alexander may well have subscribed to the same view, but once on
campaign in Asia he integrated foreigners into his army and administration. Such actions were motivated by practical reasons at the time, and do
not mean he had changed his mind about the 'acceptable' relationship (in
Greek eyes) of Greek to non-Greek.

For three years Aristotle taught Alexander in the Gardens of Midas, and
it must have been close to an idyllic life for both of them. However, as a
member of the Argead line of kings, Alexander's education and training
were directed to the day that he would become king – and represent the
king in his absence. In 340, as Philip prepared to leave on campaign again
(against Byzantium this time), Aristotle's teaching came to an end. Philip
ordered Alexander, then 16, back to Pella, and appointed him regent in
the king's absence. The general Antipater would remain with him to act
as adviser. The regent had various civic duties. He carried around the
royal seal to use on state documents, and he protected the state's security.
He also performed the daily religious sacrifices on behalf of the state.
These were to Heracles Patrous (Heracles the father), the ancestor of the
Temenids (see below).

Not long after Philip left, the Maedians revolted. These were a Paeonian
tribe on the upper Strymon River, close to Thrace. A 16-year-old boy
might be expected to defer to the older and more experienced Antipater.
Not Alexander. He marched north and, though the details are few and
hazy, ended the revolt.[8] To keep the people in check he transplanted
people from Macedonia, Greece and Thrace to go and live in a new city
that he founded in that region, Alexandropolis. This was probably no
more than a glorified garrison post, as opposed to a city proper. However,
his first campaign, although not yet king, had been a success and he had
named a city after himself. It would be nine years before Alexander, in
331, would name another city after himself, Alexandria, in Egypt (see
Chapter 7).

We do not know Philip's reaction to Alexander's campaign or city foundation. He must have been impressed by his son's battle prowess though,
because two years later Philip gave him command of the left flank of the

Macedonian army, and of the Companion Cavalry no less, at the Battle of Chaeronea.[9] His father's frontal strategy opened a line in the Greek defence that Alexander smashed through. The fighting was fierce, but Alexander, now 18, was responsible for defeating the 300-strong Sacred Band of the Theban army. In Philip's dealings with the Greeks after the battle, Alexander, as heir apparent, and Antipater solemnly carried to Athens the ashes of its citizens who died in the battle. Alexander had now proved himself in battle and in diplomacy. His father in turn had given him tasks that clearly showed he was grooming him to be king and trusted him.

The young heir would only have to wait for two more years before he became king. However, in those two years relations deteriorated drastically between the two of them. The seeds of what later motivated Alexander as conqueror and how he would see himself were sown.

Alexander was brought up to believe in the Homeric notion of personal success for the sake of honour and glory, and his life was based on gaining these. He always strove to emulate his two heroes Heracles and Achilles, as we will see during his campaigns. They were more than mere heroes, though, they were also his ancestors. The Macedonian royal house had as its founder Argeas, son of Macedon, who was a son of Zeus. A new dynasty came from Argos in Greece, the Temenids, the first king of which was Perdiccas. On his father's side Alexander, therefore, could trace his lineage back to Zeus and, via Temenus of Argos, to the hero Heracles (himself a son of Zeus and a mortal woman), who had been deified on death. On his mother's side, Alexander's ancestors were Achilles (son of the goddess Thetis and a mortal man) and Andromache. Once he invaded Asia, he seized every chance he could to outdo these divine ancestors, and he made the connection with Zeus far more emphatically – and ominously. He saw himself as not merely a descendant of Zeus, but an actual living son of the god.

As well as his ancestors' exploits there were those of his father, Alexander's greatest role model. Philip was the warrior king par excellence, who was 'ready to sacrifice to the fortune of war any and every part of his body', as even his arch enemy Demosthenes[10] had to confess. And it was true, for Philip fought without any regard for his own safety. At the siege of Methone in 354, an archer from the ramparts shot an arrow at him that pierced his skull around his right eye and cost him his sight in that eye. In battle against the Triballi (who lived in the Danube basin) in 339, he maimed a leg and a hand. Alexander's similar disregard for his own safety was no coincidence.

However, despite Alexander's obvious grooming as heir apparent, he seems to have resented his father. The turning point probably came once

Alexander had had a taste of action, especially at the Battle of Chaeronea. He believed that he would never be able to surpass his father's exploits, especially if he lived to a ripe old age. After the defeat of the Greeks, Philip had shown no signs of slowing down and had formed plans for an invasion of Persia. Who knew when he would stop where he would stop, and what he would have accomplished by then? Alexander used to say to his friends, apparently, that his father would be the first to do everything and leave him with nothing great to do.

He seems also to have been unduly influenced by his mother Olympias, who disliked Philip intensely. Perhaps this was one of the reasons why Philip sent Alexander away from Pella to study under Aristotle. As the mother of the heir to the Macedonian throne, Olympias probably enjoyed a superior position in Philip's collection of seven wives.[11] She was not afraid of making her opinion known or of meddling in political affairs (as was the case after the death of her son). As he grew up at Pella Alexander had the most contact with her, for Philip was on campaign almost every year of his reign. He spent little time with his father, and the relationship of the two is illustrated by those who called Leonidas, the physical fitness tutor, his foster father.[12] The attribution could not have been lost on Alexander.

That does not mean that Alexander never spent time with his mother and father together, or that when he did it was always a sombre occasion. An ivory figurine from Vergina may depict Philip, Olympias and a young Alexander as Pan in Bacchic revelry (see Plate 8). Moreover, there was no move on Philip's part to marginalise Alexander. None, that is, until the last two years of his reign. After the trust that Philip had placed in him, Alexander probably expected to play a greater role in state affairs, especially in military life. He was certainly ready to do so after Chaeronea, and he had shown that he could meet any challenge. He probably expected his father to see him in a different light too, but that was not the case.

Olympias also had her concerns about Philip, but for different reasons. She may have given birth to the heir to the throne, but she was not a full-blood Macedonian. That did not present a problem until now, for Philip's five other wives were non-Macedonian. However, in 337, Philip married Cleopatra, the niece of Attalus. This was his seventh marriage, the only one in which he was said to have married for love. Cleopatra was a commoner, but Attalus was a powerful Macedonian noble, and trusted by Philip. Moreover, Attalus became Cleopatra's guardian when her father died. Olympias resented the new queen and seems to have been concerned about Alexander's succession. At first sight, there were no grounds for this fear. Even if Cleopatra had borne Philip a son, Alexander's age and designation as heir meant that he would inherit the throne.

Or would he? Unlike the other wives, the young Cleopatra was a full-blood Macedonian. At the marriage feast of Cleopatra, Attalus drank too much, and prayed that Macedon might at last have a legitimate heir. That comment showed where his loyalty, and perhaps that of other nobles too, lay. Alexander was already nearly 20, but there was no reason to suppose that Philip would not be king for another 16 or so years. He was, after all, only about 45 by then, and he showed no signs of slowing down despite his wounds.

Attalus's comment infuriated Alexander. He threw his drinking cup hard at Attalus's face, and called on his father to reprimand him. Philip did not. To make matters worse he drew his sword against Alexander, and then fell over a table in a drunken stupor. Alexander is supposed to have said contemptuously that the man who planned to cross from Europe to Asia could not even navigate around a table. The heir to the Macedonian throne and his mother then left the court in disgust.

It is a significant indication of how strained relations were between Philip and his son that Alexander fled first to Epirus with his mother, as we would expect, but then to Macedonia's old enemy Illyria. There was no love lost between the Illyrians and Philip, so Alexander's flight there posed a problem for Philip. Olympias, back in her home state, could also raise support against Philip. That probably explains why he recalled his son (but not Olympias) to the court within a year. It may also explain why he arranged for his daughter Cleopatra (from his marriage to Olympias, hence Alexander's sister) to marry the King of Epirus. That marital pact would, Philip hoped, offset anything Olympias was trying to do against him.

On Alexander's return there was a reconciliation of sorts, but bad blood still existed. Attalus had not been punished for his remark, and he was appointed one of three commanders of the advance force to Persia in 336. Moreover, Philip decided that Alexander would be Regent of Macedon and Deputy *Hegemon* of the League of Corinth while he was campaigning in Asia. Obviously, Philip needed someone whom he could trust to be in charge of Macedonia, and Alexander had proved his worth. We should also not overlook the danger to the empire of king and heir coming to grief in Asia if both went there. However, Philip's decision may well have been the final straw. Alexander was already anxious about what he could do to establish his reputation. Staying behind would do nothing. He wanted to march with his father, to battle the Persians, to conquer and to win.

Later in 337 (the timing is controversial), Pixodarus, the ruler of Caria in Asia Minor, wanted a marriage pact with Macedonia to support his plan to break away from Persia. Although ruler, he was still subject to the authority of the Great King and he wanted to sever the tie completely. He perhaps decided on this course of action when news of Philip's proposed invasion of Persia became known. The Macedonian king was not averse to an alliance with Pixodarus, and he put forward Arrhidaeus, Alexander's half-brother, who played little if any role in state affairs, as the potential husband. Alexander, for some reason, became furious that Philip had overlooked him. He sent Thessalus to Pixodarus with the news that Alexander wished to offer himself as husband.

Philip refused Alexander's wish. He wanted a better marital tie for the heir to the Macedonian empire, and that made perfect sense. Tempers between Philip and Alexander flared, and an angry Philip exiled four of Alexander's close friends as a warning.[13] These were the later imperial treasurer Harpalus, Nearchus, who was to sail along the coast of the Indian Ocean in an epic voyage, the general Ptolemy, whose eyewitness account of Alexander's exploits is the basis of at least Arrian's narrative history, and Erigyius, who would be an army commander. We see how Alexander later rewarded his boyhood friends for their friendship and loyalty. Negotiations with Pixodarus were now abandoned and the rift between father and son grew immeasurably wider.

Alexander's later teen years, then, were marred by Olympias's suspicions and his feeling of being disregarded and belittled. Sixteen year olds who are trusted with the regency of Macedonia, and who go on to defeat a tough enemy in battle and name a new city after themselves, are not the type to handle being overlooked readily. The Pixodarus incident showed Alexander who was king and who was heir. Attalus's taunt and his father's allowance of it showed him how much Philip thought of his hurt feelings. A potential baby brother, born of full Macedonian parents, showed his succession might not be set in stone after all.

Finally, and perhaps the most important for Alexander at that time, Philip was denying him the chance to march against the Persians and to consolidate his own military renown. Instead, Alexander would have a 'desk job', albeit an enormously important one, administering a pacified Greece, while his father fought battles and conquered new territories.

Something needed to be done. Given the concerns of Alexander and Olympias, it is not beyond reasonable doubt that they were implicated in Philip's assassination at Aegae in summer 336. Is it merely a coincidence that Philip was murdered the day after the wedding of his daughter Cleopatra to Alexander of Epirus (see Chapter 2), as part of a plan to limit Olympias's influence at the Epirote court? Is it merely a coincidence that when Alexander visited the oracle of Zeus Ammon in 331 he was told that his father's murderers had been punished? Of course, we only have Alexander's word for this, as no one else was present with him when he spoke to the priest. However, patricide was a heinous crime. If some suspicion were still sticking to him, then his visit to the oracle may also have been to exculpate himself.

Perhaps if more of Alexander's childhood had been spent with his father than in the formal relationship of king and heir, matters would have been different, but who knows? Certainly, his love–hate relationship with his father affected him greatly. His attitude of admiration and rivalry may well have changed to resentment.[14] This is not a novel argument in Alexander studies, but it needs to be stressed more than it usually is. He was the heir to a growing empire, eager for glory himself, but denied this because he was, after all, only the heir. I believe that this explains his motivation to eclipse Philip's exploits. Military conquest was not enough, for Philip had done that. Alexander needed more. Here we see his ambition to establish an absolute monarchy and especially his pretension to personal divinity.

Philip may have been deified in the last year of his reign, though this is controversial (see Chapter 14). He certainly was accepted as a god on his death. Alexander, however, wanted deification for himself while alive. This delusion is the pattern to his reign (see further, Chapter 14). The turning point came in 331 with his visit to the main sanctuary of the oracle of Zeus Ammon at Siwah (see Chapter 7). There, 'the prophet immediately told him that he was not Philip's son but the son of Zeus Ammon himself. Alexander recalled the account of his mother Olympias that a snake once prevailed over her at the time of his birth.'[15] Alexander the man decided that he was the son of a god.

Given Alexander's successes, it is easy to understand his delusions of self-grandeur, and how his attempts to be recognised as a god while alive are the key to so many of his actions. These actions are meant to outdo those of his father. In fact, Alexander could not even bear to hear stories of Philip's greatness. No time is this more obvious than when he murdered Cleitus, who had been singing Philip's praises over his own (see Chapter 10). Yet Alexander could never shake off Philip's influence, and so often in his reign we see him taking a leaf out of his father's book. Philip's ghost indeed.

Alexander had done everything that Philip asked of him and more. However, those last two years of his father's life and the plans he devised for him, showed him how his father really saw him. The shock turned admiration into resentment, and then, when king, into wanting to leave Philip far behind. He did so, but at what cost?

4

King at Last

Not everyone was in favour of Alexander's accession. When Philip II was assassinated, Alexander's friends armed themselves expecting trouble, and 'all Macedoniaia was seething with discontent, looking to Amyntas and the sons of Aeropus'.[1] Amyntas was Philip's nephew, the son of Perdiccas III who was killed in battle in 360. He was the true heir to the throne in 360, but had been bypassed in favour of Philip because of his youth and the threats to Macedonia at that time (see Chapter 2). In 336 he was still around and an adult. He probably posed the greatest threat to Alexander's position because of his legal right to succession, in 360 and now in 336.

The three sons of Aeropus of Lyncestis were Arrhabaeus, Heromenes and Alexander. Philip had exiled their father, and they may even have been involved in his assassination. Certainly, Alexander thought so, although he may have been using them as scapegoats. There was also Attalus himself. Philip had sent him with Parmenion at the head of an advance force to Asia in 336, but he was still influential. In fact, Demosthenes in Athens had sent letters to him calling on him to revolt. Finally, there was Parmenion, Philip' senior general, one of whose daughters was married to Attalus.

No trouble came, at least from the Macedonians. Perhaps this was because Antipater and Parmenion stayed loyal to Alexander. Antipater was present with Alexander, and Parmenion's loyalty to the heir never seems to have faltered, despite his son-in-law. Antipater probably led Alexander before the Macedonian people in their Assembly soon after his father's murder. Macedonian custom was for the people to acclaim the heir king and then swear an oath of loyalty to him. In this Assembly, with Philip's body lying in state, they shouted and the men under arms clashed their spears on their shields. The king was dead, long live the king.

Constitutionally, anyone trying to usurp the throne or who opposed a new king was a traitor, and could be executed. Under Macedonian law a traitor's family was also executed. Alexander thus had right on his side in moving not only against his immediate opponents but also their families. He immediately executed the three sons of his father's assassin, Pausanias, although they were not implicated in the murder.

In a series of purges that lasted for over a year, Alexander got rid of the opposition.[2] The king named several men whom he suspected of complicity in his father's murder. They were tried by the Assembly, as was the law, and found guilty. Arrhabaeus and Heromenes of Lyncestis were the first to be executed, and were dispatched at Philip's funeral (see below). The third brother Alexander was spared. This was not because he was Antipater's son-in-law, and Antipater was immensely important at this critical time, but because he read the writing on the wall. He recognised Alexander as king and vowed his loyalty to him. He was a general in Thrace for a time, and then accompanied Alexander to Asia, later receiving charge of the Thessalian cavalry under the overall command of Parmenion.

Nonetheless, Alexander of Lyncestis did not stay loyal to Alexander for long. A little after the first defeat of the Persians at the battle of Granicus in 334, Parmenion intercepted a letter to him from the Great King of Persia. It offered him 1,000 talents to kill Alexander the king. He was arrested, and he remained under close guard until 330, when the king engineered his death in Phrada (see Chapter 9).

Amyntas, the true heir to the throne, was put to death for treason, though probably not until after Alexander returned from a campaign against the Illyrians (see below). The powerful Attalus was next. Alexander sent his friend Hecataeus to Parmenion with orders to try Attalus for treason. If he resisted, he was to be killed. Attalus protested his innocence and tried to make amends, but in vain. Parmenion obeyed the king's orders without question.

There are two final murders in which Alexander did not play a part. Taking advantage of Alexander's purges, Olympias (who returned to Pella when Alexander became king) had Philip's last wife Cleopatra and her baby daughter (born in the last year of Philip's life) horrifically murdered. They were roasted over a brazier. Olympias would show her murderous, scheming self again in the years after Alexander's death, and no tears were shed when she was executed in 315.

Alexander spared his half-brother Arrhidaeus. He could have been used as a pawn against the king by a scheming noble or faction, especially after Alexander had left Greece, but this was not the case. Alexander would not have known that of course. We can understand why he had those who presented a threat to him executed, for it would have been impossible to cross to Asia leaving opponents at large in Greece. Yet he allowed

Arrhidaeus to live, and in doing so we see the softer side to his nature. Arrhidaeus was his half-brother; the two had grown up together at Pella, and there was a powerful bond of brotherly love and trust between them. He could not bring himself to kill his half-brother, and trusted him to stay loyal.

But Arrhidaeus was used as a pawn. After Alexander's death in 323 he was proclaimed king as Philip III by some of those generals carving up the empire for themselves (see Chapter 13). His tenure of power was short, for Olympias had him and wife Eurydice killed in 317.

Supported and surrounded by Philip's ablest generals as well as his boyhood friends, all of whom would soon find themselves in greater positions of power as a gesture of his gratitude, Alexander was secure. At an Assembly a few days after he became king he stressed that he would continue what his father had started. Thus, the Argead line of kings continued in the hands of the 20-year-old Alexander III, King of Macedonia and *Hegemon* of the League of Corinth.

Before the first round of executions, Alexander had to attend to his father's burial place. The capital of Macedonia since 399 was Pella, but royal burials and weddings were held in the traditional capital, Aegae. There, Philip's body, together with his arms and armour, were placed on a great pyre. The Macedonian army solemnly marched past it in full armour. Then Arrhabaeus and Heromenes of Lyncestis were put to death next to the pyre, as were the horses to which Pausanias the assassin had tried to flee. The horses' harnesses, some of the arms of the two men, and the dagger that killed Philip were put on the pyre. It was then set alight.

When the fire had died down, Philip's bones were washed in wine, wrapped in a purple robe, and placed in a gold *larnax* or casket. On its lid was the Macedonian sunburst, the royal emblem, and rosettes. Alexander had already ordered the construction of a large tomb, and the king's body was interred in it. The *larnax* was put inside a stone sarcophagus, to be deposited in state in the tomb (see Plate 9).

Precious gold and silver vessels were also placed in the tomb, as were some of the king's arms and armour. On a wooden bench was a series of small ivory heads of the members of the royal family (see Plate 10). The tomb would be sealed with earth covering it in the form of a large mound or tumulus as protection. On top of the tomb were placed the objects from the pyre, and the corpses of Arrhabaeus and Heromenes were put into the soil that covered it. For a while, the crucified body of Pausanias was hung in front of the tomb entrance, but then taken away as the soil covered it.

As the centuries passed, the location of Philip's tomb was forgotten, as indeed was the site of ancient Aegae. In 1977 the Greek archaeologist Manolis Andronikos excavated a large tumulus at Vergina, which N.G.L.

Hammond identified with Aegae. Inside, he discovered several chamber tombs, some of which had been looted. One had not been touched, which is called Tomb II. It was of a barrel vault construction, and had two chambers, a large one and a small one. When he penetrated the large (main) chamber, a sea of glittering gold and silver greeted him.[3] These were art works of the highest quality, including an exquisite gold wreath that alone proves the high skill of the Macedonians in metal working. A stone sarcophagus and several ivory heads, each about one inch high, scattered on the floor were also inside. When he removed the top of the sarcophagus he saw a gold *larnax* with the royal sunburst on the lid.

Andronikos knew that he had discovered a royal tomb, but he was still unsure whose it was. Two of the ivory heads though had a striking resemblance to Philip and Alexander. The skeletal remains in the *larnax* were subjected to analysis, and found to have traces of purple cloth and wine on them. Forensic scientists in England reconstructed the skull, which showed severe damage around the right eye (see Plate 11).[4] This was consistent with Philip's being wounded by an arrow there during the siege of Methone in 354. After lying undisturbed for almost two millennia it seemed that Philip's tomb had been found.[5]

Or had it? Almost as quickly as the occupant was identified as Philip came a wave of scepticism.[6] For one thing, the tomb had two chambers, the main chamber, with the *larnax* in it, and an ante-chamber, in which were the bones of a young woman. The main chamber has no elaborate decorations on the wall, which are just rough stucco, in contrast to rich paintings in the ante-chamber. Further, the main chamber was hastily sealed, and some armour was left lying against the door on the outside. It has also been argued that a fresco of a Royal Hunt scene painted above the door of the tomb postdates Philip's death by a considerable time.[7] Not even the reconstructed skull of Philip II, with the clinching trauma to the right eye, was accepted. As occupants of the tomb Philip III Arrhidaeus and his wife Eurydice (killed in 317) were put forward.

However, the ante-chamber was built onto the main chamber. In other words, it postdates it. Philip III and Eurydice were buried together in a planned double burial – thus, we would expect both chambers of their tomb to have been built at the same time. The female bones could just as easily be those of Philip's last wife, Cleopatra, who died after him. Hence, her chamber would postdate that of her husband. The fresco on which so much weight is rightly put is badly deteriorated, and could well depict not Alexander's successors but Philip on horseback about to kill a lion, with Alexander in the centre galloping to help him. In front of them and on foot are the Royal Pages, the youths who attended the king from the ages of 14 to 18.

The obvious signs of haste in closing the main tomb and the lack of decoration on its walls tie in with the situation of the time. Alexander had to bury his father quickly so that he could attend to the threats to his position and to a revolt of the Greeks (see below). Further, one of his last plans was to build a magnificent tomb to his father to rival the greatest pyramid. He died before he could set that plan in motion. However, it clearly shows that he did not intend the tomb at Vergina to be Philip's final resting place, hence there was little point in finishing it properly. After his death, of course, it was left as it was.

The controversy will never be solved, and the brief and select treatment above hardly does it justice. The finds are stunning, and no photograph can do them justice. They were originally housed in the Museum, at Thessaloniki, but have now been moved to the new museum on site at Vergina.

Alexander may not have faced any trouble from his own people, but it was a different story with the Greeks. An Athenian general operating in the north, Charidemus, was the first to send news of Philip's death to Athens. Exactly what Charidemus was up to is anyone's guess, but he seems to have been involved in some sort of guerilla warfare to protect Athens' interests. The story goes that when Demosthenes heard of Philip's death he dressed himself in his best festival clothes and rejoiced openly in the streets. We should not be so surprised at his behaviour given his fervent patriotism and staunch resistance to Philip. However, his only daughter, on whom he doted, had died a week earlier. Normal custom was to mourn for a month, but Demosthenes broke it. His action gives us a real insight into the hatred that he felt for Philip.

When news of Philip's death was confirmed, the Greeks revolted from the League of Corinth. Some states like Athens merely voiced discontent, while others took militant action. Thus the Thessalians seized the Tempe Pass and prepared to resist Alexander if he marched on them. The Ambracians expelled the Macedonian garrison and oligarchy installed by Philip as part of his 337 settlement. The Greeks' action cannot have come out of the blue. Philip had imposed Macedonian rule over Greece. He had enforced a Common Peace agreement to control them. Greek states did not want to be in this situation, for they believed absolutely in their autonomy.

Alexander could not allow this attack on the Macedonian hegemony of Greece. Anyone who doubted his abilities now that he had graduated from heir to king did not do so for long. Once he had gained the support of the army and established his position in Macedonia, he turned to deal with the Greeks. His father had believed in diplomacy rather than fighting first, but Alexander was no Philip and in any case he did not have the time to waste on diplomacy. He had to show the Greeks that he was king.

Our sources are frustratingly quiet about the details of this revolt, perhaps because it did not last long. They tell us that he won over some cities by diplomacy, others by striking fear into them and the remainder by the use of force. Alexander marched south from Pella along the coast road through Methone and Pydna and into Thessaly. There he faced his only serious resistance, when his route was blocked by the Thessalians' control of the Tempe Pass (between Olympus and Ossa). Alexander simply marched around them, climbing Mount Ossa, and came down on them from the rear. That was the end of Thessalian resistance.

In the pro-Macedonian town of Larissa he held a meeting of the Thessalian League. It acknowledged him its President (as his father had been) and promised him cavalry. Then he pushed on to Thermopylae, where he convened a meeting of the Amphictyonic Council. This council was composed of a number of Greek states and was primarily responsible for the management of the Delphic oracle. It wielded considerable political power, and it too pledged its support. In return, Alexander made concessions. For example, when an apologetic embassy came to him from the Ambracians, he did not punish the city but allowed it to return to a democracy.

Alexander had won the support of the northern and central Greeks. The southern Greeks, especially the Athenians, were next. The Athenians sent an embassy to him with an apology and pledged their support. He decided not to go there, but instead travelled directly to Corinth. It was crucial to reimpose the League of Corinth and so reunite all the Greeks under his hegemony. At Corinth he called a meeting of the Greek states and the League was resurrected. At the same time, he announced that his father's last plan, the invasion of Persia, would go ahead and for the reasons that Philip gave.[8] The Greeks had little choice but to endorse his decision, and Megara went so far as to confer honorary citizenship on him. Its action would have pleased Alexander, for the Megarians had done the same thing for his ancestor Heracles.

Within a few months of his accession, Macedonia was again in control of Greece.

Only Sparta refused to join the League of Corinth, again refusing to acknowledge Macedon's hegemony. Alexander, like his father, left it alone. If he thought that Sparta was a spent force he miscalculated. In 331 the Spartan king Agis III went to war against Macedonia and appealed for help from all the Greeks. Although almost no one responded and Agis was defeated and killed the following year, Alexander was not going to miscalculate again. Probably after Agis' defeat Sparta was forced to join the League.

At Corinth Alexander made a point of meeting one of the most famous men of the time, the Cynic philosopher Diogenes. He had chosen to give up a normal lifestyle and to live as simply as possible, to get back to nature. He wore no, or very little, clothing and lived in a barrel. For his manner of living, he was nicknamed the dog, *kuon*, because he lived 'like a dog'. From this Greek word comes the term Cynic. Diogenes used to walk through city streets with a lighted lamp by day looking for a 'good man' – one that was morally good, that is. He was very quick with witty and often deprecating remarks. For example, when he was asked which wine he preferred the most, he replied 'someone else's'. When a man was boasting of his swimming ability Diogenes wondered why he boasted about what 'any good dolphin could do'.

When Alexander met Diogenes he asked what he could do for him. The philosopher was not in his barrel at the time, but was lying on the ground sunbathing. The king was standing in the sun, and so casting a shadow over him. Diogenes replied that Alexander could move as he was blocking the sun. Alexander is reported to have said that if he were not Alexander he would want to be Diogenes. Whether Alexander actually met Diogenes is not known for certain; the account could be the product of a later writer. However, it is a nice story, and again has been a source of illustrative fodder, as a lithograph of Alexander and Diogenes by H. Daumier in 1842 shows (see Plate 12).

With Greece secure, Alexander returned to his capital at Pella for the winter and presumably to hone the plan for the invasion of Persia. He also planned a campaign in the spring against the Triballi, who lived in the Danube basin. The purpose for this was twofold. First, revenge. Philip II had clashed with the Triballi during his conquest of Thrace. As he returned from a campaign in Scythia in 339 they had attacked him, wounding him severely, and seized some of his booty. Whether Philip planned a revenge mission against them is unknown, but Alexander certainly did. It would also help prepare his troops for more formidable fighting in Asia.

Another, more pressing, reason was personal. It was necessary for Alexander to win the confidence of his men in battle. True, at the age of 16, as heir to the throne, he had defeated the Maedians on the upper Strymon. But now he was king, and there had been potential opposition to his accession. Hence the present campaign would suit his purpose well, and assert his authority as king before the invasion of Asia. That Alexander was exploiting this campaign for these ends is shown by the composition of the force he took with him: about 20,000, including 5,000 cavalry, and almost all Macedonian.

Alexander set out from Amphipolis in spring 335, leaving Antipater behind as his deputy in Macedonia. This act foreshadowed the role given to Antipater when Alexander left for Asia the next year, and perhaps Alexander even at this stage intended that Antipater would remain behind when he left for Asia. The king also took advantage of this campaign to deal with some tribes in Thrace who had reasserted their independence. They occupied a pass over Mount Haemus, and as the Macedonian army approached they developed a deadly plan of attack. They set up wagons to roll from their superior position on the pass down on the army below. The Thracians would then take advantage of the ensuing disruption in the ranks of the phalanx to attack.

It was a good plan, but they were facing Alexander, whose quick thinking was extraordinary. He realised what the Thracians intended to do with the wagons, and immediately hit upon a plan so that his army would escape harm from them. As the army marched into the narrow pass and the wagons thundered down towards it, the ranks of the phalanx opened where they could to let the wagons rumble through, harming no one. Where the line could not open up because of the narrow terrain, the men, following Alexander's orders, lay flat or knelt on the ground, locking their shields over their heads. The wagons rolled harmlessly over them, apart from causing a few headaches.

Alexander's plan was a bold one, and in 331 at the Battle of Gaugamela he would employ a similar one of opening up the line against the Persian scythed chariots. His strategy required the men to stand fast as they saw death and destruction bearing down on them. That they did so is not merely a testament to their training and fearlessness, but also a tribute to their confidence in Alexander as commander.

With the threat from the wagons over, Alexander led the charge against the Thracians. He was at the front with the Agrianians (a tribe in the Upper Strymon region, around Sofia) and the hypaspists (the special corps of Macedonian shield-bearing infantry). Against that front, and with the phalanx's wall of deadly sarissas bearing down, 1,500 of the enemy were killed. Those who did not die fled, leaving behind their women and children. These Alexander captured and sent back to Macedonia as slaves, along with a substantial amount of captured booty.

Pushing further north, the Macedonian army met the Triballi a few days' march from the Danube. It was necessary to defeat the Triballi in pitched battle, for which he needed open ground, but they were ensconced in various defensive positions. He sent a small contingent of archers and slingers to fire at them in the hope of luring them out. His hope was realised. The Triballi rushed this contingent in force, and so fell neatly into Alexander's trap. There, on open ground, they found the full army waiting.

Another battle ensued in which 3,000 of the enemy were killed thanks to the power of the Macedonian infantry and cavalry. Alexander's army was reputed to have lost a mere 11 cavalry and 41 infantry. The Triballi fled for refuge to one of the islands on the main stream of the Danube called Peuce, where they found a force of Thracians already there. The island was naturally protected by rocks, and the fast-flowing river and high banks made a frontal assault difficult. In fact, Alexander tried to land on Peuce and was beaten back by the natural defences. The last thing he could afford was a costly loss of men, so for the moment he had to wait. Since he had the Triballi blockaded on the island he could prevent supplies reaching them, so it would only be a matter of time before they surrendered.

About this time, the Getae from the north Danube plain came down to the far bank of the Danube. They did not seem to be intent on attacking Alexander, although the force was large: 10,000 infantry and 4,000 cavalry. Since it was harvest time, there were plenty of crops to be had, and Alexander decided the Getae would try to get supplies to those on Peuce. He crossed the Danube one night with 4,000 infantry and 1,500 cavalry prepared to do battle, but they fled at his approach. His men then destroyed the crops, and Alexander offered sacrifices to Zeus the Saviour, Heracles and the Danube itself.

The Getae did not formally confront Alexander, as the Triballi had, and there was plenty of distance between them and the Macedonians. Also, it would have been hard for them to send supplies to those on Peuce. Why then did Alexander go after them? Was he so active that he could not wait patiently for the Triballi to surrender? Perhaps. However, Philip's ghost may play a part. Philip had campaigned in the same areas as Alexander was in, but he had not crossed the Danube. Alexander did, and significantly he offered sacrifices for his success. If Alexander intended to eclipse his father's achievements, then he was already on his way.

When Alexander returned to his camp he was greeted by embassies from the surrounding areas and farther afield. These included Celts from the Balkans, as well as from the Thracians on Peuce and Syrmus, king of the Triballi. Evidently, the siege of Peuce had proved too much for those on the island. Alexander responded favourably, and a treaty of peace and friendship was agreed. Under this, Macedon would receive an annual tribute and troops when needed. The Triballi remained allies of Macedon from then on, even committing soldiers for the invasion of Asia the following year. Philip's son had proved himself, as an avenger of his father and as king in battle and in diplomacy.

Alexander's first campaign as king had been successful. It was the shape of things to come. He had moved with a speed reminiscent of that of his father: another shape of things to come. And, like his father, he had shown that he could think fast on his feet and adapt as circumstances demanded. He had learned well. On his way back to Pella he stayed with his ally Langarus, king of the Agrianians, in the Upper Strymon region. These tough people time and again proved themselves loyal to Alexander, and the king was always careful to court their favour.

As Alexander and his troops were enjoying the success of their two-month campaign, there came the worrying news that the Illyrians in the north and west had revolted and were poised to invade Macedonia.

The Illyrian revolt had a personal element to it. It was centred in the region of Lyncestis, and less than a year earlier Alexander had executed Arrhabaeus and Heromenes of Lyncestis. Cleitus, the formidable King of the Dardani (around Kosovo), and one of his father's old enemies, was behind the revolt, and he had made an agreement with Glaucias, King of the Taulantii (around Tirana) and with the Autariatae (around Bosnia). Cleitus had persuaded the Autariatae to attack Alexander on his march to meet him, so the Macedonian army faced two hostile and powerful forces. In the meantime, an army from the Taulantii would march to Cleitus, so that the Macedonians would eventually have to face this larger, combined one. Alexander's very kingship depended on his defeating the Illyrians. He knew it, and so did they. And he rose to the challenge.

Speed again characterised Alexander's campaign. He foiled Cleitus's plan of blocking the army between the Illyrians and the Autariatae by having his ally Langarus invade the territory of the Autariatae and defeat them. He was well rewarded, Alexander even promising his sister Cynnana to him when he returned to Pella. At that time, she was still married to Amyntas. However, Alexander had earmarked him for execution when he returned, and hence he could unscrupulously promise this soon-to-be widow to the Agrianian king. Langarus never took his reward, for after returning home he grew sick and died.

Alexander drove through Paeonia (Skopje) and then south to the plain of modern Florina, the centre of ancient Lyncestis. Cleitus had occupied a fortress in Pelium, close to the western border of Macedonia. Alexander duly besieged it, but was forced to withdraw when troops from Cleitus's other ally, the Taulantii, arrived on the scene and occupied the surrounding mountains. Alexander's speed was shown by the fact that the Taulantians, who had been approached by Cleitus well before Alexander knew of the Illyrian threat, arrived *after* the Macedonian king. Moreover, he had foiled the second part of Cleitus's plan because he prevented the two forces joining together.

Alexander's withdrawal was understandable, not least because the siege of Pelium was getting nowhere. He also needed supplies, and so he sent Philotas, the son of Parmenion, with some troops to get corn from the fertile plains of the north. Then the king discovered from scouts that the Taulantians had not posted sentries around their camp. They could be caught off guard, and so he decided on a surprise attack. Two days after he had broken off the siege he led a night attack on their camp. They were caught completely by surprise, and either fled into the mountains or managed to struggle to Pelium. Resistance collapsed, and Glaucias surrendered. He was allowed to keep his throne, but became a vassal to Alexander.

There was no time to capture Cleitus or to negotiate a treaty with the Illyrians because Thebes in Boeotia suddenly revolted and called on the Greeks to end Macedonian rule. Alexander was forced to deal with that potentially dangerous revolt immediately. Cleitus managed to escape, but he did not regroup his forces and the Illyrians remained on amicable terms with Macedon for the rest of Alexander's reign. They even sent a contingent of troops for the invasion of Persia. The sight of the Macedonian army in action, along with the tactical skill of Alexander at its head, was enough of a deterrent to ensure Illyria remained passive. Alexander may well have allowed Cleitus to retain his throne, but as his vassal.

Now we move to the darkest episode of Alexander's early reign.

Under Philip's settlement of 337 a pro-Macedonian oligarchy and a garrison had been installed in Thebes and many democrats had been exiled. A rebellious (and clearly democratic) faction in Thebes brought the exiles back in September 335. Exploiting a rumour that Alexander had died in Illyria, they persuaded the Thebans to overthrow the oligarchy, besiege the garrison on the Cadmea (the Acropolis of Thebes), and solicit help from the Greeks to liberate Greece and to bring down the 'tyrant' of Greece.[9]

The revolt was supported by several Greek states, including Athens at first, and was backed by money from Darius III, the Great King of Persia, who had come to the throne in the same year. Evidently, he saw in Alexander's planned invasion of Asia a threat too serious to ignore. The revolt was not something that Alexander could afford to take lightly. It was an attack on the constitutional machinery of the League of Corinth and its panhellenic invasion of Persia. A signatory of the Common Peace could not legally revolt, and if it did it could face a combined League army bearing down on it. Alexander thus had legality on his side. He was also impatient to invade Asia, and Thebes was defying him and so costing him time. For that it had to be punished. The guilty party in his mind could never redeem itself.

From Illyria Alexander rushed south, with some 30,000 infantry and 300 cavalry. He was suspicious of Athens and wanted to stop the Theban revolt becoming more widespread. Certainly, if the Athenians and

Thebans joined forces the coalition would have interfered with his invasion plan. In the end, Athens did not support Thebes, and only Elis and Aetolia offered positive aid. Arcadia deployed an army, but it waited at the isthmus to monitor events.

Alexander marched 250 miles in 13 days,[10] through Mount Grammus, Mount Pindus and Mount Cambunia, stopping for only a day at Pelinna in Thessaly to give his army a respite. In those days, and especially through that rough terrain, that was fast. So fast, in fact, that the Thebans did not believe it was actually him when he stood before their gates. At this point, if not a little before, the Athenians withdrew their support (unscrupulously keeping the money from Darius), leaving the Thebans to fend for themselves.

The Macedonians outnumbered the Thebans, but the latter were in an excellent defensive position. The Cadmea formed part of the city's southern wall and the Thebans had also enlisted the support of slaves and metics (resident aliens) to boost their numbers. The Macedonian garrison was still besieged on the Cadmea, so the Thebans took steps to prevent Alexander getting to it. They reinforced the southern section of the wall by the Cadmea with a double palisade, one behind the other. If they could hold off Alexander there was always the chance of reinforcements arriving from other Greek states and of the garrison being used as a bargaining tool.

Exactly how the Macedonian attack began is controversial. Some sources say that Alexander himself attacked the palisade with a substantial force of archers and two battalions of the phalanx. Another source has it that Perdiccas jumped the gun and attacked first, thus forcing Alexander and the Macedonians to follow him. Whichever is true, the Theban infantry drove back the Macedonians; they lost 70 archers, and Perdiccas was seriously wounded in the space between the two palisades.

Then Alexander himself with his hypaspists and royal guard (agema) joined the action. The Thebans fought hard, and with substantial losses, against the Macedonians, but were eventually overcome and retreated inside the gates. That allowed the Macedonians to clear the walls of defenders and then smash their way through them and into the city. As more Macedonians entered the city a contingent liberated the besieged garrison on the Cadmea. The initial panic turned to horror as the Thebans realised their end was in sight. After some street fighting they prepared for a last stand at the Temple of Amphion.

Carnage ensued as Alexander's men and his Greek allies, namely the Phocians, Plataeans, and other Boeotians who had suffered at Thebes's hands in the past, went on the rampage. Five hundred Macedonians were said to have died in the Thebans' last stand, but 6,000 Thebans were killed and 30,000 were taken prisoner and enslaved that day. Worse was to come.

Alexander referred the punishment of Thebes to those state representatives of the League of Corinth who were with him at the siege. They urged Thebes's total destruction on the grounds that during the Persian Wars Thebes had allied with Persia, Greece's common enemy. This was a topical charge given the upcoming panhellenic invasion of Persia.

At face value, Alexander's referral showed that he treated the revolt not as a personal attack on him or on Macedon, but as a breach of the terms of the Common Peace. The League of Corinth, by which Macedon controlled Greece, had to be taken seriously, especially with Alexander so close to departure for Asia. The Theban revolt would allow him to set an example to other Greek states that they had to adhere to the Common Peace – or else. The ancient sources indicate this was his motive in destroying Thebes. His action, says Diodorus Siculus, writing in the late first century BC, 'presented possible rebels among the Greeks with a terrible warning'. Plutarch, in the late first century AD, states that 'Alexander's principal object in permitting the sack of Thebes was to frighten the rest of the Greeks into submission by making a terrible example.'[11]

Behind the scenes, Alexander did take Thebes's revolt as personal. While he was concerned to make an example to other states, he did not refer Thebes's fate to the entire League Council but only to those states that were with him. These states were Thespiae, Phocis, Plataea and Orchomenus, all of which had suffered terribly at the hands of Thebes in the past. Plataea, Thespiae and Orchomenus had been destroyed by Thebes in the 370s and 360s (but revived by Philip II after Chaeronea), and Thebes had been Phocis's bitter enemy in the Third Sacred War of 355–346. It was clearly payback time, and Alexander knew those states would react as they did. His use of the League, then, was cynical and manipulative.

He razed Thebes to the ground, sparing only the house of the poet Pindar (who had been dead for over a century) and his descendants. Perhaps this was because of Pindar's encomium on his ancestor, Alexander I Philhellene. Thebes's territory was then divided among neighbouring states, those Thebans who had fled were cursed, and the king seized the treasury.

Tales of Thebes's fate are found in a variety of sources from Alexander's time to the reign of the emperor Diocletian in the fourth century AD. The effect that Alexander's action had on the Greeks is vividly demonstrated by the third-century historian and orator Hegesias of Magnesia. He has several references to Thebes's destruction, but one stands out:

'Alexander, in sacking Thebes you acted no differently than if Zeus took away the moon from its share in the sky. There is left to me the sun, Athens. These two cities were the eyes of Greece. Hence I am anxious about the one left now. One of these two eyes, the city of Thebes, has been plucked out.'[12]

Alexander's punishment, though, did the trick. Apart from the abortive war of Agis III of Sparta from 331 to 330, Greece remained passive until the king died in 323.

The story goes that during the looting of Thebes the captain of a Thracian company, 'neither civil nor sober but rude and mad' according to one source,[13] entered the home of a Theban lady, Timoclea. Her brother Theagenes had commanded the Theban phalanx (perhaps even the Sacred Band itself) at the Battle of Chaeronea. After eating her out of house and home he raped her, and then threatened to kill her unless she handed over her valuables to him. She calmly told him that she had ordered her maids to throw her silver bowls, gold and money down a well so that they would not fall into Macedonian hands. She led him to the well, and when he had clambered down to the bottom she and her maids stoned him to death.

When she was brought before Alexander she remained defiant and justified her actions:

'Theagenes was my brother, who was a general at Chaeronea. He died fighting against you in defence of Greek freedom so that we might not suffer an outrage such as this. Seeing I have suffered an outrage unworthy of my rank, I refuse not to die. It is better to do so than to experience another night like the last, which awaits me unless you forbid it.'

Those who heard her apparently burst into tears, except Alexander, who was so impressed by her spirit and eloquence that he spared her life (see Plate 13).

Alexander did not need to make any moves against those states that had supported Thebes. The Arcadians executed those who had spoken in support of Thebes; the Eleans welcomed back the pro-Macedonians they had exiled and the Aetolians sent embassies to him begging his forgiveness. That left the Athenians.

They too resorted to diplomatic means, sending an embassy to Alexander to congratulate him for his successes in the Illyrian campaign and, contemptibly, for his punishment of the Thebans. A disgusted Alexander demanded that several Athenian politicians, including Demosthenes, Lycurgus and Hyperides, be handed over to him. Demosthenes in no small panic made the analogy of sheep surrendering their dogs to the wolves, 'comparing himself and his fellow orators to dogs fighting to defend the people, and calling Alexander "the Macedonian arch wolf" '.[14] The rhetoric might have been successful, but the general Phocion bluntly advised the people to hand over the men or the city might face Alexander's wrath. It was fast becoming common knowledge that Alexander did not take kindly to those who defied him, and the destruction of Thebes shocked and panicked the Greeks.

Fortunately for Demosthenes another orator, Demades, went to Alexander and persuaded him to rescind his demand. However, Alexander did insist on the surrender of Charidemus, the general who had been operating against his father at the end of his reign and who had sent news of his death to Athens. His action could be interpreted as a sign of his willingness to compromise. In reality, however, he could afford to retract his demand, for with Thebes destroyed and two of the 'fetters of Greece', Corinth and Chalcis, cities of great strategic importance, in his hands, Athens was isolated.

He had also sown some seeds of fear into the minds of his opponents in Athens, especially Demosthenes. He had asked for their surrender, and the people were prepared to hand them over to him. Then he changed his mind. However, there was always the danger that Alexander might demand their surrender again. Perhaps this explains why Demosthenes was not as outspoken as he was during Philip's reign. It was a deterrent that the Athenians were prepared to use as late as 323 against Demosthenes in an effort to curry favour with the king (see Chapter 13).

Alexander could finally return home. On the way there, he spent nine days at Dium, the Macedonian religious centre in the foothills of Mount Olympus. There he celebrated a magnificent festival, founded by Archelaus, in honour of the Muses and Zeus Olympus. One of the highlights was a number of banquets held in his royal tent, which was so large that it could accommodate 100 couches. When he finally got to Pella, he held games in honour of Zeus Olympus at Aegae. It must have been a sobering time for him, for it was at this festival in 336 that his father had been murdered.

No one could now doubt Alexander's mettle as king. However, he did one more thing to cement his position and how he saw himself. He issued coinage in his own name. Coinage was essential for the Macedonian economy, and Alexander continued his father's gold and silver coinage with Philip's name on them. In 335 coins with Alexander's own iconography on them began to be struck. There was a small-denomination silver coin, which had on the obverse the head of a young Heracles and on the reverse an eagle standing on a thunderbolt. The eagle and thunderbolt were associated with Zeus. Bronze coins also appeared with the head of a young Heracles on the obverse and Heracles's quiver and club on the reverse. The symbolism is obvious: Alexander was setting himself up as a new Heracles under the protection of Zeus.

Asia was next. Alexander spent the winter in final preparations, probably with Antipater and Parmenion, whom he had recalled from the advance force in Asia. By spring he was set to go.

One thing he did not do was to marry and produce an heir. There is no question that he neglected his duty here as king, and, if we can believe the story, both Parmenion and Antipater advised him to delay the invasion of Asia until he had an heir. Alexander ignored them. At age 22, the Homeric Alexander was more eager to fight and to gain glory than to think about his dynasty. His failure to marry (until too late) helped his empire to disintegrate on his death.

5

The Very Gates of Asia

In spring (probably May) 334 Alexander was ready to invade Asia. Antipater was to be guardian (*epitropos*) of Greece and Macedonia, and to act as deputy *Hegemon* of the League of Corinth, in Alexander's absence. He was certainly the best choice and, as events would show, more than competent to handle the task. There were no guarantees that once Alexander had left Greece would remain passive. Antipater was not Alexander, and at least half of the Macedonian army would leave with the king.

In Athens, Demosthenes was still intent on a policy of opposition. He had sent letters to Attalus in Asia when Philip was killed, calling on him to revolt. Now his policy switched from Athenian-led resistance, as in the days of Philip II, to the hope that Alexander would be defeated in Persia. The contemporary orator Aeschines tells us that Demosthenes had hoped that 'Alexander would be trampled under the hoofs of the Persian cavalry at Issus'.[1] He continued in this belief after the Battle of Issus (in 333), but saw it die at the Battle of Gaugamela in 331.[2] If Alexander died in Persia, then the Macedonian hegemony of Greece would die with him. Thus, Antipater had to live with 'worst-case' scenarios every day of his life, and he did so brilliantly.[3]

Alexander's departure had originally surprised Demosthenes, who had said that he would never leave Macedonia. Alexander may not have had any choice if Macedonia were on the verge of bankruptcy at the end of his father's reign. We are told that on the eve of his invasion money was in short supply: 'He had not more than seventy talents. Duris speaks of supplies for only thirty days, and Onesicritus says he also owed two hundred talents.'[4] Moreover, the recent campaigns in Greece, the Balkans and then against Thebes must have cost him dearly. He may even have had to borrow from his Companions – his presents of tracts of land in Macedonia to them may not reflect his generosity but his giving the only thing he had left to secure loans.[5]

It was of course not cheap to maintain an army. A Macedonian hypaspist (an elite shield-bearing infantryman) was paid one drachma a day and a cavalryman three drachmas. A Greek hoplite was paid slightly less, five obols per day (one drachma = six obols), as was a Greek cavalryman at two drachmas and three obols per day. Alexander would have paid the Macedonians and Balkan troops himself, while the Greeks paid their own troops. A mercenary soldier was paid monthly, but the rate of pay is not precisely known. In his first speech against Philip (*Philippic* 1) of 351, Demosthenes called for a force of 8,000 mercenaries, and at half-pay gave the cost as 240 talents per year. One talent is 6,000 drachmas, and so one mercenary would receive 15 drachmas per month (half rate) or 30 at the full rate. That figure is approximate, and the rate of pay surely increased by 334, but at least it gives us some idea.

Thus, the wealth of Persia may have been seen as the only hope of salvation by Philip as his expenditure increased and income decreased, especially from the Macedonian mines. Economic reasons, then, were important, but we must not discount Alexander's personal lust for glory and his love of a good fight. Plus, here was his chance to win the military renown he so desperately sought and to outdo his father. The bottom line is that if Macedonia had been the wealthiest state in the known world, Alexander would still have invaded Persia.

The king must have felt his heart quickening when he surveyed his large invasion force of about 48,100 soldiers and 6,100 cavalry.[6] The Macedonian contingent of 12,000 infantry and 1,800 Companion Cavalry was less than half, so the reliance on the allies and on Greek mercenaries (5,000 of these) was obvious. There was also a fleet of 120 warships and transport vessels, with a total crew complement of about 38,000. Sixty of these were Macedonian, and their crew of 6,000 came from the Chalcidice. In addition, there would have been merchant and other support vessels.[7]

Although Alexander's own troops numbered less than half of the entire army, he had still depleted much of the available Macedonian manpower. He left Antipater with about 1,500 cavalry (1,000 of which was Companion) and 12,000 infantry, which would put him under pressure. If he were faced by another insurrection from Greece his resources would be severely stretched. That, in fact, was the case for a time when Agis III of Sparta went to war in 331 (see Chapter 8).

The king set off from Pella for the Hellespont (Dardanelles), separating Europe from Asia, as it does today, covering the 300 miles in 20 days. The entire army did not set off from Pella with him. Contingents from the Balkan regions met up with the Macedonians at Amphaxatis, and further east at Amphipolis it was joined by Parmenion with the contingent from

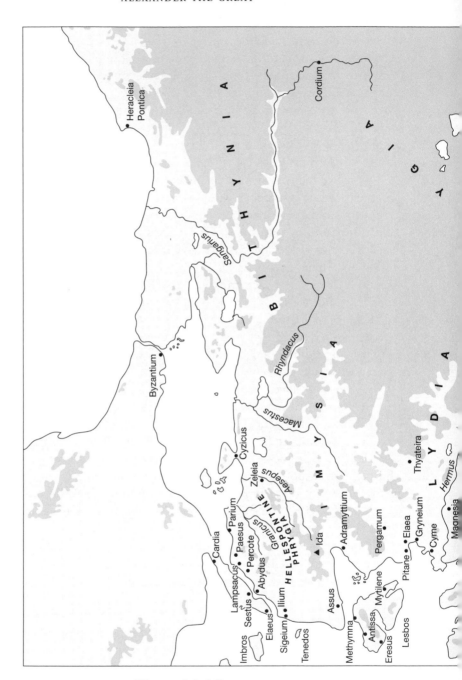

Western Asia Minor
Redrawn from Bosworth, A. B. (1988) *Conquest and Empire: The Reign of*
Alexander the Great (pub Cambridge University Press), Map 2 © Cambridge
University Press 1988, reproduced with permission.

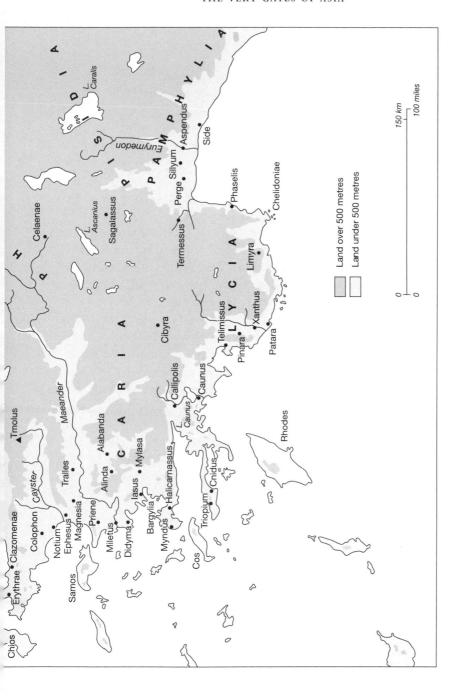

Land over 500 metres

Land under 500 metres

0

150 km

0

100 miles

Greece and the Greek mercenaries. The fleet also linked up with the land force at Amphipolis. Then the combined army marched to Sestus on the Hellespont.

A force as large as this one took a while to cross the Hellespont, during which it was at the mercy of the numerically larger Persian fleet – if the latter had been there. The Persians missed an excellent opportunity to severely damage the invasion force. Was this an indication that they underestimated Alexander? Or, as was the case before the Battle of Granicus, was this the result of confusion and contradiction between too many Persian commanders (see below)?

Alexander never liked to waste time. While the bulk of his army was making its crossing he sped off to Elaeus (the 'Place of Olives'), on the southern tip of the Thracian Chersonese (Gallipoli). From here, centuries earlier, the Greek army under Agamemnon had sailed to recapture Helen from Troy, thus sparking the fabled Trojan War. At Elaeus he sacrificed at the tomb of Protesilaus ('First-jumper'), who had commanded the contingent from Thessaly in the Trojan War. He had been the first to jump onto Asian soil and the first to be killed by a Trojan, hence his name. After setting up an altar, the king sailed across the Hellespont. Halfway across it, Alexander sacrificed a bull in honour of Poseidon and poured a libation from a gold cup to the Nereids, the Nymphs of the sea.

Alexander's sacrifices were not random acts to pass the time, and, typically, combined political symbolism with heroic symbolism. Among other things, in 480 the invading Persian army had ransacked the shrine of Protesilaus, and then gone on to loot Athens. The invasion now was to seek revenge for Persian actions against Greece, especially Athens. Moreover, there was a story that Protesilaus had voluntarily sacrificed himself for the good of the mission because he knew that the first Greek to land was fated to be killed. This was a heroic story that appealed greatly to Alexander. That is why, when he crossed the Hellespont, he jumped out of his ship in full armour, like Protesilaus before him, and threw a spear into Asian soil.

More significantly, his action and the words he is said to have uttered, 'I accept Asia from the gods', showed that he saw Asia as spear-won territory. He was out for more than just revenge. The young king wanted all Asia for his empire, a significant difference from the mandate of the League of Corinth: liberate the Greeks of Asia Minor and punish the Persians. Nowhere were Alexander's aims more obvious than a year later at Gordium, when he undid the fabled Gordian knot (see below). Whoever did that was destined to be ruler of Asia.

When he had crossed safely, Alexander set up altars to Zeus, Athena and Heracles as a thanks offering. He was now in Homer's country of the

Trojan War, where his heroes had fought and died. And Alexander had come as a young Achilles. He continued to court the favour of the gods and his heroic ancestors by sacrificing with oil at the tombs of Achilles and Ajax, said to have been just outside Troy (modern Hisarlik). He and Hephaestion, his most trusted of boyhood friends, then ran a race in the nude around the tombs of Achilles and Patroclus, cut their hair and laid a wreath. For Alexander, the adrenaline rush from being at Achilles' tomb must have been enormous. It would have heightened his resolve to be another Achilles in the fighting that lay ahead.

Alexander's sacrifice at Achilles' tomb became a model for heroic piety in the Renaissance and later periods, and was an inspiration for artists such as Fontebasso in the eighteenth century, whose painting of Alexander sacrificing at Achilles's tomb is magnificent (see Plate 14).

In the Temple to Athena in Troy itself Alexander sacrificed to the Trojan Athena and to Priam, who had been king during the Trojan War. When the Greeks took Troy, Priam had fled for refuge to the Altar of Zeus, but had been sacrilegiously slain by Neoptolemus. Alexander's actions were important. Athena was the goddess of war, hence it was imperative to have her on the side of the invaders. It was also imperative for Priam to smile favourably on the venture, for Alexander was descended from Neoptolemus. If Priam were to seek revenge on a relation of his murderer, then the entire Macedonian invasion would be in danger, hence Alexander's sacrifice (at the same Altar of Zeus) was to appease him. Alexander may have genuinely believed in the motive for his action. At the same time, we cannot rule out that it was a gesture to alleviate any fears on the part of his men, for they would know of their king's connection to Priam's assassin – and its possible implications for the invasion.

Inside the temple hung arms that were said to be those of Achilles. In the *Alexander Romance* they were apparently nondescript, but it was their symbolism that was important. Alexander took Achilles' shield, putting his own in its place. Then it was time to do what he had come to do: defeat the Persians.

The Persian army, including 20,000 cavalry and 20,000 Greek mercenaries at its core, was camped close to the river Aesepus, near Zelea (Sarikoy), about 20 or so miles from Alexander. This was in the area known as Hellespontine Phrygia, controlled by the Persian satrap Arsites.

Because of the size of the Persian empire, the Great King (the formal title of the Persian monarch) ruled through an administrative structure called satrapies. The empire was divided into a number of regions (satrapies), each one controlled by a satrap. He ruled over his satrapy, and had his own little court. However, he was subservient to the Great

King. Native princes, however, ruled the easterly regions. They had more autonomy but still acknowledged the power and authority of the Great King.

In the Persian camp, strategy was discussed, but for a while it was a case of too many cooks spoiling the broth. The Great King, Darius III, was not present, and so the various generals proposed numerous different strategies. These ranged from fighting a pitched battle to devastating the crops, on which the invading Macedonians were so dependent. The scorched earth plan was put forward by Memnon of Rhodes, who led the Greek mercenaries. He had spent time at the court at Pella, and so had some personal contact with Alexander already. His plan was probably the best, given what he knew of Macedonian fighting tactics; however confusion reigned. Finally, Arsites, who was naturally against crop devastation in his satrapy, convinced a majority of generals to vote for battle. While the Persian infantry was not as well trained as the Macedonian, it did have 20,000 mercenaries. Moreover, the Persian cavalry of about 20,000 was stronger, and so there must have been some confidence of victory.

The Persians moved to a defensive position west of Zelea, above the plain of Adrasteia, through which ran the Granicus River. There it camped on the river's east bank. This strategically effective position blocked Alexander's further advance. Here, at the 'very gates of Asia',[8] the Persians dared Alexander to risk battle. The king in fact was not far away, at a base in Abydus. A reconnaissance mission reported the Persian position to him, and he marched to it, arriving at the Granicus in the evening. He did not take the full complement of his army, but about 13,000 infantry and 5,100 cavalry. Initially, when he reached the west bank of the river, he must have been dismayed by the Persian position and battle line.

The Granicus River was about three feet deep and 80 feet wide (like today), but its western and eastern banks were very steep and around 12 feet high.

There were areas on the banks that had a slope of gravel down to the water, something akin to a ramp. To engage the Persian army Alexander had to lead his army down the west bank, across the flowing river, and up the east bank, with the Persians all the time raining down arrows and javelins on the Macedonians. Had part of the Macedonian phalanx stumbled and fallen, then the entire line would have been in disarray. The invasion, not just the battle, would have been over. There was also the danger that the Persian cavalry, probably situated a little way away behind the infantry line for maximum charging effect, could force back any Macedonians who did manage to cross the river and attack the Persian line. Had Alexander already met his match?

Some of those in the Macedonian army voiced their concern, including the powerful general Parmenion. He advised caution and, since it was almost dusk, to wait until the next day when a plan could be formulated properly. This implies that Alexander had first thought to rush the enemy, a tactic that could have terrible repercussions if it failed – in winter 331 Alexander, then in Persis, rushed an opposing force led by the satrap Ariobarzanes and was beaten back (see Chapter 8). Parmenion's caution, then, was well advised. However, Alexander allegedly responded with the remark that he would never be able to live down the shame from halting at this tiny river after crossing the Hellespont. After this exchange, some sources say that he then dashed into the Granicus, exhorting his army to follow, while others say that he did wait until dawn. Whichever is true does not matter in the end, for Alexander decisively defeated the Persians.

Alexander's strategy was to move fast and to protect the phalanx on both flanks by the cavalry. He stationed himself at the head of the Macedonian cavalry, including most of the Companion Cavalry, on the right. The Thessalian, other Greek and Thracian cavalry, under Parmenion's command, were on the left, and the battalions of the phalanx were in between. The cavalry was arranged ten horses deep, and the infantry line eight men deep. The whole line stretched for a little over a mile (Fig. 2).

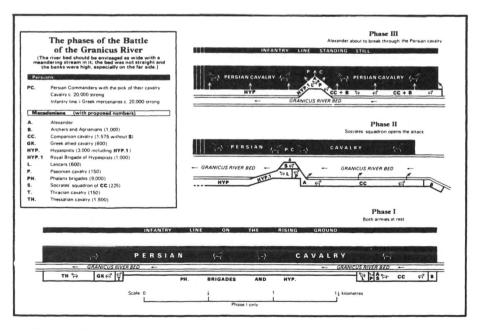

Figure 2. Battle of Granicus: Persian and Macedonian battle lines. From N.G.L. Hammond, *Alexander the Great: King, Commander and Statesman* (1989), p. 76. Reproduced by permission of Duckworth Publishers

The king adhered to this line in the river crossing. Amyntas was sent across first with a battalion. His mission to keep the Persian cavalry at bay. This was the first instance of a new stratagem in battle, the pawn sacrifice.[9] A small cavalry force was used as a pawn to split up the enemy's ranks. Alexander knew that Amyntas would suffer losses, and he did. However, sacrifice was needed to win. Amyntas's force was able to distract the Persian cavalry, allowing Alexander and the right wing to cross the river. It did so in a diagonal line, left to right, so that as it pushed its way up the river bank to the top it was able to regroup as one continuous line. Parmenion, on the left flank, in a mirror-image manoeuvre, achieved the same result. In just a few minutes, the superiority of the Persians' elevated position was gone.[10]

The superb drilling of the Macedonian army now showed itself. Without pause, Alexander led a frontal attack on the Persian army. Never one to hold back, he engaged in the fierce hand-to-hand fighting as the two sides met. Meanwhile, the Persian cavalry succumbed to the Macedonian advance; their commanders were killed, and the cavalry was routed. This left only the Persian and mercenary infantry, which must have been in shock and confusion from the Macedonian onslaught and then the cavalry's flight. Now, the tidal wave of the Macedonian battle line swept towards it, with the infantry phalanx ready to hit it head on and the cavalry surround it on both wings. The commander offered to surrender, but Alexander refused terms. The enemy fought vigorously, but to no avail.

When the carnage ended, 'of the Barbarians, we are told, twenty thousand infantry fell and twenty-five hundred cavalry. But on Alexander's side, Aristobulus says there were thirty-four dead in all, of whom nine were infantry.'[11] The Persian dead included eight commanders, including the son-in-law of Darius III himself. Arsites later committed suicide for the defeat. The odium attached to Greeks fighting against fellow Greeks was shown by the fate of the 2,000 surviving mercenaries. They were sent to work in chains in the Macedonian silver mines for the rest of their (short) lives.

During the fighting, Darius's son-in-law, Mithridates, boldly singled out Alexander, and led a contingent of troops directly against him. As they clashed, Alexander's helmet was shattered, thus exposing a bare and vulnerable head. The Persian Spithridates seized the opportunity to try to kill him. As he raised his sword Cleitus the Black, Commander of the Royal Squadron of Companion Cavalry, slashed off his right arm. It would not be the first time that Alexander's impetuosity or thirst for a fight almost cost him his life. Heroism was one thing; foolishness, another. Who would have commanded the army, and who, given that

Alexander at the time was unmarried and childless, would have succeeded as king?

However, Alexander did not die then. After the battle, he buried his
dead and visited the wounded to listen to their exploits. He must have
heard the same stories time and time again, but that did not stop him from
listening to each. Twenty-five Companion Cavalry had fallen, and
Lysippus was ordered to cast bronze statues of them that were to be set
up at Dium, the Macedonian religious centre in the foothills of Mount
Olympus. Alexander sent gifts to his mother Olympias, and significantly
300 Persian panoplies (sets of armour) to Athens for its patron goddess
Athena, together with a short dedication: 'Alexander son of Philip and all
the Greeks except the Spartans won these spoils of war from the barbarians living in Asia.'[12]

Thus we have a combination of piety and pragmatism. After all,
Alexander had invaded Persia seeking revenge for Athenian losses 150
years previously. The deliberate exclusion of the Spartans in the dedication would further isolate them in Greece. The Battle of Granicus was
fought only against Persian generals and not the Great King. However, it
was Alexander's first victory over the enemy, and his army had proved its
ability on Asian soil.

Alexander was eager to press south, not least because of the potential
danger to Greece from the Persian navy. His own fleet of about 160 ships
was sailing south along the coast of Asia Minor to Ephesus. Rather than
march inland, Alexander made as the basis of his strategy the seizure of
the coastal cities and erosion of Persian power from the west. He quickly
installed his own satrap, Calas, at Dascylium, the capital of Hellespontine
Phrygia, which Parmenion had taken when Arsites committed suicide. He
also saw to it that the tribute previously paid to Darius would now come
to him.

A march of nearly 200 miles followed to Lydia and its capital Sardis.
This was the major city in the western part of the Persian empire. News
of Alexander's victory at Granicus travelled faster than he did, for when
he was still about ten miles away from Sardis its commander, Mithrenes,
surrendered to him. Sardis and (significantly) its treasure were now
Alexander's. If he had needed an abundance of money at the start of his
expedition, he now had it.

Alexander made a point of treating well those who did not defy him.
Mithrenes was not harmed, and he declared Lydia free from Persian rule.
But freedom from Persian rule did not mean autonomy. Alexander could
not allow those areas through which he passed to remain subject to Persia.
Thus, that region, as so many would in his reign, simply swapped the devil
for the deep blue sea. Alexander also gave orders for Lydian youths to be

trained in Macedonian tactics so that they could fight in his army. He would do the same in Lycia, Syria and Egypt. This was one way that he could ensure troop reinforcements, and by 330 these youths were sufficiently well trained to join the army. The gods were not neglected either, for he saw to the building of a temple, and eventual cult, to Zeus, Macedonia's chief god.

Those in Lydia thus continued to be subject to another ruler and to pay tribute to that ruler, like the other places that Alexander liberated from Persian rule. They had their freedom, but at a price now payable to Macedon.

After a short stay in Sardis Alexander headed to Ephesus, travelling the 60-odd miles in about four days. Ephesus already had a history of amicable relations with Macedon, and had erected a statue of Philip II in its temple. The city surrendered to him and Alexander declared its freedom, expelling the pro-Persian oligarchy in favour of a democratic government. He did not leave the people to their own devices though. When some democrats started to kill their opponents, he intervened to end the bloodshed. Ephesus stayed loyal to him. The message was getting through to Persian-controlled cities that surrender meant entry into Alexander's favour. The message was helped a lot by the king's directive that he would replace oligarchies by democracies with an amnesty to all. These towns probably became members of the League of Corinth, hence subject to the Macedonian hegemony. But at least it was not the rule of the 'barbarians'.

The tribute that Ephesus paid to the Great King now went to Alexander. He used part of it to rebuild the Temple of Artemis, which was said to have burned to the ground the same day as he was born (see Chapter 3). He also sacrificed to Artemis and held a religious procession in her honour. The favour of the gods could not be lost.

While he was at Sardis several other cities in Lydia and Caria surrendered to him. So far so good. However, not every city would welcome him with open arms, as he was about to discover.

Still moving southwards, Alexander left Ephesus and arrived at the powerful coastal city of Miletus. For the first time, he was faced with resistance, made even more worrying by the fact that its harbour offered shelter to the returning Persian fleet of 400 ships. Fortunately, the Greek fleet, despite being numerically inferior, was able to take up a position by the island of Lade. This prevented the Persian fleet anchoring at Miletus. Frustrated, it had to sail ten miles away to Cape Mycale. Parmenion, it seems, was anxious to take on the Persian fleet, but Alexander wisely refrained. The fleet was larger than his own, and its Phoenician and Cyprian contingents were not only the strongest but also the best trained.

A Macedonian loss would undo all that had been won to date, and jeopardise his chances of securing the Levant.

Miletus was prepared to open its gates to Alexander only if it could be independent and so make its own arrangements with the Persians and Macedonians. The precedent that this would create was not acceptable to the king. He refused, but the Milesians were adamant. That resistance meant their days were numbered. Alexander now, as so often in his reign, took resistance as personal, and he wanted to even the score. Thus began the siege of Miletus.

The Macedonians charged the city but were easily repelled. Alexander then turned to his siege engines. These were high towers with archers on their tops, who were protected behind reinforced low walls. They fired down a rain of arrows on the defenders of Miletus (or any besieged city), killing them with systematic precision. There was no escape. The Greek fleet had blockaded Miletus from the sea by a line of triremes that stopped the Milesians escaping and prevented the Persian navy helping. Although it sailed to Miletus it could do nothing, and Alexander later sent a force to Mycale, so denying the fleet its safe base. Miletus capitulated relatively swiftly. Philip's sieges had been generally unsuccessful, but Alexander would make sure that either he never failed or he ended a siege on his terms.

The Milesians had a history of opposing Persian domination. During the Ionian revolt of 499–494 Darius had captured the city. Plus, they had surrendered to Alexander before the siege grew protracted. These factors earned them some mercy. The civil population was spared. However, almost all of the military force, which had opposed Alexander from the outset, was put to death. Almost all: an incident occurred that showed Alexander's respect for military valour. About 300 Greek mercenaries were ready to fight to the death. Alexander was impressed. He would have remembered the '300 Spartans' who fought to the last man against the Persians at the Battle of Thermopylae in 480, so he conscripted them into his army. Miletus had to accept a Macedonian garrison and pay tribute to Alexander – for the time being.

It was now autumn, but before he moved further south, Alexander visited Didyma. It was home to the oracle of Apollo and had a spectacular temple to him (see Plate 15).

During the Persian Wars, the priests who administered the site, the Branchidae, had declared their loyalty to Persia and surrendered the treasury to the Great King. The cult statue of Apollo was taken from the temple to Susa, and the Branchidae were moved to an area by the Oxus River in Central Asia. From that time, the oracle at Didyma had fallen silent, and the sacred spring of Apollo there had dried up. When Alexander arrived, the story goes, the spring began to flow again and the oracle's silence ended. Alexander installed a new priestess, who prophesied his future victory over the Persians. His visit to Didyma later played a role in his belief in his own divinity (see Chapter 14). By a twist of fate, in 329 Alexander came upon the descendants of the Branchidae when he was in Central Asia: he put them to death (see Chapter 9).

Alexander made a startling decision as far as his fleet was concerned. He sent it home. The Persian Wars had changed the nature of Greek warfare by showing the importance of naval warfare. Naval ascendancy brought with it immense power, as the Athenians had found in their Delian League of the fifth century and their Second Athenian Naval Confederacy of the fourth. A navy was vital in any line of communications. One reason why Philip II had courted the Athenians so much was because of their naval strength and expertise, both of which he needed for his invasion of Asia. Why did Alexander do such a strategically unsound, even rash, act?[13]

The answer is twofold: a navy's dependency on a harbour and impotence. At Miletus, the large Persian fleet had been rendered ineffective easily. With the harbour at Miletus blocked by the smaller Greek fleet, the Persian ships could do little more than watch. At the same time, the Greek fleet, because of its smaller size, could not engage the Persian at sea. Denied a safe harbour, the Persian fleet was forced to find another one, some distance away. When that harbour was made inaccessible, the fleet had to find yet another (after Cape Mycale, this would be Samos). If the Persian fleet had been rendered impotent, then so could the Greek. Alexander could not afford that. Nor could Alexander afford a fleet that was so numerically inferior and dependent on the army that it could do little anyway. One move would be to increase the size of the Greek fleet so that it was a match for the Persian. Instead, Alexander sent it home, keeping only a small number of ships as bulk transport vessels, including 20 Athenian triremes.

However, with no Greek fleet to worry it, the Persian navy could operate wherever it wanted, whenever it wanted. It had the potential to force cities in the north that had surrendered to Alexander to declare allegiance to Persia again. Strategically, Alexander's dismissal of his fleet was a bad move, one that he would realise within a year.

On to Halicarnassus (Bodrum). This was the home of the 'father of history', Herodotus, who lived in the second half of the fifth century. He wrote about the Persian Wars, though his account, which survives today, is more than that. It tells us of the history, customs and geography of many countries (one entire book is devoted to Egypt) and states. Halicarnassus was also home to one of the seven wonders of the ancient world, the Mausoleum. This was named after Mausolus, the powerful satrap of Caria, and was completed by Artemisia, his wife, after he died in 353. It was also the main Persian arsenal in south-western Anatolia, under the command of the satrap Orontobates, and heavily fortified. Its defensive wall was six feet thick, with high towers and battlements. Behind it lay not only the city itself but also two citadels (Mausolus's palace was in one of them, Zephyrium). In front of the wall was a wide, deep moat, and the harbour allowed easy access to supplies.

It was not Orontobates who faced off Alexander, but one of the generals who had fled from Granicus, Memnon of Rhodes. Darius himself had entrusted Memnon with command of the whole fleet and sole responsibility for the defence of southern Asia Minor. The lesson of multiple cooks spoiling the broth had been learned from Granicus. Memnon was more than capable of discharging his duties effectively; Alexander would have his work cut out for him.

Memnon prepared a large force to face Alexander on land and protected the harbour with his own triremes. The latter was unnecessary, as Alexander had disbanded his own fleet. The Macedonians began with a frontal assault but this failed. As at Miletus, they then turned to the siege towers. The archers picked off the defenders on the walls with ease, but this time, the first time in Macedonian sieges, Alexander arranged for the towers to catapult stones at the besieged city. These would smash down parts of the wall or houses inside. Alexander also had the moat in front of the defensive walls filled in so that he could ram the bottom of the walls in the hope of breaking them. Undaunted, Memnon's force rebuilt the walls where necessary with brick and tried hard to set fire to the siege engines.

Halicarnassus was holding its own. One night in a fit of drunken folly two members of Perdiccas's force tried to scale its defensive wall, causing others to follow suit. That led to fierce fighting, in which the Macedonians were pushed back, unable to recover their dead because of blazing arrows from the defenders. Alexander was forced to make a truce with the enemy so that he could bury his dead men.

Finally, Alexander's men breached the defensive wall. It was discovered that the defenders had retreated behind a semi-circular inside wall, made of brick, on top of which was their own siege tower. The Macedonian soldiers fought on, disregarding the numbers of their fallen comrades that fell to the defenders' catapults. Realising that victory was possible, two contingents of Memnon's forces engaged the Macedonians on two fronts. They were gaining the upper hand when the Macedonians, in a last-ditch effort, pushed them back. Memnon, sensing defeat, pulled his troops back and together with Orontobates took refuge in the two inner citadels. The city was left to Alexander.

The Macedonian king did not like to be resisted or waste time. He had experienced both at Halicarnassus, and now it was payback time. At the same time, there were innocent civilians in Halicarnassus, who were no match for the Macedonians. Memnon had set fire to his defence equipment and the houses closest to the walls before he had fled to the citadels. Under cover of the smoke, he then fled to the island of Cos. There he linked up with the Persian fleet, and turned his attention to the northern Aegean sea.

Alexander ordered the fires in the city to be put out. The next day, after moving the population, he levelled the city's houses and its walls. As with the razing of Thebes in 335, his action must have sent a clear message to other cities planning defiance.

It was now early in the winter of 334/3, time to take stock of his situation. To the satrapy of Caria Alexander entrusted Ada, the deposed ruler, who had established herself in the town of Alinda. She had been deposed by her brother Pixodarus. As Alexander marched to Halicarnassus she came to him and surrendered. Some mutual flattery evidently went on, for Alexander allowed her to adopt him as her son (he referred to her as his 'mother'). Now she was satrap of Caria again, although Caria's sphere of influence was taken away. The adoption also meant that Alexander gained the support of Caria and became part of the ruling household.

However, it was significant that a Macedonian officer remained in Halicarnassus with 200 cavalry and 3,000 Greek mercenaries. The siege of Halicarnassus had been costly, lengthy and strategically ineffective, for the garrison force that Alexander left in Halicarnassus was no match for the Persian forces. Alexander knew this, but he could not deviate from his strategy or route.

Those of his men who had married just before the army marched from Greece were now sent back to Macedonia so that they could spend time with their wives. They would not rejoin the Macedonian army until late spring 333 at Gordium. On the one hand, Alexander's measure had the mark of a general thinking of his troops; on the other hand, it showed the downside of the invasion. Alexander was already in need of more men, and the commanders of these troops had a charge to levy more from the homeland. Another officer was sent to the Peloponnese to hire mercenaries from there. Alexander may even have hoped that once the men and their wives had reunited there would be a rise in the birth rate – after all, a Macedonian winter was cold, and during this season there was not much in the way of fun.

As Alexander marched further south to Lycia, he encountered more resistance, although we do not know all the details. For example,

Hyparna was besieged and quickly fell to him, and there was some fighting against people in the interior. Macedonian victories paid off: the cities of south-east and then south-west Lycia surrendered to him. In midwinter Alexander stopped off at the coastal city of Phaselis, in eastern Lycia. There he helped its people in a campaign against Pisidia. As in Lydia, Alexander ordered that Lycian youths be trained in Macedonian tactics for his army. Then he pressed on into Pamphylia.

On this leg of his march, an event happened that would be exploited, then and later, by the king's propaganda machine. Sending the bulk of his army on by a mountain route, Alexander and a small contingent marched along the Pamphylian Sea by Mount Climax. They were buffeted by large waves that impeded progress. Suddenly the waves ceased, and a path across the beach became clear and dry. The sea itself was bowing to Alexander, Callisthenes would later say.[14] In reality, the wind had changed from south to north, hence the calm. But Alexander was not interested in any natural explanation.

Pamphylia was soon his, despite low-level resistance from some towns, Aspendus in particular. It had voluntarily surrendered to Alexander but asked that no garrison be imposed in it. Then it decided to resist after all. Alexander did not want to waste time and so negotiated terms. In spring 333 he was ready to leave, and Nearchus of Crete was appointed satrap.

Speed characterises Alexander's march. He had probably heard by now that Darius had started to form a great army in Babylon, about 600 miles to the east, intent on bringing the invaders to battle. The king could not afford to delay any longer. He travelled north into Phrygia, heading to Gordium (close to Ankara). It was important for symbolic reasons, as will be seen, that he went there, plus the place was a logical one to link up with Parmenion's force. Some time earlier Alexander had sent him to deal with the satrap of Phrygia, who had been in diplomatic contact with Darius. Parmenion expelled him.

Alexander's route would take him through hostile Pisidia. At Termessus, which controlled a communications route, Alexander experienced resistance. He was able to push his way through the pass, but the terrain prevented his siege engines from attacking the citadel of Termessus. Rather than waste time, he left a rival town, Selge, to keep Termessus in check. Next, the town of Sagalassus defied him. A force from there, supported by some people from Termessus, occupied a hill in front of the town. Alexander charged frontally, and routed the enemy. No punishments were imposed, for Alexander was keen to press on to Gordium. Four days later he was at Celaenae, on the Royal Road (the most important of the Persian roads, stretching from Sardis to Susa), the capital of Phrygia. It defied him, and he wasted only ten days in besieging it before agreeing to terms. Thus, not every siege prosecuted by Alexander was successful.

This was a very different Alexander from the one who had besieged Miletus and Halicarnassus, and the reason is that he had his eyes set on Gordium. About a month or so later, in March or April 333, he arrived there, to be soon joined by Parmenion. While there, the men he had sent back to Macedonia for the winter and the requested reinforcements, 3,000 infantry and 650 Macedonian and allied cavalry, reached him. The Macedonian army was whole again.

Gordium was home to the mythical founder of the Phrygian dynasty, Gordius, who was believed to have been originally Macedonian. At some stage he left Macedonia in a wooden wagon and travelled to Gordium. The wagon, dedicated by Gordius' son Midas, to Zeus, was still there in Alexander's day. It also held the key to who would rule Asia, and its story was well known:

'It was said that Gordius was a poor man among the ancient Phrygians, who had a small piece of land to farm, and two yoke of oxen. He used one of these to plough and the other to draw the wagon. On one occasion, while he was ploughing, an eagle settled upon the yoke, and stayed sitting there until the time came to unyoke the oxen. He was alarmed at the sight, and went to the Telmissian soothsayers to consult them about the sign from the god. The Telmissians were skilful in interpreting the meaning of divine signs, and the power of divination was bestowed not only upon the men, but also upon their wives and children from generation to generation.

'When Gordius was driving his wagon near a certain village of the Telmissians, he met a maiden bringing water from the spring. To her he related how the sign of the eagle had appeared to him. As she herself was a prophet, she instructed him to return to the very spot and offer a sacrifice to Zeus the king. Gordius asked her to go with him and tell him how to perform the sacrifice. He offered the sacrifice in the way the girl suggested, and afterwards married her. A son was born to them named Midas.

'When Midas had become a man, handsome and valiant, as the story goes, the Phrygians were harassed by civil discord. Consulting the oracle, they were told that a wagon would bring them a king, who would put an end to their discord. While they were still deliberating about this matter, Midas arrived with his father and mother, and stopped near the assembly, wagon and all. They compared the oracular response with this occurrence, and decided that this was the person whom the god told them the wagon would bring. They appointed Midas king. He put an end to their discord, and dedicated his father's wagon in the citadel as a thank-offering to Zeus the king for sending the eagle. In addition the following saying was current about the wagon, that whoever could untie the cord of the yoke of this wagon was destined to rule Asia.'[15]

Alexander, then, had to undo the knot.[16] However, it was tied in such a complicated and intricate manner that the ends were hidden from sight. The same author tells us how he did it:

'It is said by some that when Alexander could find no way to loosen the cord and yet was unwilling to let it stay tied, in case this caused anxiety on the part of the people, he struck it with his sword, and cutting it through, said that it had been untied. But Aristobulus says that he pulled out the pin of the wagon-pole, which was a wooden peg driven right through it that held the cord together. Having done this, he drew out the yoke from the wagon-pole.'

It is more in keeping with Alexander's character (patience not being one of his virtues) that he severed the knot with his sword to expose the ends!

Anyone who might have queried whether he had actually undone the fabled knot was silenced that night by thunder and lightning. Zeus himself was greeting Asia's new master, and Alexander was quick to sacrifice to him the next morning.

In the meantime, Memnon, who had escaped from Halicarnassus, was wreaking havoc with the Persian fleet in the northern Aegean. During the early summer of 333, he won over the island of Chios (where previously Alexander had established a democracy and recalled its democratic exiles), as well as almost all of Lesbos. Mytilene, in eastern Lesbos, resisted stoutly, supported by a force of mercenaries from Alexander. During its siege, perhaps in June, Memnon died. The god was said to have smiled favourably on Alexander. Memnon's nephew Pharnabazus succeeded him, and Mytilene capitulated some time later. Soon after, Miletus took advantage of the change in Macedonian fortune and revolted. Others must also have followed suit.

There was also worrying Persian activity in the vital Hellespont region, where a base was established at Callipolis, and the Persian fleet under Pharnabazus actually made it to Siphnos in the western Cyclades. The potential was there for an occupation of Euboea and then an attack on Macedonia itself. Agis III, the Spartan king, seized the chance. Shortly before the Battle of Issus, he opened negotiations with Pharnabazus. Agis wanted Persian help, ostensibly to promote Spartan ascendancy in the Peloponnese, and that made war with Macedon inevitable.

Alexander's Asian successes to date were now compromised, and to make matters worse he was far from home and with no fleet. Therefore, he took steps to rectify his earlier, and premature, decision of disbanding his fleet. He immediately called for the fleet to go on the attack. To Amphoterus was entrusted the task of reversing the Persian successes in the Hellespont, and to Hegelochus the recapturing of the islands. To build up naval strength he spent the massive sum of 1,100 talents, split between these two admirals and Antipater, and also ordered contributions from the member states of the League of Corinth. Some in Athens, always the centre of resistance to Macedon, refused, but the general Phocion was able to persuade the people to accept reality.

Luckily, Memnon's death and the siege of Mytilene prevented serious conflict in the Hellespont. Then the Macedonian fleet was unwittingly aided by the Persian King. Darius was mustering a big army and he needed Greek mercenaries at its core. He issued an order that Greek mercenaries from everywhere go to him in Syria, to prepare for what would be the Battle of Issus in 333.[17] The Persian fleet was thus denuded as its commanders complied with the royal directive.

The symbolism of Alexander's act in untying the Gordian knot was obvious. It would have rallied his men and boosted their morale as they prepared to meet Darius. With any luck, it would have caused consternation in the Persian camp. It can also be connected to Alexander's casting a spear into Asian soil at the time of his landing. From the start, Alexander saw his mission to Asia as more than revenge for Greek losses during the Persian Wars. Asia was handed to him as spear-won territory by the gods. Gordium confirmed that he was intent on permanent conquest, and that he believed he was fated to do so. Eventually, he would even think of moving the Macedonian capital from Pella to Babylon, regardless of the reaction of his own people. For now, though, Alexander had undone the Gordian knot: he was the man who would be ruler of Asia. It was time to make this a reality.

6

A Bridge of Corpses

In the summer of 333 Alexander left Gordium and marched across Anatolia and Paphlagonia. The latter was made part of Hellespontine Phrygia, but did not have to pay tribute. A swift campaign in Cappadocia, east of Paphlagonia, took place, which Alexander followed with another satrapal appointment. When news came of Memnon's lucky death – lucky for Alexander – and of the disruptions in the Persian fleet, he decided the time had come to go after Darius.

By the end of the summer Alexander had arrived at the Cilician Gates. This was the main pass on the Golek-Boghaz hills through the Taurus mountain range on the road from Anatolia to Syria. At points the pass was so narrow that the army of 40,000 men could only march four abreast. A lacklustre resistance was offered, as Arsames, Satrap of Cilicia, slashed his crops to deny the Macedonian army needed provisions. As the army drew closer to him he fled from his capital, Tarsus, setting fire to the palace as he did so. It was imperative that Alexander took the capital to use as a base, so with a contingent of cavalry and light infantry he marched from the Cilician Gates to Tarsus in one day. His speed left Arsames's plan dead in the water, and the fire damage was minimal.

Then, as so often in his reign, Macedonian successes were placed in jeopardy by the king himself. A Macedonian summer was hot, but nothing like the temperatures that the army was then encountering, and in full armour too. It is hard to imagine what the marching and the camp conditions must have been like. The fierce heat, insects, thirst and constant marching, and with no end in sight, must have affected the spirit of the army immensely. However, as proof of its discipline, not to mention faith in Alexander, it did not falter. That would come later.

In these conditions, with Darius and a huge army already en route from Babylon, a hot Alexander jumped into the River Cydnus, which flowed through Tarsus, to bathe. The river had crystal clear water that was doubly seductive on a hot day. However, even in summer it was icy cold,

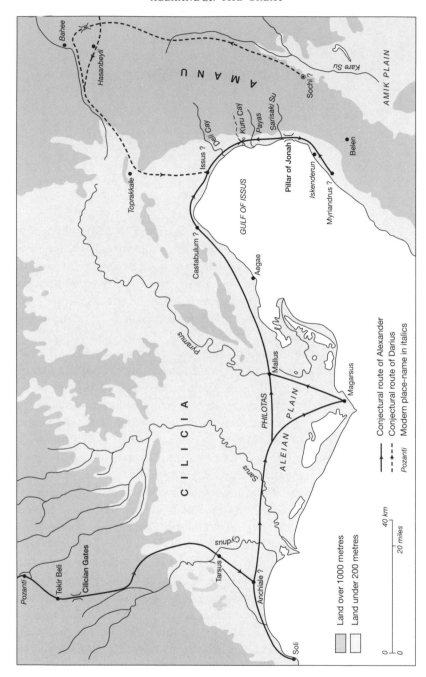

Cilicia and Northern Syria
Redrawn from Bosworth, A. B. (1988) *Conquest and Empire: The Reign of
Alexander the Great* (pub Cambridge University Press), Map 3. © Cambridge
University Press 1988, reproduced with permission.

thanks to the snows of the Taurus range. Alexander caught a chill and could not stop shaking. It developed into a full-scale tropical fever, which lasted several days, and put his life in danger. He may even have caught malaria, which was prevalent there. On the seventh day, he was saved by the intervention of his doctor, Philip the Acarnanian, who gave him some type of medicine in the nick of time. Alexander's recklessness almost cost him his life: it would not be the last time.

There is a story connected to the medicine given by Philip. Just as Alexander was about to drink it, 'Parmenion, who had a quarrel with Philip, wrote to Alexander and warned him to beware of Philip. He heard that Darius was offering him a thousand talents and his own sister in marriage as the price of the king's death. Alexander received the letter and putting it aside it drank the medicine.'[1] The story goes further that Alexander handed the letter to Philip while he drank his medicine so that those present would know its contents. Presumably he did so to be on the safe side: 1,000 talents and a royal marriage were a high price for a contract, and would have swayed lesser men.

The fact that their king almost died but recovered probably made the army euphoric for many reasons. They were far from home, so if he had died who would lead them back? Since Alexander was still unmarried and had no heir, what would happen to the Macedonian throne? The latter was presumably less important to the army than the former. As news of Darius's immense army filtered through to the men their worries can only have increased. It would not be too long before the two sides met in battle. The uncertainty of the situation perhaps manifested itself in the flight of the financial officer, Harpalus. He was one of Alexander's boyhood friends, promoted to this important position when Alexander became king. Harpalus had some kind of physical deformity that precluded him from military duty, but Alexander's loyalty to his friends was such that if Harpalus could not be given a high-level military post he received an administrative one.

Harpalus repaid that loyalty, not to mention friendship, by fleeing. His motive was unknown. Embezzlement cannot be ruled out, for Harpalus was not the most upright of men as his later career would show. Also, he was aided and abetted by an unscrupulous character called Tauriscus, for whom the lure of money would have been too much. However, we cannot discount that Harpalus's flight is an indication of the mood of the army, that it thought there could well be a defeat at the hands of Darius, and what would happen then? Harpalus decided to put plenty of distance between himself and the battle just in case.

Alexander did not lose, of course, but Harpalus stayed in the Megarid area of the Greek mainland for a year before Alexander recalled him (spring 331). Characteristic of Alexander's loyalty to his friends is that Harpalus was reinstated in his post. Whether he was guilty of embezzlement or of a faint heart, or both, the king was prepared to forgive and forget. Indeed, he exercised even more power when he moved to Babylon to oversee the imperial treasury. This seems to have been an administrative rearrangement of the existing Persian financial system. Harpalus repaid his trust by living a luxurious and corrupt life at Babylon. He fled a second time in 324 to escape Alexander's wrath (see Chapter 12), but there would be no mercy that time.

Darius was on the move. In early summer 333 he had led his vast army west from Babylon. Precise figures are not known but the Macedonians, who had about 26,000 infantry and 5,300 cavalry, were certainly outnumbered – the Greek mercenaries alone in Darius' army numbered 30,000, and Persian casualties from the Battle of Issus were said to be as high as 100,000. However, the very size of the Persian army would be its downfall, especially in retreat.

Accompanying the Persian army was the royal baggage train, groaning with treasure, as well as Darius's wife and daughters – it was always good to see one's husband and father do battle. The size of the army and its baggage train made progress slow. Even though Darius picked up speed when he heard of Alexander's illness the Persian army still took about three months to travel from Babylon to Sochi, in Syria, close to the Amanus (Nur) mountain range. This was inland from the Gulf of Iskenderun, separated from it by the Amanus Mountains. The plain there was spacious, and so suited the big Persian line well. Most of the baggage train was sent to Damascus about 200 miles to the south, which took about three weeks. Some of it, along with the royal family, stayed with Darius. It was now September.

Alexander did not stay long in Tarsus after he recovered. After a series of brief campaigns in Cilicia, probably as a test to make sure that he had fully recovered more than anything else, he started to move east. He had already sent Parmenion and a force south to the Pillar of Jonah, a narrow pass separating Cilicia from Syria. Darius was already at Sochi, two days from the Pillar, and Alexander pressed on to link up with Parmenion. His idea was to draw the Persians from their position onto a narrower, coastal plain, between the Amanus Mountains and the sea. That would hamper their battle line.

Darius's strategy was to stake everything on one pitched battle. This was by no means a panic measure. Darius was a skilled strategist and tactician, and so his plan, given his numerical superiority, made sense. It was some time before actual fighting began, probably because each side was cautious of the other and wanted to double-check enemy positions and strengths.[2]

In the end, it was Darius who made the first move. In doing so, he took Alexander completely by surprise, for he led his men not at Alexander but around him. Marching some 100 miles the Persian army crossed the Amanus Mountains by the Bahçe Pass and came to the coast at Issus, which was on the Gulf of Iskenderun. He had neatly outflanked the Macedonian camp and severed Alexander's lines of communication through Cilicia.

The Macedonian sick and stragglers had been left at Issus. They were defenceless, but that did not stop Darius using them to send a warning to the Greeks: he cut off their hands, cauterized the bloody stumps with pitch, and sent them to report to Alexander that he had arrived.

Alexander did not believe the Persians had rounded his army until he had sent a ship along the coast to verify the rumour. His position was suddenly serious. The Persian army had come down to him, as he had wanted, and it was camped on a narrow coastal plain south of the Pinarus. However, there was no guarantee that another contingent of it was not ready to attack his rear from the other direction, via the southern passes, the direction from which he had expected Darius to march. He was forced to split his army so that part of it could turn back to guard these passes. The night before the battle was spent at the Pillar of Jonah: the men's mood can only have been grim.

The exact location of the Battle of Issus is unknown, but it was probably around the Kuru Çay River or perhaps the Payas River, which separated both armies. The Persian battle line was stretched across the narrow coastal plain. It had the bulk of its cavalry to the right, by the Gulf, next to which was a force of Persian archers. The Greek mercenary contingent was massed in the middle, next to which stood another force of Persian archers. On the left was allied cavalry and the Persians' own infantry. Darius, surrounded by his own 3,000-strong Royal Bodyguard of infantry and cavalry, was roughly in the middle but behind the mercenary line. The entire line was so long that it stretched to the foothills of the Amanus, and its dog-leg position at the left outflanked the Macedonian right wing. This was a formidable battle array, one that would test Alexander's strategic skill to the utmost.

The Macedonian army had started to move to the plain even before dawn. Having to travel through the narrow passes from the higher ground was cumbersome and time-consuming, and probably took up most of the morning. By midday, though, the battle line was assembled. The Thessalian and allied cavalry were on its left, by the Gulf, next to which, in the middle, were the various divisions of the phalanx each led by one of Alexander's top generals. Behind them was a line of allied and mercenary infantry. Next to the middle was the Royal Brigade of hypaspists led by Alexander, and on the right, by the Amanus Mountains, was

Macedonian and allied cavalry. Archers and light infantry reinforced the right wing to prevent the uncomfortably close Persian left from breaking through and outflanking the Macedonians. It was a long line, and it must have been daunting to the Persians (Fig. 3).

The Macedonian army charged first, in the late afternoon, led by Alexander. His cavalry easily repelled the Persian left and got behind the Persian centre. Then he fixed his attention on Darius himself. Elsewhere, the Macedonians were running into trouble. The Persian cavalry was forcing back the Thessalian cavalry on the Macedonian left, and, worse still, the Macedonian cavalry had moved so quickly that the infantry were left behind. Into the gap that had opened between cavalry and infantry poured the Persians' mercenary troops, who attacked the Macedonians not face on but from the side. The Greek mercenaries had killed 120 Macedonian phalanx troops and were probably pushing the Macedonian line back. This deadly attack rendered the phalanx's massed sarissas, which could only point forward, useless. The Macedonian line was suddenly in disarray and faltering.

Luck saved the day for the Macedonians. For one thing, the Greek mercenaries suddenly realised that the Macedonian cavalry had managed to come around their rear and encircle them. They backed off, perhaps hoping that this action would save them from the fate that had befallen

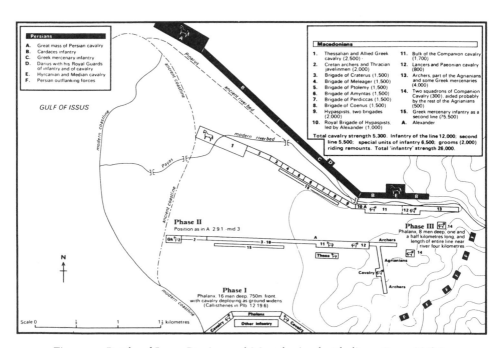

Figure 3. Battle of Issus: Persian and Macedonian battle lines. From N.G.L. Hammond, *The Genius of Alexander the Great* (1997), p. 88

those after Granicus. Also, Alexander did not abandon his push towards Darius. The Great King and the Macedonian king did not fight each other, although there was bitter hand-to-hand fighting around them. There is a story that Alexander wrote to Antipater describing 'with all sincerity' how Darius had wounded him in his thigh with a sword.[3] This is embellishment on his part. Darius, seeing his personal bodyguards dying before him, and as his own capture was imminent, fled from the scene of the battle to Thapsacus. The rest of his bodyguard followed suit.

Darius's last minutes on the battlefield are brilliantly depicted in the famous mosaic found at the House of the Faun at Pompeii and known as 'the Alexander mosaic' (see Plate 16).[4] It was modelled on a contemporary painting (perhaps by Philoxenus of Eretria), and vividly depicts Alexander, on a rearing Bucephalus, and Darius, looming in almost superhuman size above Alexander in his high war chariot, and about to flee. Their eyes are locked on each other, victory in those of Alexander, desperation in those of Darius, as the Persians are surrounded by the huge sarissas and Darius's bodyguard fails him. The painting would become part of the battle's own tradition, in keeping with the embellished accounts of it put out by Alexander's court historian Callisthenes. That embellishment included stories such as Darius fleeing as soon as the Macedonians attacked, or the Persians losing 100,000 men and over 10,000 cavalry in the battle to Alexander's 500.

Luck, then, rather than superior battle tactics on the part of Alexander gave the Macedonians victory, and Darius threw his chance of victory away. Once news of his flight reached his men, their morale was broken. Alexander turned his force to the left to support his hard-pressed army on that flank. As he did so, the Macedonian phalanx regrouped itself, and against the wall of sarissas the Persian line stood no chance. The battle was over. The Persians were routed, and fled. Who could blame them?

The Macedonian attack became a pursuit, which lasted until night fell. Nothing could save the Persians, who found out to their horror that a huge force was also a huge liability when on the run. For one thing, it was slowed down and obstructed by the terrain, especially rivers. For another, the Persian infantry fled first, before the cavalry. That meant the cavalry, in its effort to escape, rode through the infantry mowing many down. The number of Persians who fell in the retreat, either at the hands of Alexander's men or as victims of their own cavalry, was great. So great in fact that one source vividly states: 'The men who were with them in the pursuit of Darius, coming to a ravine, passed over it upon the corpses.'[5] By no stretch of the imagination, a bridge of corpses shows the extent of the slaughter.

One person who was not killed or captured was the Great King himself. This would turn out to be a blunder on Alexander's part, for Darius was able to escape and regroup his forces, bringing Alexander to costly battle again two years later at Gaugamela. For now, Alexander basked in the relief of his victory. The element of luck in the battle's outcome was downplayed by court historiography. The battle became the sort of one found in the Homeric epics, and the painting of it (see above) gave it a tradition of its own.

While Darius did flee from the battle, leaving behind his family, we should not underestimate his bravery and fighting prowess. The sources for the battle are Greek, and clearly would paint him in a demeaning light. However, we should not forget that before the battle he had outfoxed Alexander by coming around to his rear, and caused the king considerable worry. However, once the battle was underway and Darius was actually facing Alexander, it was a different story. As Great King, Darius was a very capable administrator, but he was not a great general. He did not follow through with his strategy in the battle, and ought to have forced Alexander's cavalry into the water, rendering them useless. For that he can be blamed, but then his opponent was second to none.[6] As the Macedonians surrounded him, Darius realised that to continue the battle was futile, so he decided to flee in order to fight another day. The act of leaving his army and family becomes, then, not one of a coward, but one of putting his kingdom above all else.

Not long after the battle, Alexander entered the Persian king's tent and was struck by the magnificence of what he saw. Gold cups, pitchers, sofas, tables laid out in anticipation of the Great King's dinner, and everywhere was the smell of incense.

More was to come. He sent Parmenion to Damascus to seize the royal baggage train. This netted him enormous wealth, some 3,000 talents, as well as a Persian noblewoman called Barsine, the daughter of Artabazus. She had been married to Mentor of Rhodes, the brother of Memnon. When he died, she married his brother, only to see him die during the siege of Mytilene. She was brought to Alexander, who was captivated by her beauty and intelligence. She had also received a Greek education. Apparently, he lost his virginity to her, for he 'did not know any woman before marriage except Barsine'.[7] The two were soon in a de facto relationship. They did not marry, but Barsine did bear Alexander's child, a boy named (no surprise) Heracles in 328/7.

Alexander had also seized the baggage train that Darius had brought to Issus. This included members of the royal family: the Queen Mother Sisygambis, the royal princesses, Darius's six-year-old son, and Darius's wife Stateira. She was his sister but the two had been married for almost 20 years, and had three children. They presumed he was dead, and were in mourning. Alexander, ensconced in Darius's tent:

'heard the weeping of women and other similar noises not far from the tent. He therefore enquired who the women were, and why they were in a tent that was so near. He was answered by someone as follows: "O king, the mother, wife, and children of Darius are lamenting for him as dead, since they have been informed that you have his bow and royal cloak, and that his shield has been brought back." When Alexander heard this, he sent Leonnatus, one of his Companions, to them. He ordered him to tell them: "Darius is still alive. In his flight he left his arms and cloak in the chariot; and these are the only things of his that Alexander has." Leonnatus entered the tent and told them the news about Darius. Moreover, he said that Alexander would allow them to retain the status and retinue that was in keeping with their royal rank, as well as the title of queens. He had not undertaken the war against Darius from a feeling of hatred, but had conducted it in a legitimate manner for the empire of Asia.'[8]

It is important to note Alexander's response. While it was necessary to defeat Darius, his family would not suffer because the war was not a personal one against Darius, but for the rule of Asia. The king did treat the royal ladies as befitted their noble stature (when Stateira died in 331 she was given a royal burial), and he also promised that he would protect the princesses and arrange marriages for them.

Sisygambis, by then in her sixties, went to Alexander's tent the following day to thank him. It was perhaps at that meeting that she mistook Hephaestion for Alexander because he was taller. She went up to him and curtsied to him. Embarrassed, Hephaestion probably mumbled that he was not the king. Alexander apparently told her not to worry for Hephaestion was also an Alexander. He obviously endeared himself to her, for when he died she went into mourning and starved herself to death.

In Lydia and Lycia he had given orders that youths be trained in Macedonian tactics. Now he gave orders that the princesses were to be taught Greek and educated in Greek culture. This was the start of the spread of Greek civilisation among the 'barbarians', something that would occupy Alexander for the rest of his reign and change the face of the territories through which he marched forever. When he later took Susa, the princesses were left there. They were waiting for him when he returned to Susa in 324, and by then had learned Greek (see Chapter 12).

Darius III was still alive, so technically the prophecy of the Gordian knot had not yet come true. However, it was getting there. Alexander's treatment of the royal ladies is especially significant in the battle's immediate aftermath. His actions and orders showed that he had taken over Darius's role as father and husband. Though he would never formally call himself Great King, Alexander thus saw himself as that. This was a clear message to the Persians and to his own men.

So too was his minting of silver and gold coinage after the seizure of the baggage train at Damascus. Issus was celebrated by a commemorative gold coin, which had the head of Athena on the obverse and Nike on the reverse. Alexander also put out a silver tetradrachm, with the head of a young Heracles on the obverse and on the reverse Zeus sitting on a throne, sceptre in his left hand and an eagle on his right hand. This coin is truly symbolic of how Alexander was seeing himself. Heracles was an ancestor of Alexander's and a god worshipped in other forms by those in Asia. The young Heracles was the young Alexander. The seated Zeus called to mind the Persian coins minted at Tarsus that showed a similar seated figure, in their case the god Ba'al. Hence, Alexander's seated Zeus worked on two levels. For the Greeks, he was the Macedonians' chief deity, ruler of the gods, helper and protector of the king. For the Persans, he was Ba'al, who was performing a similar function. Both were condensed in and around Alexander.

After Issus, many thousands of Darius's force of Greek mercenaries saw the writing on the wall and left his service. A group led by a Macedonian deserter, Amyntas, son of Antiochus, sailed to Egypt. He declared himself the new satrap appointed by Darius, but did not last long. A number of other mercenaries were hired by the kings of Cyprus. Yet another group, of 8,000, made its way to the great mercenary base at Taenarum, on the southern tip of the Peloponnese. These large numbers showed how decisive a defeat Issus had been for the Persian army.

The Persian fleet returned from its base at Siphnos to Cyprus when news of Issus broke, but defections within it to Alexander's side made it a shadow of its former self. The new Macedonian fleet was on the offensive. Over the next few months, the Persian base at Callipolis in the Hellespont was captured and the Persian force expelled. The towns and islands of the coast of Asia Minor that had so recently been lost to Alexander sent embassies to the king begging his pardon. No reprisals were taken, and later, from Egypt, Alexander rewarded Mytilene with land on the Asian coast for its gallant resistance to Persia. Macedonia again had the upper hand in Asia Minor and at sea.

The Persians may have been defeated, but they were not broken. Nor had all the Greek mercenaries deserted. Four thousand of them joined Darius in Thapsacus. Another group of survivors continued north through the Cilician Gates and launched an offensive against Macedonian influence in Cappadocia and Paphlagonia. It took over a year for Antigonus Monophthalmus, Alexander's satrap of Phrygia, to defeat this threat, in the process waging three hard-fought battles. Even so, Cappadocia would be for a hotbed of discontent for decades.

Rather than pursue Darius to the end, as strategically he ought to have done, Alexander let him go and continued to march south. He had his eyes set on Egypt for a number of reasons (see Chapter 7). To get there, he first had to march through Syria.

Leaving two Companions, Balacrus and Menon, in charge of Cilicia and northern Syria Alexander entered Phoenicia (Syria and Lebanon), marching south. Its major city in the north, Aradus, surrendered to him. At Marathus ('Amrit), he apparently received a letter from Darius offering to treat Alexander as a friend and ally and to ransom his family. Alexander refused. The mandate of the League of Corinth had not yet been fulfilled, but more importantly for him Darius did not speak of surrendering any territory. That meant Darius saw Alexander only as an invader while he remained Great King. While Alexander never called himself Great King, he could not allow another to hold that title. He responded to Darius's letter saying that he was only prepared to negotiate if Darius acknowledged himself as subject to the Macedonian king. Now it was Darius's turn to refuse – as Alexander must surely have expected. Another battle was inevitable.

As he continued through Phoenicia, Byblos and Sidon surrendered to Alexander. The people in Sidon even went as far as deposing their king, Straton II, because he was Darius's friend. Next, Alexander came to Tyre, arriving there at some time in late January or early February 332. Tyre was a powerful commercial and naval city. In antiquity, unlike today, it was an island, about half a mile offshore. The Tyrians acknowledged Alexander's power, and gave him money and gifts.

Then Alexander decided to sacrifice in the Temple to Melqart, who was a local equivalent of Heracles. The Tyrians refused because of the sacrilegious nature of a Macedonian sacrificing in their temple, especially at this time, for they were about to celebrate a festival in Melqart's honour. Instead, Azemilk, the King of Tyre, proposed a compromise. Tyre would become Alexander's ally, but he should sacrifice on the mainland at Old Tyre, opposite the island. An angry Alexander sent envoys to say this was unacceptable and that the Tyrians had to surrender. They murdered the envoys and threw them off their walls. He then ordered its siege.[9]

There is no question that control of Tyre was essential since Alexander could not afford a revolt of the Phoenician cities as he pushed on to Egypt. Tyre could also have been used as a base by the Persian navy, given its strongest contingent was Phoenician. The navy was currently using Cyprus and Egypt as bases, but to allow it access to Tyre when Alexander eventually marched inland after Darius was dangerous. Moreover, this was the time when Agis III of Sparta was fighting Macedonian troops in Crete. Agis had sought Persian help for a rising in the Peloponnese, and had received money and ten triremes from Pharnabazus, admiral of the Persian fleet, about the time of the Battle of Issus. For some reason Agis turned to Crete rather than the Peloponnese, but the potential for that fight to turn into a war on the mainland was there. If that happened, together with the Persian fleet's presence and ability to disrupt his lines of communication, then Alexander's kingship would face serious problems.

However, there was no love lost between the various Phoenician towns, and so no guarantee that the Persian fleet, or just its Phoenician contingent, would support Tyre. In fact, as news of Alexander's victory at Issus spread, there were defections in the fleet, and Tyre would not receive naval support. Alexander would not have known this when he began the siege of course. What he must have known, however, was that the Persian fleet was a fraction of its former self, and hardly in a position to wage an effective war at sea.

Strategy played an important role in Alexander's decision to besiege Tyre, but for him the more important reason was personal. He wanted to punish the Tyrians for their open defiance of him as king. He could easily have left a garrison on the mainland to keep Tyre in check. That would have been the sensible thing to do, given that Darius was regrouping his forces and that Alexander was intent on going to Egypt. After all, the Tyrians had originally surrendered to him, so it would have been the mark of a wise and diplomatic king to retract his demand to sacrifice in the Tyrian temple.

Reason often gave way to emotion when Alexander had been personally affronted, and the siege of Tyre is a classic example of this. Besides, Alexander had the gods on his side:

'During this siege he had a dream in which he saw Heracles stretching out his hand to him from the wall and calling him. Many of the Tyrians dreamed that Apollo told them he was going away to Alexander, since he was unhappy at what was going on in the city. At that point, they encircled his huge statue with cords and nailed it down to its pedestal, as if the god had been a deserter caught in the act of escaping to the enemy, and called him an Alexandrist. In another dream, too, Alexander thought he saw a satyr who mocked him at a distance, and eluded his grasp when he tried to catch him. Finally, after much coaxing and chasing, he surrendered.'[10]

The siege, which lasted for at least six months (and would be the longest he ever prosecuted), was also a classic example of Alexander's superior skills at siegecraft. Attacking by boat across the straits separating Tyre from the mainland was costly and strategically unsound, so Alexander decided to attack it by land. First, he destroyed Old Tyre, and then, with the earth and stones, and with wood he brought in from the Lebanon, he began construction of a causeway 25 feet or so in width across the straits to connect the island to the mainland. The plan was feasible, for the water was shallow until close to the island, where the depth was about 15–20 feet. The army would then attack over the causeway.

It was an audacious and bold plan, one that was entirely in keeping with Alexander's character. Work on the mole began, under the supervision of the military engineer Diades of Thessaly, and at first it went smoothly. However, the closer the work force got to Tyre, the more it came under attack from the Tyrian archers stationed on the 150-foot high defensive wall. Casualties grew. In an effort to solve this problem, Alexander brought in two enormous siege towers, set on the far end of the causeway, to protect the workers there. On top of each was a torsion-powered catapult that bombarded the enemy with huge stones. In addition, there were archers who kept the Tyrian archers at bay and so acted as a defence force for the Macedonian workers.

It was imperative to destroy the Macedonian siege towers so that the Tyrians could then pick off the workers on the mole. They thus changed their tactics. They packed a ship with wood and attached two long masts to its bows that stuck out a little way. On each were fixed containers of bitumen and sulphur. Heavy rocks were placed in the stern so that the ship's prow was well out of the water. Then, taking advantage of the strong south-west wind, they sailed the ship directly towards the closer end of the causeway to them – and the siege towers. When it reached its target, the wood and the flammable contents of the containers were set alight. As the wind carried the ship to the mole, the crews jumped to safety. When it smashed into it, the two protruding masts broke off and dumped the flaming contents onto the mole and the siege towers. Everything was engulfed in flames, and to make matters worse, the causeway itself was damaged by even stronger winds. The resilient Tyrians had gained the upper hand, and the siege became something of a stalemate, dragging on into the summer. Still, Alexander refused to end it, and ordered Diades to build more engines and start work on another causeway.

A breakthrough for the Macedonian king came in midsummer with the return of the Phoenician contingent of the Persian fleet, which anchored at Sidon. Eighty ships were from cities other than Tyre, and a short while later 120 ships from Cyprus put into Sidon, bringing with them Cyprus's surrender to Alexander. The Phoenicians and the Cyprians were enemies of the Tyrians, so the arrival of their armada of ships was a godsend for Alexander. The Macedonian king returned to the siege with vigour. He used some of these ships to keep the Tyrians at bay by blockading their two harbours (to their north and south) and to protect his work force on the mole. New siege towers were also constructed, but not the fixed, static ones as before. The new ones were mounted on ships, and were equipped with stone-throwing catapults and scaling bridges. It was hard to imagine anyone or any city resisting such massive and powerful equipment.

The Tyrians did not abandon hope yet. They dropped rocks into the sea at the foot of their walls to prevent any breach of them. They dropped boiling sand from cauldrons on the besiegers. They strengthened their walls with skins stuffed with seaweed in preparation for the onslaught. They even attached revolving wheels to the ramparts to deflect Macedonian arrows aimed at the defenders. During the siege they built an inner defensive wall, and filled in the gap between the two walls with rocks and soil. Thus, even if the outer wall were breached by the Macedonians, as was likely, the Tyrians would still be well protected.

The Tyrians' defiance was also seen in their murdering captured Macedonians and, in full view of the Macedonian camp, dropping the bodies into the sea. It was not the best scenario for the Macedonian army, and on top of the frustration arising from the length of the siege must have been a burning desire for revenge. That desire was realised by the men when Tyre did capitulate.

Alexander brought up his men and prepared to attack. A Tyrian fleet of 13 ships had previously sailed out to hamper the Macedonians. It had almost defeated the Cyprian fleet before Alexander's ships had turned the tables. Next, Alexander worked to breach the walls. The causeway was finished and a road of sorts built on top of it for the army. Rams were attached to ships to hammer at the walls, and the southern section of the outer wall was breached. However, the Tyrians were able to fend off the attackers, at times using grappling hooks, sharp poles and nets to drag the Macedonians off the walls, and when night fell hostilities ceased. The winds that had wreaked havoc with the mole some time earlier had returned and prevented renewal of the attack for two days. The dawn of the third day brought sufficient calm for Alexander to launch what would be his final attack.

He used the Phoenician fleet to attack the remaining Tyrian ships in the south harbour while the Cyprian ships captured the north harbour and attacked the city from that side. While this two-pronged assault was going on, his siege engine ships continued to attack the wall. As more sections of it fell, confusion and disarray reigned. Alexander then took a force of hypaspists and a division of the phalanx and secured a landing spot where the wall had fallen. That spelled Tyre's doom, for the rest of the army was able to enter the city and the Tyrian defence collapsed completely.

The siege of Tyre became a famous and often-told story. So much so, that it was a scene on the illuminated manuscripts of the mediaeval period; for example, there is this Flemish copy of the *Alexander Romance*: see Plate 17.

Carnage followed, which was condoned by Alexander. Three hundred Macedonians died and 3,000 were wounded, but the city was all but destroyed. The Macedonians slaughtered over 8,000 of the Tyrians and enslaved the rest (about 30,000). Perhaps some Tyrian nobility, including the king, and certainly 30 visiting ambassadors from Carthage, who had fled as suppliants to the Altar of Heracles, were allowed to live. This was not so much piety on Alexander's part but pragmatics. The Tyrians had requested military support from Carthage; the Carthaginian embassy did not agree to their request, but had sympathised with their plight. Alexander sent it home with a grim message: Carthage was now his enemy, and he would deal with it in the future. In 332 the future was anything but certain, and the Carthaginians probably took the threat lightly. In 323, as Alexander returned to Babylon, a Carthaginian embassy was waiting for him: that future time had come (see Chapter 13).

As an example to cities that defied him, Alexander ordered that 2,000 of the Tyrians be crucified along the Syrian coast. While his order was being carried out, he finally sacrificed to Melqart. The army processed in full armour, and he held athletic contests and a torch race. He also dedicated to the god the Tyrian sacred ship and, cynically, the first of the battering rams that had breached the walls and so brought about Tyre's destruction.

Leaving a garrison in Tyre, which was repopulated by settlers from surrounding regions, Alexander could finally continue his journey to Egypt. During the siege Darius had sent another letter to Alexander, again wanting to ransom his family, but this time offering to surrender Asia Minor from the Hellespont to the Halys. Alexander refused: he was after everything.

Ultimately no real gain came from the cost in time, money and manpower expended on the siege, except to repair Alexander's damaged ego. Indeed, the message of the crucified Tyrians failed because as he marched south Alexander met further resistance. At the old Philistine city of Gaza, of great importance on the route from Palestine into Egypt, the commander, an Arab named Batis, and a group of Arab mercenaries defied him. They must have known about Alexander's siege of Tyre, and of the massacre of the population, but Gaza stood on a hill about 250 feet high and was enclosed by a fortified wall. That may have lulled them into a false sense of security and superiority. Again, Alexander prosecuted a siege.[11]

He ordered the building of a mound the same height as the city walls. On top of it, facing the part of the defensive wall that he thought was the weakest, he set up his siege towers from Tyre.

The assault began, and it lasted from September to November 332. At first the Macedonians were unsuccessful, and during one assault

Alexander was shot in the shoulder by a catapult bolt and lost much blood. The power of these bolts cannot be underestimated. This particular one penetrated both Alexander's shield and cuirass before lodging itself deep into his shoulder. He recovered, but the injuries that both sides sustained in any siege must have been terrible.

While Alexander's siege engines continued to bombard the walls of Gaza, the king gave the order to weaken the walls by digging under them. This was an easy task in the soft sand, and this tactic, plus the massive onslaught of the stones, signalled the end. Three Macedonian charges failed. Then a large section of the wall collapsed, and a fourth assault, led by Alexander, smashed through and into the city. The king though was wounded in the leg, and was forced to retire from the fighting.

The siege of Gaza lasted only two months, and the Macedonian army went on another murderous rampage. The fighting men of Gaza were wiped out, perhaps as many as 10,000, and the women and children sold into slavery. As in Tyre, a new population was put in place in Gaza from the surrounding regions. Batis was taken alive, though wounded. Alexander ordered a punishment akin to that inflicted by Achilles on the Trojan prince Hector when Troy fell. Batis's heels were pierced and a rope was run through these holes. This was then fixed to the back of a chariot. Naked, he was dragged behind a chariot around the walls of Gaza:

'Racked by pain, as his body passed over many rough pieces of ground, he began to scream. And it was just this detail that I now mention that brought people together. The torture was agonising, and he kept shouting out outlandish yells, asking mercy of Alexander as "my lord"; and his talk made them laugh. His fat and bulging figure suggested to them another creature, a huge-bodied Babylonian animal.'[12]

Batis was an obese eunuch and so the subject of ridicule. At some point while he was dragged alive and screaming around the walls he died.

Achilles, Alexander's hero, had done the same thing to Hector, so Alexander had a model to follow. Hector, however, was already dead when Achilles dragged him.

The punishment imposed on Tyre had not done the trick, for Gaza had defied Alexander. The punishment imposed on Gaza (and on Batis) repeated the terrible message of what would happen to anyone who lay on Alexander's route and defied him. Resistance seemed all the more futile.

7

Son of Ra, Son of Zeus

After the best part of a year, Alexander could finally swing west to Egypt. The sieges of Tyre and Gaza had cost him dearly in time as well as manpower, and he sent Amyntas, commander of the phalanx corps, to Macedonia for more troops. The winter timing of Amyntas's mission showed the desperate situation. It was doubly dangerous in the ancient world to travel by sea in winter, but so urgent was Alexander's need for men that Amyntas's safety came second.

Egypt is an exotic country today, and it was in antiquity. The Greeks knew about it, above all from traders. There was also Herodotus' fascinating description of its history and customs in the second book of his *Histories*. Alexander intended to go to Egypt for a number of reasons, including its wealth and trading connections. It was also controlled by Persia and it needed to be Macedonian. More importantly, it was home to the oracle of Zeus Ammon, situated in the Oasis of Siwah. Alexander's visit to this oracle was to be the turning point in his pretension to personal divinity.

Alexander's arrival in Egypt in 332 spelled the end of Persian rule, for the country surrendered to him. Egypt would never be its own master again in the ancient world. After Alexander's death in 323, Ptolemy seized Egypt and founded the Ptolemaic dynasty. That lasted until Cleopatra VII, when she and Antony fought Octavian, the future Emperor Augustus, at the Battle of Actium in 31. Thereafter Egypt became part of the Roman Empire, and was the emperor's personal possession.

After seven days of marching from Gaza, the Macedonians reached Pelusium (Port Said) on the Egyptian border. The fleet sailed alongside the army, probably carrying rations and water, and anchored safely in the harbour. There was no resistance, and the Egyptians at Pelusium turned out in force to welcome the Macedonian king, so great was their hatred of Persian rule. Memphis, which had already been capital of Egypt for 3,000 years, was next. The fleet sailed up the Nile while Alexander took

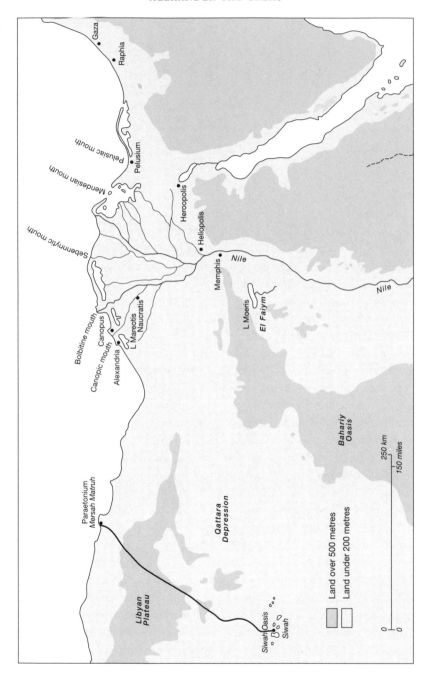

Northern Egypt and Siwah

Redrawn from Bosworth, A.B. (1988) *Conquest and Empire: The Reign of Alexander the Great* (pub Cambridge University Press), Map 4. © Cambridge University Press 1988, reproduced with permission.

a different route, via Heliopolis. There he visited the sun temple, before continuing to Memphis. The satrap of Egypt, Mazaces, had been in diplomatic contact with the king during the siege of Tyre. He surrendered Memphis, and thus Egypt, to him.

The Egyptians' reaction to his arrival pleased Alexander. It must also have been no small relief for his men too since winter was now upon them. Alexander celebrated with a sacrifice, athletic games, and musical contests, attended by competitors from all over the Greek world. This panhellenic event had a non-Hellenic element for there was a sacrifice of one of the bulls sacred to the Egyptian god Apis. Alexander used this sacrifice for propaganda reasons. Two previous Persian rulers of Egypt had impiously killed the sacred bulls. Alexander wanted to show that he would be tolerant of native religion.

Afterwards, Alexander received the formal titles of the Pharaohs: King of Upper and King of Lower Egypt, Son of Ra (the supreme god), Beloved of Ammon and Selected of Ra. As Pharaoh he performed the official sacrifices to the gods, and as Horus he was a god on earth. The *Alexander Romance* has Alexander crowned with these titles in a formal, Egyptian ceremony at Memphis. In other words, he was crowned actual Pharaoh. More likely is that Alexander accepted the titles but without a formal investiture.[1] In any case, he did not need the formality, for in reality as conqueror he was Pharaoh. That would set a pattern for the future Ptolemaic kings of Egypt until 196, during the reign of Ptolemy V (203–181). In an effort to counter threats to the Ptolemaic dynasty and recapture Egyptian loyalty, this king, at the age of 12, was crowned Ptolemy V Theos Epiphanes not in Alexandria, the capital established by Alexander, but in the traditional capital, Memphis.

Alexander's deference to local religion was far different from his attitude at Tyre, but the difference between the two places needs to be borne in mind. Egypt was a large country, with a population of about four million. It was very wealthy, and easily defended from outside attack. These were reasons why Ptolemy was so quick to take that country when Alexander died. Egypt was important to Alexander, and it was necessary to remain popular with the Egyptian people.

The titles as Pharaoh and especially Alexander's deference to Egyptian religion helped to reconcile his rule with the native people. He was now a god on earth, according to the Egyptians. While in Egypt, he heard that the oracle of Apollo at Didyma, with which he had earlier contact (see Chapter 5) had pronounced him a son of Zeus. Now the time had come for him to get divine ratification of that from Zeus himself. The dividing line between man and god was growing blurred, and not just in his own mind.

The oracle of Zeus Ammon in the Oasis of Siwah in Libya was the main sanctuary of the god in the Greek world. The Libyan Ammon was identified with Zeus, and as a boy growing up in Macedonia Alexander probably visited the temple to Zeus Ammon at Aphytis in the Chalcidice (see Chapter 14). Now it would be fitting to visit the god in his main sanctuary to give thanks for the successes so far.

But there was more to it than this. Alexander was struck with a 'longing' to go there. The Greek word for 'longing', *pothos*, now becomes a fixture in our accounts of Alexander's motives for his actions. It is more than a mere wish to do something that is desirable rather than essential. It means a real urge to go somewhere or do something; an aching, a personal need that has to be met. When Alexander wanted to march further east after he defeated Darius it was because of his *pothos*. However, while his men would follow him because of agreed policy, would they continue to follow him because of his *pothos*?

Alexander, then, really longed to go to Siwah for his own reasons, not because the Macedonian army needed to go there. His personal agenda was to learn 'his own origin more precisely, or at least that he might be able to say that he had learned it'.[2] The last part is ominous, for we have no record of exactly what the priest told Alexander, only the king's word (see below). And what Alexander would say clearly illustrated his pretensions to personal divinity.[3]

The oracle was in the middle of a desert, and stories abounded about it and its magical qualities:

'It is full of cultivated trees, olives and palms; and it is the only place in those parts which is refreshed with dew. A spring also rises from it, quite unlike all the other springs that come out from the earth. For at midday the water is cold to the taste, and even more so to the touch, as cold as cold can be. But when the sun has sunk into the west, it gets warmer, and from the evening it keeps on growing warmer until midnight. Then it reaches its warmest point. After midnight it starts to get gradually colder. At daybreak it is already cold, but at midday it reaches the coldest point. Every day it undergoes these alternate changes in regular succession.'[4]

The journey across the desert to Siwah was notoriously difficult. Cambyses was reported to have lost an army when going there. It was well known that Alexander wanted to eclipse the deeds of those before him. Thus, the men would have expressed no surprise at his intention to go there.

After a short stay in Memphis, Alexander set off with a small contingent of men and sailed down the Nile. They passed by the centuries-old Greek trading post of Naucratis, and reached Lake Mareotis. The site with its narrow isthmus between lake and sea was perfect for trade. Alexander decided he would found a new city on that isthmus, connected by a canal to the Nile, so that it would have two harbours. Thus was born Alexandria. This would become the premier city of the Hellenistic period, the second city of the Roman empire and a city of great trading importance today. Alexander only seems to have identified the site at this time. He did not lay the actual foundations until his return.

Siwah was a long way to the south-west. Alexander travelled 180 miles to the coastal town of Paraetonium; from there his route was due south – and over 150 miles of desert, and only desert, all the way. Apparently, the distance could be travelled in five days, but the Macedonians took longer, perhaps eight days, because of the hostile environment of the Libyan Desert, with its heat and sudden torrential downpours.

The actual details of the march are unknown. What we do know has been exaggerated as part of the Alexander legend. Callisthenes has this to say: 'When he got lost on the road, he escaped being overcome in a sand storm by a shower of rain, and by the guidance of two crows, which directed his course.'[5] 'But there was plenty of rain for Alexander,' says Aristobulus, 'a fact that was attributed to the god's influence.'[6] When Alexander got lost again, the same writer tells us:

'Ravens appeared and took over the direction of their march. They flew swiftly in front of them when they followed, and waited for them when they marched slowly and lagged behind. Moreover, what was most astonishing of all . . . the birds by their cries called back the men who got lost in the night, and cawed until they had set them back on the right track.'[7]

Ptolemy on the other hand has Alexander saved by two snakes: 'Two snakes went in front of the army, speaking in a human voice. Alexander ordered the guides to follow them, trusting in the divine portent. He says too that they showed the way to the oracle and back again.'[8] Ptolemy and Aristobulus also accepted Callisthenes' version of the two ravens as the most plausible.

Lucky rainstorms to save the men from dehydration, and ravens (or talking snakes) to guide the lost army back on the right path, admittedly make a great story. Then again, sudden rainfalls, sand storms that cover landmarks, crows by oases, and of course the heat, were, and are, found throughout the desert. Aristobulus even says so:

'Whenever a south wind blows in that region, it heaps up sand upon the route far and wide, rendering the tracks of the road invisible. It is impossible to discover what route one needs to take in the sand, just as if one were at sea. There are no landmarks along the road, no mountain anywhere, no tree, no large permanent hills, by which travellers might be able to work out the right course, as sailors do by the stars.'[9]

The story of the march has a kernel of truth to it, but the supernatural element can only have arisen thanks to court historiography (perhaps at the instigation of Alexander himself) out to make the king superhuman even before his visit to Siwah.

Finally, the men with Alexander saw Siwah. They must have stopped in their tracks at the sight. There, in the middle of nothing, was an oasis that was over 50 miles long and in parts 15 miles wide. Michael Wood's account of his journey there helps to bring to life the impact of the oasis on people even today:

'We entered a magical world ... It is an amazing sight surrounded by absolute desolation. Towards the sunrise are the dunes of the Western Desert. . . . To the south, lunar ridges, gravel beds, and the burning salt wastes of the Great Sand Sea stretch towards the Sahara, with scarcely a fixed habitation between there and Timbuktu. At our feet, shaded by a quarter of a million date palms, was boundless fertility. No wonder it was a sacred place for so long, a place where the divine was believed to speak directly to humankind [see Plate 18].'[10]

The oracle itself was situated inside a mud-brick fortress in the centre of the oasis. Alexander alone was admitted into the inner sanctum, a small room about 10 by 20 feet, for a consultation with Zeus's priest. He did not shed his clothes and put on the loincloth that those asking questions of the god wore. He was, after all, Pharaoh, and that allowed him latitude even with the god.

The priest would relay his questions to the god, interpret the divine responses and report back. Unlike the oracle of Apollo at Delphi, for example, where the god seems to have given his responses vocally to the priest, who then communicated them to the Pythia, the Egyptian god communicated by movement. Eighty priests hoisted onto their shoulders a golden boat on which was the jewelled image of the god. The god would then influence them to move one way or another, and perhaps also to shake the boat any number of times. They may have sung as well as part of the ritual. The priest would interpret the movements and deliver the answers. These were 'not given, as at Delphi and at Branchidae, in words, but mostly by nods and signs, as in Homer: "the son of Kronos nodded with his sable brows", the prophet imitating Zeus'.[11]

The priest may well have tried to greet Alexander as 'my boy', which would be in keeping with the fact that Alexander was Pharaoh and Son of Ra (Zeus). In Greek, 'my boy' would be O paidion. However, he seems to have slipped in his pronunciation (he was an Egyptian-speaking Greek after all) and greeted Alexander as O pai Dios, which means 'Son of Zeus'. A big difference, and one that Alexander eagerly took up. This was the first official word that he was not merely a descendant of Zeus.

Later tradition would have Alexander asking a barrage of questions, from how he should run the empire to whether the murderers of his father had been avenged. The latter might indicate that Alexander was still under a cloud for alleged complicity in an assassination conspiracy. The king apparently wrote to his mother Olympias to say that the priest had told him certain things that could only be related to her, and this he could only do when he returned to Macedonia.

During the exchange, the priest allegedly told Alexander that Philip II was only his mortal father, and that his real father was Zeus. The historicity of this part of the visit is likely to be false. So too are the divine predictions of Alexander's victory over Darius at Gaugamela in 331, Darius's death, and the enigmatic 'political changes at Sparta'. However, what is common to all accounts is that after the consultation Alexander called himself Son of Zeus.

Siwah is the turning point in Alexander's belief in his own divinity. As Pharaoh he was divine, but the priest called him Son of Zeus, and that was what counted. Alexander was alone with the priest, and so we have no way of knowing whether he reported the exchange accurately to his men – we are simply told that he 'heard what was agreeable to his wishes'.[12] However, as was quoted above, Alexander always *intended* to get this answer, and if he had to manufacture it then so be it. This shows the real reason for his visit to the oracle: whether the priest confirmed it or not, Alexander wanted divine parentage. From that time, Alexander always called himself son of Zeus as opposed to descendant of Zeus. The distinction is important. He was a descendant of Zeus through his Argead lineage (see Chapter 3), something his men accepted. But as time continued they came to resent the king who thought his father was Zeus, and that he himself was a god on earth. In 324 when the army mutinied at Opis, the men mocked his association with Zeus Ammon. Alexander, as a king and commander, ought to have known better.

Soon after, Alexander returned to Memphis. At the site of the proposed Alexandria, dream became reality:

'[He] ordered his architects to trace the circuit of the city to be founded. Since they had no clay to do so, he happened to see a threshing-floor with wheat on it. He ordered them to place the grains around and use them instead of clay to mark out the circuit. They did so. The following night birds came and ate up the grain. This seemed to be a sign. Some said that it augured ill (the new city would be captured). However, Alexander said it was a good omen (it made clear that the city would feed many people) and at once he built a large city there. He called it Alexandria, after his own name.'[13]

Deinocrates of Rhodes, the most famous architect of the day, supervised the plans. So was founded the second city that Alexander named after himself. The first was back in 340 when he had put down a revolt by the

Maedians on the upper Strymon and founded Alexandropolis. In 340 he had been only 16; in 331, when he founded Alexandria, he was still only 24.

On 7 April 331 Alexandria was officially founded. It would become much more of a multi-cultural city than the ordinary Greek state. It would be 'the crossroads of the world', the centre of trade, and of intellectual life in the Hellenistic period that followed Alexander's death down to the Roman occupation of the Greek east. Egyptians were free to live in Alexandria. They paid taxes, but could practise their own religions and customs, and were subject to Egyptian law. They could not take part in the administration of the city, however, which was firmly in the hands of Alexander's appointed officials. Only soldiers could carry arms and it was they that maintained law and order. Thus, we see two distinct tiers in the population of Greek and non-Greek. What is interesting, and deliberate policy on the part of Alexander, is that if the native Egyptians learned Greek language and indulged in Greek culture, they could become Greek citizens.

After Alexandria, it was back to Memphis, where Alexander held a sacrifice to Zeus the King. The son had returned safely.

The question remained, how long would Alexander be safe with Darius still on the loose? After a short stay in Memphis, Alexander moved north in perhaps April 331. He left behind a Macedonian fleet of 30 triremes and 4,000 troops to hold Egypt, with garrisons in Pelusium and Memphis. The commanders of these forces were subservient only to Alexander. Egyptians were responsible for collecting taxes in Upper and in Lower Egypt, which were sent to the king's finance officer, Cleomenes. He too was subservient only to Alexander. Thus, the king's control of Egypt was total.

Alexander's route lay across the Sinai, through Phoenicia to Tyre, which he reached in the summer. It was a very different arrival from his first time, and the cultural pull of the Macedonian court – and of the King of Macedonia, Son of Ra, and Son of Zeus – was shown.

At Tyre, Alexander held a celebratory festival to Heracles, attended by many dignitaries and royalty throughout the ancient world, including an embassy from the League of Corinth and the kings of Salamis and Soli on Cyprus. That island had already voluntarily surrendered to Alexander when he was besieging Tyre. Now, in an effort to show the island's loyalty and earn his goodwill, these kings funded elaborate and spectacular games and plays. Two kings in particular, Nicocreon of Salamis and Pasicrates of Soli, tried to outdo each other. They brought in the most celebrated performers of the time, Thessalus and Athenodorus. Thessalus had been a personal friend of the king for years. When he was still heir to the throne Alexander had used him in marital negotiations with Pixodarus, the satrap of Caria (see Chapter 3). Athenodorus was booked to perform at the City Dionysia in Athens, a festival of major cultural importance. It was created by Pisistratus in the mid-sixth century, and at it Thespis performed the first tragedy (hence the word thespian). In the fourth century it attracted people from all over the Greek world. Athenodarus broke his contract so that he could perform at Tyre, and was heavily fined. Alexander paid his fine.

Politics also occupied Alexander's mind while at Tyre. He received an embassy from the League of Corinth, which congratulated him on his achievements and voted him a golden crown. So too did the Athenians, who sent their own embassy. There was of course no love lost between Alexander and the Athenians. Evidence of this can be seen in a reference in one of the orator Aeschines' speeches that Demosthenes, the leading anti-Macedonian during Philip's reign and that of his son, had hoped that Alexander would be trampled under the hooves of the Persian cavalry at Issus. The Athenian embassy to Alexander had its own agenda: to keep in the king's good books and to plead for the release of Athenian captives from Granicus.

Alexander was not so naive as to misread the intentions of the Athenians. However, he granted their request. For one thing, trouble was brewing on the mainland due to the activities of the Spartan king Agis III. Sparta had refused to join the League of Corinth, and Agis was currently embroiled in a war against Macedonian troops in Crete. Alexander sent Amphoterus with the fleet there, and ordered Antipater to be on full alert in case Agis started to court mainland cities. The last thing he wanted was a war in Greece, or to alienate the Greek cities any more than he had to by enforcing the League of Corinth. Hence, releasing the prisoners from Granicus would appease the Athenians, and, he probably hoped, offset any sympathy for Agis.

As events turned out, the theatre of war did switch to Greece as Agis sought support from the Greek states in a war against the Macedonian hegemony. Almost all refused, including the Athenians, though not just because Alexander released their prisoners. Antipater would defeat and kill Agis a year later at the Battle of Megalopolis (see Chapter 8).

Another embassy met with far less success, and that was the one from Darius. The chronology is not certain, but it met Alexander either at Tyre or not too long after he had left the city in search of Darius. The Great King was now building on his earlier offer to Alexander. Now he would surrender all territories west of the Euphrates, become the friend and ally of the king, pay the colossal sum of 30,000 talents for the return of his family, and give one of his daughters in marriage to Alexander. This was unprecedented, and at least Parmenion thought the offer too good to refuse. Alexander disagreed, for he wanted unconditional surrender. This prompted the famous exchange between the two Macedonians in which Parmenion is alleged to have said that if he were Alexander he would accept the terms, and Alexander replied that if he were Parmenion he would.

The authenticity of this exchange is probably suspect. However, every story has a kernel of truth. This one indicates that at least some of his generals thought the invasion had achieved enough, that more fighting was needless given the worsening situation back on the mainland, and were unsettled by Alexander's cavalier attitude, especially towards the succession. He was still unmarried, and so without a legitimate heir. For a Macedonian king, this was a signal failing. Sometime in 332 Alexander had started a relationship with the Persian noblewoman Barsine, whom Parmenion had captured at Damascus (see Chapter 6). They did have a son, Heracles, but he was illegitimate for they did not marry.

If the Son of Zeus were aware of his men's attitude, he chose to ignore it. As Alexander expected, Darius rejected his demand of unconditional surrender. The final battle loomed.

8

Lord of Asia

The final battle against Darius, at Gaugamela, was arguably Alexander's greatest challenge to date. Granicus had been fought against hastily levied local troops, who underestimated the Macedonian war machine. Issus ought to have been a Persian victory, given its numerical superiority, but Alexander's tactics and Darius's flight sent victory Macedonia's way. Darius had been given another chance; his empire was now at stake, and he could not afford to lose at Gaugamela.

Since Darius had lost his support base in the west, he turned to the eastern and north-eastern parts of his empire for military support. Here lived – and live – some of the toughest people in the world. First-class cavalry and infantry came from Bactria, Sogdiana and western India, brought by Bessus, satrap of Bactria (north Afghanistan), and a blood relative of the Great King. There was also a contingent from the Saca peoples to the west and north of Sogdiana, whose cavalry was on a par with the Companion Cavalry. Almost as formidable were the cavalry from the central satrapies, for example the Areians, Arachosians and Parthyraeans.

Darius also had 200 scythed chariots, each pulled by four horses. These had razor-sharp scythes attached to the wheels as well as the chassis and the yoke pole. If used properly, these chariots could cut an opposing line to pieces, gashing the men in their legs and bodies. That would open up gaps big enough for the cavalry to exploit. However, the infantry did not match the superiority of the cavalry. The training of the local contingents of infantry was far inferior to the Macedonian, and the Greek mercenaries were all but non-existent.

Precise numbers for the Persian army are not known. Some sources give 200,000 infantry and 45,000 cavalry, while others give 1,000,000 infantry and 400,000 cavalry. The Macedonian army was about 47,000 infantry and 20,000 cavalry. There is no question that it was outnumbered, and the Persian cavalry force must have been a major source of

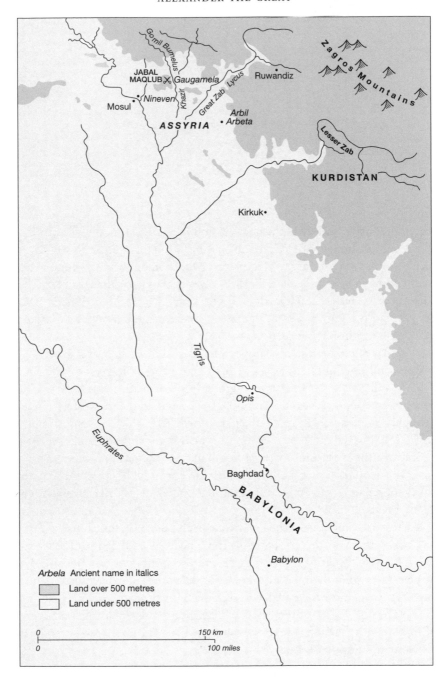

Assyria and Babylonia
Redrawn from Bosworth, A.B. (1988) *Conquest and Empire: The Reign of
Alexander the Great* (pub Cambridge University Press), Map 5. © Cambridge
University Press 1988, reproduced with permission.

concern for Alexander. Darius, moreover, was fighting for his empire. No wonder Alexander's senior generals were alarmed.

The Persian army set out from Babylon in the summer of 331, probably about the same time as Alexander left Tyre. It headed north through Mesopotamia, crossing the Tigris five days later, and then continued through Assyria (northern Iraq) to Arbela (Irbil), and finally encamped close to the village of Gaugamela (Tel Gomel). Mazaeus, Darius's former satrap of Syria, was sent with a force of 3,000 cavalry and 2,000 Greek mercenaries to keep an eye on Alexander and to disrupt his crossing of the Euphrates. Although Mazaeus prevented the construction of two bridges over the Euphrates at Thapsacus, Alexander's arrival panicked the Persians who hurriedly departed. Thus, Alexander crossed the Euphrates, near Jerablus, in mid to late summer 331.

He then marched east across northern Mesopotamia, making some incursions into Armenia, towards the Tigris, a distance of about 275 miles. It was imperative to bring Darius to battle as soon as possible rather than delay and so allow him to add to his forces. Alexander reached the Tigris to the north-west of the modern city of Mosul. After resting his army for two days he crossed the Tigris on the evening of 20 September. The date is known because of a lunar eclipse that occurred on 20–21 September, which Alexander took to forecast Macedonian victory over Persia. The eclipse was recorded in the Babylonian astronomical tablets. These and other documents written in cuneiform have only recently been discovered. They are valuable for chronology and for the Persian perspective of Alexander's invasion.[1]

Darius stationed his army in the plain between the River Bumelus (Gomel) and the Jabal Maqlub hills, between the Tigris and the foothills of the Zagros Mountains, stretching from Armenia to the Persian Gulf. He did not march to meet Alexander because the plain would allow him to use his cavalry against Alexander. He placed his hopes in his cavalry because he knew his infantry was no match for the Macedonian. He buried spikes (caltrops) in the ground to impede the Macedonian horses, and he also levelled out parts of the plain so that when he deployed his scythed chariots they would not encounter any bumps. The last thing Darius would do was to march to Alexander, and hence risk a battle on uneven terrain that would render his cavalry impotent.

After crossing the Tigris Alexander continued north-eastwards. He must have had a good idea of where the Persian army was, but it was not until four days later that he confirmed the actual location from some captured Persian scouts. Darius was less than 20 miles away. A four-day rest period for his army followed, during which Alexander sent his own scouts to spy on the Persian force and report back on its size and especially the terrain. When he was satisfied, it was time to move. He led his army to the base of the Jabal Maqlub, where he left his baggage train and non-military personnel. Mazaeus, he knew, was keeping check on him. However, the Macedonians were left alone, although Mazaeus will have reported Alexander's proximity and forces to Darius.

At night Alexander crossed to the slopes overlooking the plain of Gaugamela. He was only a couple of miles from the Persian line now, as visible to the enemy as the enemy to him. Darius had already drawn up his battle line. His immense numbers would have taken time to assemble and he could not afford to be caught off guard if the Macedonians suddenly attacked. The downside to his action was that he afforded Alexander the leisure time to study his deployment and finalise his plan of attack. We should also not devalue the psychological stress the Persian army would have felt by having to remain in battle order as the minutes ticked by and then the hours. What must have been going through their minds?

The Persian battle line was arranged in ethnic units. On its right flank, commanded by Mazaeus, were troops from Syria, Mesopotamia and from the central satrapies. In front of them were 50 scythed chariots and cavalry from Armenia and Cappadocia. Darius was in the middle of the line with his Royal Bodyguard and, on either side, whatever Greek mercenaries had stayed with him after Issus. In front of him was a small but deadly corps of 15 Indian elephants and 50 scythed chariots. On the backs of the elephants were wooden towers, in which sat armed men to shower javelins and other deadly weapons down on the enemy. Opponents were destroyed both by the men in the towers and by the elephants that trampled them underfoot.

The left wing was composed of the tremendous cavalry corps from the north-east regions together with the levies of the Saca peoples and others. In front of it were more cavalry and 100 scythed chariots. More infantry was to the rear of the long line, in an ever-deepening formation. It was Darius's intention to use the scythed chariots to open holes in the Macedonian line, through which the cavalry would pour, wreaking havoc. For that strategy to work, the Persian line had to stand fast and remain intact.

Alexander decided to attack the next day, perhaps yielding for once to the advice of Parmenion, who had insisted on a full reconnaissance of the Persian camp. His men were probably anxious to get the battle over with, and there seemed little point in delaying any longer. There was also the possibility that Darius would stand down his army, for it had been in battle formation all night. That was to Alexander's advantage for the troops would be tired and stressed, and so more likely to make mistakes. Alexander exhorted his men to do battle, and then with his right hand 'appealed to the gods, as Callisthenes tells us, praying to them, if he were really a son of Zeus, to defend and strengthen the Greeks'.[2] His wish was granted, so he said, when his 'father' sent an eagle at the Persian line.

Alexander saw that the Persian left wing, with the cream of the cavalry and the deadly scythed chariots, posed the greatest threat. He also saw that the Macedonian army would be outflanked because of the Persians' huge numbers. He decided on a strategy of having as many troops at as many points as possible to deal with the Persian push. These would disrupt the Persian lines before they disrupted his, and so allow his men to push through the gaps and encircle the enemy.[3]

The Macedonian line had the hypaspists on its right and in the centre Alexander with his infantry phalanx and Companion Cavalry. Alexander and Darius were probably facing each other almost exactly. On the left flank Parmenion led the cavalry of the Greek allies, including the invaluable Thessalians. Behind the front line was a second row of infantry, composed of troops from the League of Corinth, mercenaries and basically anyone else that was not stationed in the front line. The gap between these two lines was closed on each flank by more infantry and cavalry (Fig. 4).

The battle took place on 1 October. The details are largely unknown. This is not only because of the conflicting accounts in our ancient sources

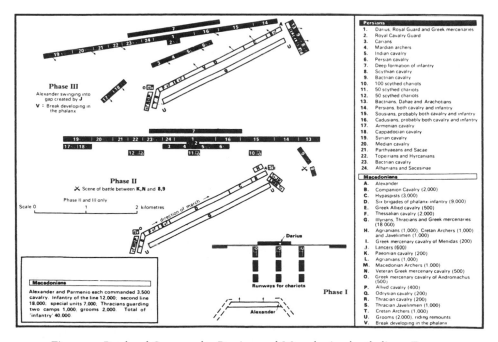

Figure 4. Battle of Gaugamela: Persian and Macedonian battle lines. From N.G.L. Hammond, *The Genius of Alexander the Great* (1997), p. 107

but also because the large number of cavalry created such a dense dust cloud that it was hard for anyone to see exactly what was going on. Dust storms were and are frequent here, and visibility can be reduced to only four or five yards.

The cavalry of the Persian left flank charged so hard at the Macedonian right that it was pushed back, forcing Alexander to wheel to his right to help to defend that flank. Fortunately for him, the sheer mass of the Persian front proved a hindrance as it could not move quickly enough to block his move, and the scythed chariots remained parked rather than veer onto rough terrain. On the left flank Parmenion was also in dire straits. His task was to stand fast and block the Persian right's advance under Mazaeus while Alexander tried to penetrate the Persian right wing. This plan came unstuck for a while when the Bactrian and Saca cavalry under Bessus blocked Alexander's advance. Some gaps in Parmenion's line opened, and contingents of Persian and Indian cavalry actually made it through. The fighting must have been bitter, the losses terrible, but Parmenion was not made of the stuff that gave way easily. The enemy advance was repelled.

At this point, Darius launched his scythed chariots. The Macedonian army was on the part of the plain that Darius had levelled so that these chariots could have a smooth and deadly ride. They should have penetrated the Macedonian line, disrupted the phalanx, and opened gaps for the Persian cavalry to crash through. They did not. The army, probably on cue, raised such an uproar that the horses were thrown off course. Then Alexander's Agrianians and javelinmen systematically shot them down, and the chariots went out of control – and everywhere except their intended destination. Some chariots did make it to the Macedonian front. As the line had done when facing the crashing wagons of the Thracians in spring 335, it created careful gaps to let them through, thus avoiding the scythes, and soldiers in the rear polished them off.

Meanwhile on the right wing of the Macedonian line the battle revolved around cavalry clashes. Bessus and his contingent had returned, and the fighting was fierce. Then the break that Alexander wanted happened. The Bactrian corps that had broken line to stop him penetrating the Persian right had opened a gap between the Persian left flank and the rest of the line. Against a commander of such daring and speed as Alexander this gap was fatal. In attempting to break through the Persian line, the Macedonian king had regrouped his men into a triangular formation. He now found himself at the head of this wedge formation, with his Companion Cavalry and phalanx streaming down one side and the Agrianians and infantry on the other. Alexander burst through the Persian line, soon followed by the Companions and the phalanx with its deadly wall of sarissas. The Persian line was breached, and Alexander now sought Darius himself. He would never find him at Gaugamela. The Great King saw that all was lost. He had already fled, to Arbela about 70 miles away.

Darius's flight was followed by the retreat of Bessus and his force, leaving the Macedonian right safe. The Macedonian left was still outnumbered and still under heavy attack, and Parmenion sent an urgent request to Alexander for help. His motive for doing so has earned his criticism in the sources:

'There is a general complaint that in the battle Parmenion was sluggish and inefficient, either because old age was now affecting his courage to an extent, or because he was envious and resentful of the arrogance and display, to use Callisthenes' words, of Alexander's power.'[4]

The king did not help, but fortunately Parmenion was saved by the news of the Persian rout elsewhere and that Darius had fled. The Persian right's spirit was dashed, and its will to fight destroyed. Thus, Parmenion, ably helped by a last-minute charge of the Thessalian cavalry that sent the remaining troops fleeing, defeated the Persian right. A considerable achievement, and one worthy of Alexander himself. The criticism of the source quoted above is unjust.

The battle that Darius should have won, needed to win, was over. Alexander's numerically smaller army had defeated the Persian one. A more competent king might have proved more of an obstacle for Alexander, but it is hard to imagine the eventual outcome of the battle being different. Darius's strategy with the scythed chariots, for example, had failed, and the battle had turned in Macedonia's favour when he fled. Alexander's strategy, which depended so much on the Macedonian right flank keeping the Persian heavy cavalry at bay and the left flank standing fast against the Persian advance, had been brilliantly successful. The precise number of casualties is unknown, but the Persians are said to have lost 56,000 to the Macedonians' 1,200.

Why did Alexander not immediately go to the aid of the hard-pressed Parmenion? For one thing, Alexander was not prepared to have Gaugamela turn into another Issus. This time, Darius had to be captured. Once he knew that the Great King had fled, Alexander pursued him immediately, regardless of the danger facing the Macedonian left. He probably gambled that once news of Darius's flight became known, Persian demoralisation would have done the rest. That in effect, was what happened. Another solution is that he never got Parmenion's urgent demand, given the confusion on the battlefield and especially the dust cloud that would have obscured vision. The messenger with Parmenion's request may never have seen Alexander, or saw that he was already too far away to be caught. There is also another possibility that, based on the growing divide between Alexander and Parmenion, the king deliberately chose not to help him. This scenario is set out and discussed in Chapter 9.

There was not the massacre as there was in the aftermath of Issus, but that was probably because the terrain allowed the survivors an easy escape. Alexander had also immediately set off in pursuit of Darius while the rest of his army was still fighting in battle. He pursued him for almost 20 miles until night fell, and then returned to camp. This made sense as he would want a full report on the battle and would need to know how his troops were doing. The fighting was not yet over, however, for as he and his Companions rode back to the main army they came across a contingent of retreating soldiers from the Persian left. An unexpected and desperate fight ensued, costing the lives of 60 Companions, before the enemy troops were beaten.

Darius was now a spent force. He fled eastwards towards the Zagros Mountains with some of his men including Bessus and his cavalry. However, the majority of the Persian survivors threw in their lot with Mazaeus. They marched south to Babylon by a circuitous route that kept them a long way from the Macedonian army. Although Alexander renewed his pursuit of Darius the day after the battle, he abandoned it at Arbela. He was anxious to press south, to the riches of Babylon and Susa (Shush). These, as Arrian describes them (3.16.2), were the 'prizes of the war'. Alexander was ready go to the heart of the Persian empire itself: Persis.

Alexander was now, in fact, Great King, but he referred to himself as Lord of Asia. The difference is important when it came to his relations with his own men. After cremating and burying his dead from the battle, the march south through Babylonia began. Any doubts that his men had before the battle about his leadership or his plans must have vanished in the light of the success at Gaugamela. Some may well have hoped for a return home, given that Alexander now controlled a vast stretch of land west of the Zagros Mountains. However, it was clear that Alexander was far from ready to return.

The men must have been aware of his desire since he had sent Philoxenus ahead to secure the surrender of Susa. They probably guessed that this would not be his final destination. If he truly wanted to avenge the Greeks for what they suffered during the Persian Wars, he would have to press on to the great palace of Xerxes at Persia's ceremonial capital Parsa (what the Greeks called Persepolis). This he would do. For now no one uttered a word of protest. He may even have enticed his men to continue on with the promise of large cash bonuses once he got to the treasuries at Babylon and beyond.

His route took him along the Royal Road to Kirkuk by the foothills of the Kurdish Mountains. Three weeks and 280 miles later, he came to

Babylon, on the junction of the Tigris and Euphrates rivers. Babylonia was the richest satrapy in the Persian empire, and Babylon was one of its most important capitals. He arrived there on 24 or 25 October. Mazaeus, commander of the Persian right wing at Gaugamela, who had fought so hard and valiantly against Parmenion – against Macedon – surrendered to the new Lord of Asia. The citadel commander Bagophanes followed suit.

Alexander would now become King of Babylon, former home of Nebuchadnezzar, site of the Tower of Babel and of course the Hanging Gardens. Iraq had enjoyed three millennia of history that had placed it (and Babylon) firmly at the centre of civilisation. Now it was Alexander's. The young monarch had come a long way in terms of distance and imperial acquisitions. His exploits are all the more amazing for it had only been a little over three years since he crossed the Hellespont. Now the Great King had been convincingly defeated, and Alexander controlled almost all of the mighty Persian empire. He was about to penetrate to the very heart of Persia, Persis, and its capital Persepolis. No one, not even Alexander, could have foreseen his spectacular successes when he first set out for Asia.

Alexander entered Babylon through the magnificent Ishtar Gate like a Roman general celebrating a triumph. Cheering crowds threw rose petals in his path, and the air was thick with the smell of incense. The Babylonians had endured two centuries of oppressive Persian rule, and they were ready for a change. As might be expected, Alexander made the great palace with its 600 rooms his home for the duration of his stay in Babylon. If it was good enough for Nebuchadnezzar, then it was good enough for him.

He also seized the treasury, and saw to it that his long-suffering troops finally received a bonus. Each Macedonian cavalryman was given 600 drachmas, each Greek cavalryman 500 drachmas, and each Macedonian infantryman 200 drachmas. A Greek mercenary infantryman was given two months' pay, about 60 drachmas. The other allied troops received donatives of a similar amount. The cash bonuses may not have been a reward for the mere sake of reward, but Alexander keeping up his end of a deal struck after Gaugamela. It would not be the first time that Alexander would use money to lure his army further east.

Alexander then sacrificed, in local tradition, to the patron deity of the city Belus (Ba'al). One thing he did not do, and that was to rebuild Egasila, site of a great temple complex to the god Marduk that had been run down during Xerxes's reign in the fifth century. The local priests probably expected their new King of Babylon to rebuild the site, not least to ingratiate himself with them and to gain the popularity of his subjects. They would be sorely disappointed. Alexander was not against the rebuilding project, but it was the Babylonians who had to foot the bill and perform the labour. When he returned to Babylon in 323, he found they had still not done so (see Chapter 13).

Alexander had his sights set on higher things. The army spent a month enjoying the pleasures of Babylon (though prostitution with crocodiles is probably far-fetched!), and set off for Susa (Shush) on 25 November 331. This was the winter capital of the Persian empire, where the court went to escape the searing heat of Babylon in the summer. It is now in Iranian Khuzestan, about 350 miles to the south-east of Babylon, close to the head of the Persian Gulf.

During this time, Amyntas had returned with reinforcements from the mainland. This was the man whom Alexander had sent to Greece a little over a year ago, after the siege of Gaza, when he was in need of men. Amyntas brought with him 15,000 troops, of which 13,500 were infantry (Macedonian, Thracian and mercenary), and 1,500 were cavalry (Macedonian, Thracian and Peloponnesian). In view of the losses at Gaugamela, the new men could not have come at a better time. The Macedonian army was probably not as large as in the initial invasion in 334, when it numbered about 40,000, but at least those who had died at Gaugamela were replaced.

Also travelling to Alexander with the reinforcements were 50 sons of Macedonian nobles, intended for use as his bodyguard. They were the Royal Pages, and so would have been 17. The age is known because from the time they turned 14 the Pages spent four years in various academic and physical pursuits before graduating at 18, when they became permanent fixtures in Alexander's retinue. The last year of their 'course' was spent on location with the king or another high-ranking Macedonian. Callisthenes and other intellectuals at the court were responsible for the Pages' instruction.

The Royal Pages had traditionally attended the king at his court in Pella. Alexander was now a long way from there, so it made sense for him to summon the boys to wherever he (and his court) happened to be, rather than have them train for their final year under Antipater's direction. There may be more to it than this, though. Later in his reign, Alexander seems to have become fixed on making the capital of his empire not Pella but Babylon, to the discontent of his army and people at home. The new venue for the completion of the Pages' training could be part of this new direction in the Macedonian kingship. In 327 some of the Pages hatched a plot against Alexander's life that almost succeeded (see Chapter 10).

Before Alexander left Babylon he made some administrative arrangements. The Persian system of satrapies had been operating for centuries, and it made sense for Alexander to exploit it. He appointed Mazaeus as satrap of Babylonia, the first Persian to be given this title and power. Almost in the same breath, he appointed Mithrenes, commander at Sardis, satrap of Armenia. His actions must have caused consternation among his men, but Alexander was intent on treating the enemy well if that enemy voluntarily defected from Darius. Mazaeus had faced him at Gaugamela, but he had redeemed himself by surrendering Babylon without protest. Others would do the same as news of Alexander's policy became known. This political agenda had an equally important pragmatic one. Native satraps were already conversant with local customs, laws and religion; they could speak the native language and local dialects, all of which were necessary for the smooth running of the administration.[5]

At the same time, Alexander could not give Mazaeus total power. Hence, two Macedonians were given power. Apollodorus was made commander of 700 Macedonian and 1,300 Greek mercenary infantry, and Asclepiodorus was the collector of the tribute. Mazaeus's power lay only in the civil sphere, while Macedonians controlled what really mattered: the army and the treasury. This arrangement became the lynchpin of his imperial administration. The Persian administrative system of satrapies and satraps owing allegiance to the king was already in place and had been working well for over a century. It made perfect sense for Alexander to adopt, and adapt, it. It also showed how Alexander was setting himself up as King of Asia, not merely the conquering King of Macedonia.

Philoxenus had already secured Susa, the satrap Abulites surrendering to him without incident. All Alexander had to do was to march along the Persian Royal Road from Babylon to Susa, which lay close to the Persian Gulf. It took him about 20 days. He was now on the border between Iraq and Iran. So civilised the regions, yet so bloody given their long history of warfare that extends down to today.

Abulites met him at the river Choaspes, a mile or so from Susa, with gifts including Indian elephants and racing camels, and ceremoniously escorted him into Susa. It was now 15 December 331. Once in Susa, second capital of the Persian empire, home of the tomb of the prophet Daniel, Alexander took control of its vast treasury. He netted 40,000 talents of gold and silver bullion and 9,000 talents of Persian gold coins, the most money he had captured in one hit.

The Persian kings lived in a state of great luxury:

'At the head of the royal couch there was a supper-room laid with five couches, in which there were always kept five thousand talents of gold. This was called the King's pillow. And at his feet was another supper-room, prepared with three couches, in which were constantly kept three thousand talents of silver. This was called the King's footstool. And in his bedchamber there was also a golden vine, inlaid with precious stones, above the King's bed, and this vine, Amyntas says in his *Stages*, had bunches of grapes, made from the most valuable precious stones.'[6]

For centuries the Persian king had collected vast wealth and treasures. In one room of the palace Alexander came across the art works and stat-

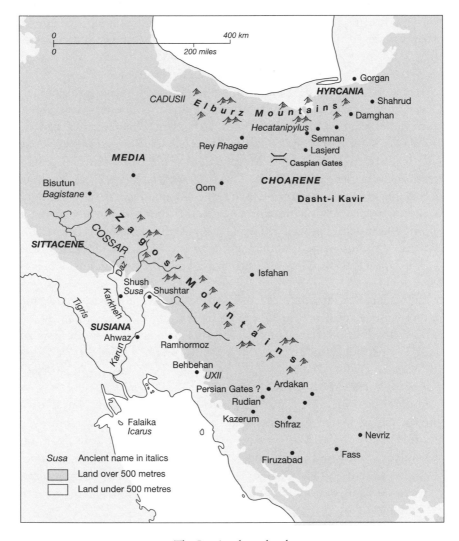

The Iranian heartlands
Redrawn from Bosworth, A.B. (1988) *Conquest and Empire: The Reign of Alexander the Great* (pub Cambridge University Press), Map 6. © Cambridge University Press 1988, reproduced with permission.

ues that the Persians had seized when they invaded Greece in the early fifth century. This included the statue of two famous tyrant slayers of the late sixth century, Harmodius and Aristogeiton, which had been set up on the Acropolis. It was meant to symbolise the importance of democracy over unconstitutional rule, specifically the rule of one man (a tyrant). Now, Alexander had it returned to the Athenians. The irony would not have been lost on him or on them.

Finding these art works brought home what the invasion was all about. While in the palace at Susa, Alexander sat on Xerxes's throne, but his feet did not reach the ground. One of his courtiers placed a table under his feet, saving him the embarrassment of dangling feet. The same table, it was said, from which Darius used to eat. Now it was Alexander's footstool. The symbolism was obvious.

The wealth and luxurious lifestyle of the Persian kings had a great effect on Alexander and on his men. In addition to availing himself of many fine works of art and pampering luxury items, Alexander gave up a completely Macedonian wardrobe for one that was a mixture of Persian and Macedonian. For example, he combined the Macedonian *kausia*, a type of wide-brimmed hat, and cloak with the Persian white-and purple-striped tunic and girdle. Indulging oneself was one thing, but Alexander went beyond mere personal indulgence. He would go even further when he started to wear a diadem around his *kausia* (see Chapter 9).

Purple was the colour of the Persian court. Now, the Companions wore purple hats and cloaks with a purple border, and they had Persian harnesses for their horses. They did not seem to object, and like Alexander enjoyed the finer things in life. They used myrrh rather than ordinary oil in the bathtub. Hagnon of Teos was said to wear silver nails in his boots while Leonnatus dusted himself before wrestling with imported powder from Egypt.

Alexander was now receiving worrying news from back home. Agis III of Sparta had taken his war against Macedonia to the Greek mainland, and was calling for aid from the Greek states.[7] Antipater at that time was occupied in Thrace. He was hard-pressed for men, the result of Alexander's call for additional troops. Accordingly, the king sent Menes with 3,000 of the captured talents to Antipater so that he could hire mercenaries.

We have to call Agis's rising a war, not a revolt, for Sparta had refused to join the League of Corinth. Although Agis was supported by only a handful of Greek states (Elis, Achaea and most of Arcadia) he had hired 10,000 mercenaries with the Persian gold given to him by Pharnabazus. The city of Megalopolis in Arcadia had refused to side with Agis and was now being besieged by Arcadian forces. Defections were not allowed by the League's Common Peace agreement, and loyal allies certainly should not be facing a siege. Moreover, there was Athens, which, thanks to its navy, was the most powerful state in Greece. If the Athenians joined Agis, then the potential for an invasion of Macedonia was very real.

There was a debate in Athens over Agis's call to arms, so at least some of the Athenians were not closing the door on him. Demosthenes, supported by the general Phocion, advised the Athenians against supporting him. His anti-Macedonian policy had been the gamble that Persia would defeat Alexander. He had seen this gamble lose at Issus in 333 and it would die the death at Gaugamela in 331. Now, Demosthenes was finally reading the writing on the wall properly. He realised that Agis's war was fruitless, and that Athenian involvement in it would lead to severe reprisals at the hands of Antipater, or Alexander himself. He probably had not forgotten his scare in 335 when Alexander demanded his surrender. If he did that once, he could do so again. Legally, any state that flouted the Common Peace of the League of Corinth could face an army of the other states led by Antipater, and there was little love lost between the various states. It must have been hard for staunch anti-Macedonians like Demosthenes to realise that no rising against the Macedonian hegemony could be successful.

In hindsight, Demosthenes's counsel was prudent. Although Sparta managed to defeat a Macedonian force led by Corragus, Antipater did not need the money sent by Alexander. In April or May 330 he took an army of 40,000 into the Peloponnese to face Agis's army of 32,000 (including the 10,000 mercenaries hired with Persian money) at Megalopolis. There, Antipater defeated and killed Agis along with 5,300 of the Spartan army. Rather than impose his own penalty on the enemy states, Antipater referred their fate to the League of Corinth. It fined Agis' allies the large sum of 120 talents, an amount that was to be paid to Megalopolis, and arrested the ringleaders for treason.

The Spartans' fate was referred to Alexander himself. Perhaps surprisingly, he pardoned them; but they were now made to join the League of Corinth. There seems little doubt that the Athenians would have been punished severely had they supported Sparta. From then until Alexander's death in 323, Greece remained passive under Macedonian hegemony. Agis's war had shown the impotency of the Greeks; Alexander could rest easier – and advance further – knowing that Antipater exerted total control over the Greeks.

Alexander had little time to enjoy Susa for he was anxious to get to Persepolis as soon as he could. It was mid-winter, probably January. The passes that he would have to traverse through the Zagros Mountains would be covered in snow, probably blocked. This was not the time to travel but Alexander had no choice. He confirmed Abulites as Satrap of

Susa, but again left a garrison of Macedonian soldiers to keep the place in check. This garrison included 1,000 veteran soldiers that Alexander could relieve from active duty because of the fresh supply of troops brought by Amyntas earlier.

The army, probably grumbling about an advance at that time of the year, set off. The march went well, showing among other things the Macedonians' competency, expertise even, in mountain travel, all the more remarkable given the inhospitable and tough conditions of winter. Then they came to Uxiana, south-east of Susa. The Uxians were an independent people, and those who lived in the upper region levied a fee in animals or goods for anyone, including Persians, who wanted safe passage through their land.

Medates and a force tried to block Alexander's passage, probably close to the northern border with Susiana, and a minor battle was fought. The Macedonian army easily crushed the opposition, Alexander attacking them head-on while a contingent of Agrianians and mercenaries went around the side of the enemy force and came out on top of it. Surrounded, Medates surrendered.

Alexander resumed his march and came to the people of the upper region, who requested their usual passage fee. The king refused to pay but offered to discuss the matter at the entrance to the pass that they controlled. While they went there, Alexander put into action a very fast and two-tiered strategy. First, he rushed into nearby Uxian villages and burned and looted them. Then he marched to the pass, and sent Craterus and a unit of troops into its heights before the Uxians arrived. A fierce battle was fought, which turned into an annihilation as the Uxians were boxed in between Alexander and his men and Craterus's force. Those that survived had to pay an annual tribute to Alexander of 600 horses and mules and 30,000 cattle, goats and sheep. The tribute in kind reflects that the people did not have a monetary economy.

The conflicts in Uxiana were minor compared to the battles fought against the Persian army of course. Nonetheless, they show us the ease with which Alexander defeated these two opposing forces and how rapidly his men could be deployed. It was a pity that more opponents in Alexander's path did not learn this lesson. Alexander realised that some people still resisted the Macedonian advance, and by extension that Darius still commanded some loyalty. His battles were still far from over.

At the modern town of Fahlian, close to the border with Persis, Alexander split the army into two. Parmenion would lead the main column, together with the baggage train, and take a slower and more circuitous route to Persepolis via Kazerun and Shiraz. The king, leading about 20,000 Macedonians, together with the Agrianians and archers, would take a different and more direct route over the Zagros Mountains to the plain of Persepolis. The reason for this split and a faster-moving smaller force is clear: Alexander needed to get to Persepolis before its treasury was embezzled. The entire army would be too slow because of the baggage train. Thus Parmenion would arrive after Alexander had established himself in Persepolis, and was in control of Persis.

Alexander's exact route is unknown, but it took him to the Persian Gates, a narrow gorge about six miles long, passable only by foot. There is no doubt that he needed local guides to steer him through. There the invader faced the defender. Deep into the Persian Gates, a Persian army, led by the satrap Ariobarzanes, was occupying the heights on both sides and was blocking the gorge. Alexander charged forward, but realised his mistake too late. He was driven back by a barrage of missiles from the heights. This had been a rash move on his part, the result of underestimating the superior location of the enemy troops as well as their reason for fighting. This was their land after all. To make matters worse, he was forced to leave his dead, an unthinkable situation for him (and his army), as he retreated.

Fortunately for him, a local shepherd (from Lycia, but who spoke Greek) told him of an arduous, rocky path about 12 miles long that would bring him out behind the Persian force. This was his only chance, and that night, in pitch black conditions, he set off. Craterus, with two phalanxes and some archers and cavalry, was left behind in the Macedonian camp. He burned extra fires in it to make it look as though the full complement of Alexander's army were there. Speed was of the essence. In a gradual loop, Alexander crossed over the Bolsoru Pass and then went south-east to the base of the Kuh-i-Rudian.

Persian scouts could be anywhere, and Alexander needed to move quickly and confuse the enemy. As Alexander reached the end of the path, and thus the rear of the Pass, Ptolemy and 3,000 soldiers were left to make their way down to the middle of the enemy by another route, this one down a deep ravine. Alexander's strategy had a twofold function: scouts might only see one contingent and report back accordingly, and when Alexander attacked the Persian camp he would be able to bring up two waves of attackers from different positions. The element of surprise was always crucial to his strategy.

It took another day and night before the Macedonians reached Ariobarzanes and his force. At dawn, Alexander came down hard from behind them, while Craterus, responding to a prearranged trumpet signal, attacked frontally. Ptolemy was waiting for them in the middle. The Persians were caught off guard, and were routed. A massacre followed. Ariobarzanes and a small force of cavalry and infantry managed to escape

li apainst en macedone en
la samblance quil li deust
aidier quil peust retornei
sain et sauf a son peuple
non mie poi lui mes poi le

sauuement deaus. Lois
a ombia la uertu diuine.
Coment alixandies se fet es
ter en la mer en j tonnel
de uoirre.

Plate 1. Alexander the Great being lowered to the sea-bed in a glass cage where the fish
crowd round him and pay homage. From 'L'Histoire du Noble et Valliant Roy
Alixandre le Grant', French, 1506, Bibliotheque Royale de Belgique, Brussels, Belgium /
Bridgeman Art Library.

Plate 2. Mount Olympus. Whole massif. AAA Collection Ltd.

Plate 3. Cobbled floor and ruins at Pella. © John Heseltine/CORBIS

Plate 4. Gold medallion with the head of Philip II of Macedonia c. 4BC. Akg-images.

Plate 5. Marble statue of Demosthenes, the Athenian orator and politician.
© Bettmann/CORBIS.

Plate 6. Bust of Alexander the Great (marble) attributed to Lysippus (fl.370–310 BC). Louvre, Paris, France / Bridgeman Art Library.

Plate 7. Two classical figures fighting a lion, early hellenistic period (mosaic). Archaeological Museum, Thessaloniki, Greece / Bridgeman Art Library.

Plate 8. Ivory group of Pan-Dionysus-Ariadne, from Vergina, perhaps showing Philip, Olympias and a young Alexander as Pan. Exhibition of the Royal Tombs at Vergina

Plate 9. Gold larnax from the casket of Philip II of Macedonia at Vergina, decorated with the star emblem of the Macedonian dynasty, 4th century BC (gold), Archaeological Museum, Thessaloniki, Greece / Bridgeman Art Library.

Plate 10. Ivory head of Alexander, from Tomb II. Exhibition of the Royal Tombs at Vergina.

Plate 11. Head of Philip II of Macedonia, from Tomb II at Vergina. © Gianni Dagli Orti/CORBIS.

Plate 12. H. Daumier, 'Alexander and Diogenes'. National Gallery of Athens.

Plate 13. L. Domeniquin (1581–1641), 'Timocleia before Alexander'. Paris, Louvre ©
1990, Photo Scala, Florence.

Plate 14. Painting by Fontebasso, 'Alexander Sacrificing at the Tomb of Achilles'.
© 2003 National Gallery in Prague.

Plate 15. Temple ruins at Didyma. David Wallace/Maya Vision International.

Plate 16. The 'Alexander Mosaic'. AAA Collection Ltd.

Plate 17. Illuminated manuscript showing the attack on the city of Tyre. From the History of Alexander the Great, France, 15th c. Dutuit 456, f. 58v. Photo: Bulloz. Réunion des Musées Nationaux/Art Resource, NY. Coll. Dutuit, Musée du Petit Palais, Paris, France.

Plate 18. Siwah Oasis. Michael Wood/Maya Vision International.

Plate 19. General view of Apadana, 6th–5th BC, Persepolis, Iran. Giraudon/Art Resource, NY.

Plate 20. Silver coin of Lysimachus showing Alexander the Great wearing the horn of Ammon. Museum of Fine Arts, Boston, Henry Lillie Pierce Fund; 04.1181. Photograph © 2003 Museum of Fine Arts, Boston.

Plate 21. Silver coin of Ptolemy showing Alexander wearing an elephant cap and a ram's horn. Museum of Fine Arts, Boston, anonymous gift in memory of Zoe Wilbour (1864–1885), 35.215. Photograph © 2003 Museum of Fine Arts, Boston.

Plate 22. Iranian tale-teller, Michael Wood/Maya Vision International.

to Persepolis, but its citadel commander Tiridates, seeing the writing on the wall, kept the gates closed. In a last-ditch effort Ariobarzanes and his force took on the Macedonian army again, and were cut to pieces.

Persepolis was now Alexander's for the taking, and he entered it on 30 January 330. Tiridates had sent a letter to the Macedonian king surrendering Persepolis and its huge treasury. His act would not save the city, however. The principal reason given for the invasion of Persia in 334 was revenge. Revenge for the Persian Wars of 480–479, sparked off by Xerxes's invasion. At the same time, it would not be forgotten that Darius I had sent a Persian army into Greece in 490. This had looted Eretria on the island of Euboea before the Athenians defeated it at the Battle of Marathon.

Now, the Macedonian army was in Persepolis, the symbolic centre of the Persian empire, 'the most hateful city in Asia'.[8] A little distance from the city (probably Istakhr) was the palace of Darius I and Xerxes (see Plate 19), with its soaring columns, audience halls, and friezes showing embassies from Ethiopia, India (people of Hindush, the Indus Valley), Central Asia and Asia Minor, bringing gifts and tribute to the Great King.

Alexander occupied the palace itself and allowed his men free range to act as they saw fit in the city. They did not need to be told twice. For one entire day they looted it. Some of them fought with each other over the valuables they found in the houses. Some cut off the hands of those who would not let go of something they wanted. They also killed the military and non-military men, and enslaved the women, after first raping them, and children. Given that the ordinary population had nothing to do with the Persian Wars and that Tiridates had opened the gates voluntarily to Alexander, there was no excuse for the slaughter of so many innocent people. Except there was, in Alexander's (and in the Greeks') eyes: revenge for what the Persians had inflicted on the Greeks 150 years ago.

Persepolis ceased to be the capital of Persis. From then on, Persis became a satrapy ruled by a new capital: Babylon. Close to Persepolis was Pasargadae, the first capital of the empire and home of the tomb of Cyrus the Great, the founder of the Persian empire. The wealth that Alexander seized from Persepolis and from the treasury at Pasargadae was enormous: 120,000 talents of gold coin as well as treasure. He arranged for an enormous train of 7,000 camels and pack animals to transport most of it to Susa. The remainder he took with him on the next leg of his campaign, to Media, where Darius III was again raising an army.

The Macedonians spent at least four months at Persepolis until the winter had passed. During that time, Alexander was involved in a campaign in southern Persis against the Mardi tribe. These people are distinct from the Mardi who lived south of the Caspian, on the south-west border of Hyrcania, against whom Alexander would presently campaign (see Chapter 9). The details of the present campaign are unknown, but the danger must have been enough for Alexander to fight them in the harsh winter conditions. Then again, it may simply have been used by Alexander to keep his army in training and to toughen it for what lay ahead. At some point during the stay, Parmenion and the slower-moving baggage train, which had taken a different route from the border of Persis, arrived. The Macedonian army was whole again.

In about May 330, with the winter behind him, Alexander prepared to leave Persepolis. Before he did so, something happened that has puzzled scholars for years. The palace burned to the ground. The real reason for the destruction is unknown, and will probably remain so unless some startling new evidence is unearthed or Alexander speaks to us on a psychic telephone hotline. There are two common explanations. The first is that after a drunken orgy the Macedonians burned down the palace by accident. The second is that Alexander deliberately caused its destruction, thereby closing the book on revenge on the Persians for what Xerxes had done, and formally ushering in a new age under his own rule.[9]

The two explanations may not be mutually exclusive. At some stage Alexander convened a meeting with his closest friends and generals to talk of the future of the palace itself. Should it be burnt down as revenge for the Persians' burning of the Athenian Acropolis? Should it be left to stand as a symbol of the new Macedonian regime? Alexander had stripped the palace of all its treasures, but this action does not mean that he intended to destroy it. On the other hand, its symbolic importance, as shown in the subject peoples of the friezes paying homage to the Great King, meant that he had to do *something* with it. However, to destroy it might cause reaction against him – Darius was still out there, and the remaining satraps were still loyal to him.

Alexander it seems was keen to destroy the palace but Parmenion urged him not to destroy it because of the resentment it would cause among the Persians. The king's dilemma was soon solved. At a banquet one night, the story goes, the drink flowed in its usual abundance and an Athenian courtesan, Thais, said loudly that the palace ought to be burnt given what the Persians had done to her Athens so long ago. Her suggestion was suddenly taken up, and those present, including Alexander, seized torches and in a macabre dance set fire to the palace. The wooden ceilings were soon ablaze. Then others from the army joined in, and before long the entire palace was a bonfire. No attempt was made to put out the fire, and by morning the palace was a mere collection of smoking ruins.

Alexander seems to have regretted what happened, but that may well have been a diplomatic reaction. There was no protest from the Persians at the destruction of the palace. This does not mean that his rule was coming to be accepted but that any such protest at that time would have been ineffectual. Indeed, the Persians saw him as evil, and today among some he is called accursed (see Chapter 15). Thais, on the other hand, later became Ptolemy's mistress and gave birth to three of his children. Presumably he kept a sharp eye on her in his palace in Alexandria.

Alexander could now exploit the propaganda of the destroyed palace, regardless of whether the fire had been accidental or not. It had been burned and gutted just as the Acropolis of Athens had been looted and burned during the Persian invasion. We should also not overlook the coincidental timing of the palace's destruction with events on the mainland. Agis III's war was in full swing, and from Susa Alexander had sent money to Antipater to use to hire mercenaries. News of Persepolis's destruction for the panhellenic reasons Alexander gave would have reached the Greeks in about March 330. It would have helped to offset support for Agis, and evidently did, for not long after Antipater brought him to battle at Megalopolis. Why would the Greek states support a war against the king who was successfully wreaking revenge on their former enemy?

Alexander appointed Persian satraps to govern Persis and Carmania, and a garrison of 3,000 was installed in Persepolis. In many respects, the Macedonians had fulfilled the mandate of the League of Corinth. There must have been some in Alexander's retinue who urged him to return home now, but Darius, though twice defeated, had not yet given up, and was still at large. With a contingent of his own troops and Greek mercenaries, he had fled north to Ecbatana (Hamadan), capital of Media, and the last of the three Persian capitals. There, some loyal satraps joined him, including the most powerful of the eastern satraps, Bessus of Bactria and Sogdiana. Darius made one more call for troops, this time from Bactria and the Caspian Sea area, and prepared to battle Alexander again.

Given the situation, Alexander could not return to Greece. It was time to hunt down Darius once and for all. In May or even early June of 330, with the Zagros mountain passages clear, he set out from Persepolis for Ecbatana. The bullion train with its vast fortune of 180,000 talents, escorted by 6,000 Macedonian soldiers, followed him to Ecbatana at a slower pace.

Darius's strategy was to bring Alexander to battle once more, evidently at Ecbatana. However, his call for reinforcements failed. Even the satraps could see the inevitable result. He had no choice but to leave Media with his own army and retreat eastwards, away from Alexander. In the eastern satrapies of Afghanistan he would gamble on his personal presence to muster more troops and so finally face Alexander.

Alexander was unaware of Darius's rapid change of plan until he met Bisthanes, a Persian prince, who was the son of the previous Great King,

Artaxerxes Ochus. This was probably in Gabae (Isfahan). He surrendered to Alexander, and told him that Darius had left Ecbatana with 3,000 cavalry and 7,000 infantry some five days earlier. Marching to Ecbatana was now pointless, and so Alexander split his army into two. The 70-year-old Parmenion, with a force of 6,200 Macedonians and 5,600 Greek mercenaries, would march to Ecbatana. His orders were to oversee Macedonian control over Media and the safe arrival of the vast bullion train. Alexander himself would go after Darius.

Accompanied by a force of less than 20,000 men, including cavalry, the Macedonian phalanx, Agrianians and archers, Alexander marched northeastwards via the corner of the Great Salt Desert to Rhagae (Rey, about six miles south of Tehran). He wanted to take Darius west of the Caspian Gates. It would take him ten days to reach Rhagae thanks to gruelling forced marches. During these, in the blistering July heat, some of his infantry collapsed and horses died from exhaustion. Even so, he arrived too late to capture Darius. The Persian King was already through the Caspian Gates. Alexander rewarded his men with a week's rest period at Rhagae – probably so that he could decide what shape his next move would take. Predictably, it depended on speed. A two-day march took him the 50 or so miles to the Caspian Gates, and into the area called Choarene (Khar), on the Great Salt Desert's shore.

There, he learned that Darius's authority ultimately now meant little to the eastern satraps. Support for Darius was dwindling fast. This was due to not only his losses and actions at Issus and Gaugamela but also the extreme geographical distance from the Persian capital. His plan to face Alexander in pitched battle fell on deaf ears, and Nabarzanes, the Persian second-in-command (*chiliarch*), said that the gods were not on his side. Then he proposed that Bessus replace Darius, but only for the time being. Once Bessus had defeated Alexander, Darius would become king again. We can imagine the reaction of both Darius and Bessus to this news! This disunity in the Persian high command had a great effect on the Persian troops, and many began to defect. As they made their way to Alexander he knew that the end of his hunt was near.

Urging his men on yet another forced march, Alexander left Choarene and moved out into the desert. At the oasis of Thara (Semnan), Bagistanes, a Babylonian nobleman, and Antibelus, a son of Mazaeus, came from Darius's camp. They reported that Darius had been deposed, arrested and bound in golden chains. Those responsible for this action were Bessus, Nabarzanes and Barsaentes, satrap of Drangiana and Arachosia (to the south of Areia, which made up much of Afghanistan). Artabazus, together with the 1,500 Greek mercenaries, fled to the Elburz Mountains, leaving only the eastern satraps in opposition. Although it was night, Alexander set off immediately with a contingent of troops including the Companion Cavalry. They marched all night and the next day until noon, rested, then set off again that evening. The day after he was within a hair's breadth of Darius and, as they were now, his treacherous captors.

Bessus, with Darius as prisoner, had already left when Alexander reached his camp on the evening of this second day. From various locals Alexander heard that there was a shortcut that would slash the time it would take to reach Bessus. The problem was that it lay through the waterless terrain of the Dasht-i-Kavir desert. Taking his army through that would have been more hazardous than it was worth, so Alexander selected 500 of the fittest infantry, mounted them on horses and led them by this route. The remainder of the army would follow Bessus's route.

It was another night operation for Alexander and his mounted infantry, and another one conducted at furious speed. But by dawn he had caught up with Bessus, close to the city of Hecatompylus ('Hundred-Gate City', so called because of its location on local crossroads). Alexander may well have intended to capture Darius alive, but the problem then was what to do with him. He could not have allowed Darius to live because there was always the danger that he would oppose Alexander again. However, having him executed might well have solidified any resistance against the invaders.

In the end, the problem was academic. As Alexander bore down on the Persians, Satibarzanes, satrap of Areia, and Barsaentes stabbed Darius and left him a wagon. He died minutes before Alexander's arrival. Though they did not take part in the actual murder, Bessus and Nabarzanes condoned it and both fled. It was mid-summer 330.

Darius III was dead, the last Achaemenid king, the last constitutional Great King. Whatever, his faults, Darius did not deserve to die as he did. We can condemn his murderers for their cowardly act. Alexander, shocked at Darius's murder, covered the body with his own cloak. The moment had to be a sobering one for him. It would have been easy for him to bury Darius's corpse ignominiously, for Darius had been a bitter and tough opponent, and many Macedonians had died at Persian hands. However, this was not Alexander's style. He respected the person of the Great King and ordered the body to be transported to Persepolis. There, Darius would be buried with the pomp and ceremony that befitted his status.

After seeing Darius's corpse Alexander took his men to Hecatompylus (Qummis), capital of Parthia, and waited for the rest of the army to catch up with him. He had captured every Persian capital, symbolically burning the palace at Persepolis, and the Great King was dead. The Macedonian king had added vast new territories to the Macedonian empire and increased its wealth enormously. He was Lord of Asia, and had fulfilled the mandate of the League of Corinth. He had done more than his father Philip. While at Hecatompylus he sent orders to Parmenion at Ecbatana that the soldiers of the League of Corinth were to be discharged with honour and receive a donative. Those who elected to remain with him also received a bonus. This action marked his recognition that he had achieved what he had set out to do, and so he could disband the League troops. His future campaigns would be for different reasons, for his *pothos*.

Alexander's personal bill for these bonuses was 12,000 talents. That enormous sum was tiny compared to the 180,000 talents that he now controlled and which were kept at Ecbatana under the control of Harpalus. This was the man who had fled before Issus but had been recalled by the king. Now, Alexander continued to place his trust in him by making him his imperial treasurer. At some point later perhaps in 330, he would move to Babylon.

Many soldiers did elect to go home. To plug the gap Alexander hired 6,000 mercenaries. His policy of training foreign youths in Lydia, Lycia, Syria and Egypt in the Macedonian style was now paying off. Not long after, in autumn 330, 300 Lydian cavalry and 2,600 infantry joined the Macedonian army. Later, in the winter of 329–328, 1,000 Lycian and Syrian cavalry and 8,000 infantry also joined him. They lacked experience in actual battle, but that would soon change.

The Macedonian invasion was now entering a different phase. The king's action brought home sharply to his own men that they were not returning to Greece. The Great King was dead; long live the new Great King, even if he called himself Lord of Asia. There had already been some dissatisfaction at Alexander's continued push eastwards, perhaps after Gaugamela, and certainly after Persepolis, but such discontent now flared up dramatically.

At Hecatompylus, his men appealed to him to return home. If the League soldiers at Ecbatana could be discharged, then so could they. An Assembly was called, and Alexander had to use all of his rhetorical powers to persuade his army to stay with him. He did so, apparently, by stressing the need to bring Bessus to justice and not to abandon Asia at this crucial time. Left to his own devices, Bessus would undo all of the Macedonian victories to date in Asia, given the forces of Bactria and Sogdiana that he commanded. What is important is that Alexander's appeal did not have at its focus revenge for what Greece had suffered in the Persian Wars – it could not, for the Greeks had now been avenged. At its focus was the need to maintain the new empire, whose stability, and hence Macedonian control of it, was threatened by Bessus.

It was a radical new line, and Alexander pitched it to his men by saying that it would only take a few more days. The thirst for more adventure, to journey into new places, knowing nothing but fighting, the need to eclipse Philip's deeds, all of these would have helped sway him to his decision. So too did geography. Alexander probably by now wanted to reach the Southern (Indian) Ocean, and Aristotle had told him that India was a small triangular promontory on this Ocean. What Aristotle (and Alexander) called India is today Pakistan and Kashmir. If Alexander subdued everywhere to the Southern (Indian) Ocean, then his new empire would have only natural frontiers (steppes, desert and ocean) as boundaries. This became his aim.

To accomplish this, Alexander would move into lands unknown to the Greeks. They were certainly known to those Asians with him, who would have told him all about them. Thus, he was aware of the dangers that lay ahead from the terrain and native peoples. Some of these he had already experienced at Gaugamela, like the Parthyaeans, Bactrians and Indians. No danger would change Alexander's mind once it was made up. His new empire would be vast, greater than anything Philip had ever envisaged. His appeal that he needed only a few days was, simply, a lie.

The men were persuaded to follow Alexander's new policy, and perhaps a concession on his part was allowing them to take their wives with them as they marched further east. Previously, at least for the rank and file, this had not been allowed. Discontent though had taken root, and it would continue to grow. Alexander himself did not help matters. He used two official seals, one that was his and one that was Darius's. More significantly, after about August 330, with Darius dead, he adopted a mixture of Persian and Macedonian dress.

The discontent was not helped by his promotion of leading Asians as his personal bodyguards, something of a 'balance' to his Macedonian bodyguard. His manner of address changed too. He called the influential Macedonians 'Friends', and the Persians 'Kinsmen', significantly allowing the latter to perform *proskynesis* (genuflection) before him. To the Greeks, *proskynesis* should only be performed before a statue of a god or dead hero, but to Alexander's Asian subjects it was a social protocol and had no religious bearings. It would help them see Alexander as their ruler, the Lord of Asia, rather than merely the conquering King of the Macedonians.

All that Alexander's own men could see was their warrior king changing before their eyes, and they did not like it. So much so in fact, that later, in Bactra in 327, when he tried to make them perform *proskynesis* before him, they defied him (see Chapter 10).

9

Conquest and Conspiracy

Alexander decided to put the pursuit of Bessus on hold for the moment. He thought it was more important to mop up the part of Darius's force that had split from Bessus and fled to the high (18,550 feet) Elburz Mountains. With this end in mind, he left Hecatompylus shortly after he had made arrangements for Darius's burial. For three days he marched the army to the mountains. There he divided it into three in order to penetrate the mountains by three different passes. One third was placed under the command of Craterus, another under his boyhood friend Erigyius, and the third under himself. Alexander took the most direct route towards the Caspian Sea by the Shamshirbun Pass. He encountered no resistance; indeed, the reverse.

When he reached the river Rhidagnus an envoy came to him from Nabarzanes, one of Darius's murderers, asking for mercy and a safe passage to the king. Alexander granted it. Soon after, Alexander reached Zadracarta (Sari?), capital of Hyrcania, near the southern shore of the Caspian Sea. He would stay there for two weeks, during which time Craterus and Erigyius joined him with their forces. Soon after, Phrataphernes, satrap of Parthyaea and Hyrcania, personally surrendered. So too did Autophradates, satrap of Tapuria. The eastern Elburz region was now Alexander's, and all without a fight. At the western border of Hyrcania, Artabazus surrendered. Alexander took no action against him. However, he refused the plea for mercy that came from the 1,500 Greek mercenaries who had served with Darius. For Alexander, Greek fighting Greek was still unacceptable.

The pattern of surrender was interrupted by the Mardi, who lived on the south-west border of Hyrcania (not the Mardi in southern Persis, against whom Alexander had earlier campaigned: see Chapter 8). They were supposed to have captured Bucephalus, which caused Alexander to wage war on them to get his horse back. Supposed to, that is, for they returned the horse immediately on his demand. More likely is that they simply resisted Alexander. It cost them dearly. The Macedonian army fought the Mardi, many of whom fled for refuge in the dense, mountain terrain. Undaunted, Alexander ordered that they be hunted until they surrendered or were killed. Within a week, the campaign was over and the area became part of Tapuria, which remained under the control of Autophradates. Alexander was determind to show that surrender to the Macedonian power should be the preferred option of his opponents.

On his return to Zadracarta, where he held games and sacrifices, he found Nabarzanes and the Greek mercenaries waiting for him. Perhaps because his march eastwards had gone so successfully, Alexander was prepared to be lenient. Nabarzanes was pardoned for his role in Darius' murder and joined Alexander's administration. He gave Alexander many presents, including the eunuch Bagoas, whose beauty took Alexander's breath away. The two soon entered into a sexual relationship. This should not cause any surprise, for bisexuality was normal for all the Greeks. Alexander's relationship with Bagoas would raise no eyebrows.

The Greek mercenaries, who expected the worst, must have been surprised (and relieved) when Alexander ordered that they join his army. Moreover, those who had enlisted in Persian service before 337, the year that Philip created the League of Corinth and announced his plan to invade Persia, were allowed to depart home unharmed.

It was here in Zadracarta, the story goes, that Thalestris, the Amazon Queen, came to Alexander wanting him to father a child. She was alleged to have stayed with him for almost a fortnight, during which time Alexander could not keep up with her insatiable sexual appetite. It is just a story, for Alexander never met her. One day it might become part of a movie.

It was also here that Alexander probably began to wear the diadem. This was something that the Great King and his royal relations had worn around their heads. Alexander now wore one. At first it may simply have been a cloth band around his *kausia* (the Macedonian flat-brimmed hat), but in time it seems to have become a metal one. It was how he distinguished himself as Lord of Asia, but this fusion of Persian dress with Macedonian was rapidly causing discontent among his men (see Chapter 8).

The new policy of marching east, into unknown territory, following Alexander's *pothos*, continued. From Zadracarta the army moved to the satrapy of Areia. This comprised the lion's share of Afghanistan, and was on the crossroads of Bactria to the north, India to the east, and Drangiana to the south. Alexander's route took the army back across the Elburz Mountains into Parthyaea. At Susia, Satibarzanes, satrap of Areia and one of Darius's murderers, surrendered to him. His recognition of Alexander's power earned him the Lord of Asia's favour and, more importantly for him, reconfirmation of his position as satrap. He would rule from the capital, Artacoana (Herat). Evidently, Alexander could overlook Satibarzanes's part in Darius's murder as and when it suited him. Eager to move on, Alexander left a Macedonian force of only 40 javelinmen to keep him in check.

Then Alexander's luck changed. He heard that Bessus had turned out to be a greater threat than he had predicted to his men at the Assembly at Hecatompylus. Instead of merely leading an army against the Macedonian invaders, Bessus had proclaimed himself Artaxerxes IV, the next Great King, and was wearing the upright tiara, the symbol of Persian kingship. Since Bessus was related to Darius, his claim had some standing. Alexander's army now numbered around 45,000. If Bessus won over the satrapies of the east, then Alexander would be outnumbered and face considerable opposition. It would also not help Alexander's cause that a 'real' Great King, one with a greater claim to the throne than Alexander, was ready to fight the Macedonian invader. The self-proclaimed Lord of Asia responded to the news about Bessus with the decision to invade Bactria at once. Would the prophecy of the Gordian knot ever come true?

The Bactrians were a very tough people indeed. They had a reputation for killing their elderly or infirm:

'Now in early times the Sogdians and Bactrians were not much different from the nomads in their life and customs, although the Bactrians were a little more civilised. However, of these, as of the others, Onesicritus does not report their best characteristics. He says, for instance, that those who have become infirm because of old age or sickness are thrown out alive as prey to dogs kept expressly for this purpose, which in their native tongue are called "undertakers". While the land outside the walls of the city of the Bactrians looks clean, most of the land inside the walls is full of human bones. Alexander ended this custom.'[1]

The custom of exposing the elderly or sick to die was unsavoury to the Greeks, who thought that the soul was in danger if a corpse was not properly covered up and buried. Yet it was a local custom, and Alexander did not have the legal right to ban it. He knew that he was going to face considerable resistance and heavy fighting, but his attitude to local customs was another reason for the locals to resist him.[2]

So eager was Alexander to hunt down Bessus as fast as he could that he ordered the burning of the transport wagons. He marched east from Susia, along the Kopet Dag massif, to invade Bactria from the west. The news about Bessus was bad enough, but worse was to come. Almost as soon as Alexander left Susia, Satibarzanes revolted from Macedonian rule, murdered the Macedonian troops at Artacoana, and declared Areia's loyalty to the new Artaxerxes IV (Bessus). Despite the danger from Bessus, the precedent that Satibarzanes's revolt set in this part of the world was too dangerous for Alexander to ignore. If the revolt were successful, then word would spread. Alexander had to act immediately.

Alexander was 70 miles away from Areia's capital Artacoana, when he heard the news of the revolt. With a small contingent of troops – including his Companion Cavalry, two phalanx battalions, the Agrianians and some lighter infantry – he marched back to it in fury and reached it after two days of forced marching. Satibarzanes, taking a leaf out of Darius's book, fled to Bessus in Bactria with about 2,000 cavalry almost immediately. Those who stayed fast against Alexander took refuge on a wooded hill close to the capital. They put up a good fight until the Macedonians started a fire, forcing their surrender. They appealed for mercy, which Alexander, pressed for time, granted. His quarrel in any case was with Satibarzanes, who had betrayed his trust. There would be no second chances.

Areia was now Alexander's again. He appointed a Persian nobleman, Arsaces, as satrap. He also founded a new city close to Artacoana called Alexander in Areia, populated by Macedonians, Greeks and Areians. This was his first foundation since Alexandria in Egypt. Where Alexandria was founded for trade purposes, this new city was an attempt to ensure Macedonian control. So too would his future ones be, setting a pattern of foundations to maintain control. Further, as part of his pattern of training foreign youths for Macedonian service, he made arrangements to train a select number of Areian youths in Macedonian fashion.

It is clear that Alexander's speed since Darius's death had saved him from fighting his opponents, for they had fled once they heard that the Macedonian army was fast bearing down on them. Alexander should be commended for his quickness of thought, commitment to a plan once devised and ability to exhort his men on long, forced marches. He was pushing them to their limit, and it is important to note that, despite their dissatisfaction with him, they followed him. True, his strategy was a gamble, for he might well have faced greater opposition if the satraps had rallied their forces. However, once the snowball effect had begun he was quick to exploit it, and to alter strategy once he knew the snowball was melting, as we shall see. That is a measure of his greatness as a general for there is no question that he was a great general.

Satibarzanes's revolt showed Alexander that he could not rely on his satraps' loyalty once he had departed from their territory. He probably already suspected this, and that is why he always ensured that Macedonians controlled the key elements of army and treasury. It had been a blunder on his part to leave only 40 javelinmen with Satibarzanes, but perhaps he thought a greater force unnecessary given that he reappointed him as satrap and expected his loyalty. The suddenness of the revolt may well have surprised him. However, he may well have understood a revolt in order to regain independence, but Satibarzanes's revolt was different. He had openly and defiantly expressed support for Bessus, the self-proclaimed Great King. If he could do it, then so could others. That forced Alexander to rethink his plan of running down Bessus at this time.

Once he had re-established control of Areia, Alexander disregarded Bessus for the moment, and moved south to the satrapies of Drangiana and Arachosia. He marched 180 miles south along the Persian road to Phrada (Fara), capital of Drangiana, and set up his central command there. It was too dangerous for him to leave the satrap of these regions, Barsaentes, alone, in case he too declared his loyalty for Bessus. Barsaentes, like Satibarzanes, was one of Darius's assassins, and had been part of the foursome that deposed Darius and engineered his death. If Barsaentes declared loyalty to Bessus after Alexander moved further east, then Macedonian control of these regions, to say nothing of the Macedonian rear, would be severely compromised. Hence, moving against Barsaentes at this time rather than Bessus made excellent sense. Barsaentes in fact put up no fight. He fled to India, leaving Phrada, the capital, to the Macedonians.

Alexander's stay at Phrada is marred by a gross example of his ruthlessness and growing paranoia. Philotas, commander of the Companion Cavalry, was executed, and his father, the senior general Parmenion, was killed for purely personal reasons. The incident has put a black mark on Alexander's reign throughout history, and it shows a significant downward spiral in Alexander's personality.

While the Macedonians were at Phrada, a soldier called Dimnus hatched a conspiracy against Alexander. He approached his lover, Cebalinus, and wanted him to join the conspiracy, but he refused. Cebalinus was too junior to have automatic access to Alexander's royal tent, and if he were to demand to see Alexander the conspirators might have been alerted. Therefore he went to Philotas, who visited the king twice daily, and told him of the plot. For some reason Philotas chose not to report the news to Alexander immediately. Cebalinus renewed his fears for Alexander's life to Philotas on the same evening and then the next day, but still he did not warn the king. In despair, Cebalinus persuaded a Royal Page to smuggle him into Alexander's presence so that he could tell his story. The king was having a bath, but evidently hopped out immediately at the news. He consulted his friends for advice, and then acted. The conspirators, including Demetrius, a royal bodyguard, and Philotas were arrested, but Dimnus committed suicide.

The next day Philotas was put on trial before an Assembly of 6,000 Macedonians.[3] Alexander accused him of organising the conspiracy, and called for the death penalty. He added fuel to his rhetoric by making the accusation over the corpse of Dimnus. Coenus, and Amyntas, both pha-lanx commanders, accused Philotas in similar fashion. Philotas, who defended himself, was guilty of not informing Alexander of Cebalinus's accusations. He confessed that 'he had heard of a certain conspiracy that was being formed against Alexander. He was convicted of having said nothing to the king about this plot, although he visited the royal tent twice a day.'[4]

His defence that he thought that the conspiracy was without foun-dation, and hence not worth bothering the king about, fell on deaf ears. In fact, Alexander even chastised him for delivering his defence in Greek and not in Macedonian. Given that his trial was heard in and by the Macedonian Assembly, we must presume that the language (or dialect) of Macedonian (see Chapter 2) was always used. With his father Parmenion still in Ecbatana and most of the cavalry, who would have supported him out of loyalty, not in attendance, the Assembly declared Philotas guilty.

Then Alexander turned to Parmenion. He disguised Polydamas, one of his Companions, as an Arab, and sent him on a fast camel across the Great Salt Desert to the generals at Ecbatana. These were Cleander, Sitalces and Menidas. The man carried a letter with orders to kill Parmenion, and Cleander saw to it that the deed was done within minutes of its arrival.

Parmenion did not have the slightest idea what was going to happen, and he was also unaware of his son's trial. The force that he com-manded at Ecbatana, 6,200 Macedonians and 5,600 Greek mercenaries, prepared to revolt on his murder. However, it was pacified when another letter from Alexander was read out to the men. Rather than leave them there, Alexander ordered them to join his army at Arachosia, a march of over 1,000 miles. If they remained discontented over the next few years, they would have been pleased to see Cleander, along with other generals from Ecbatana, put to death in 324 by Alexander in Carmania.

Not long after Parmenion was killed, the Macedonians executed Philotas and the other conspirators. They hurled javelins at them until they were all dead. A minor purge followed which included the execution of Alexander of Lyncestis, Antipater's son-in-law. He had declared alle-giance to Alexander in 336, and had later been given command of the Thessalian cavalry after Alexander invaded Asia. Then he conspired against the king. As a traitor, he had been under house arrest for three years (see Chapter 4). Now, Alexander ruthlessly took advantage of the conspiracy at Phrada and its fallout to get rid of him. He too was shot to death by javelins.

The conspiracy against Alexander's life tells us a lot about the dissatisfaction some felt with him as he continued east, adopted Asian customs and no doubt proclaimed his divine status. Yet Philotas's involvement in the actual plot is unclear.[5] If he had been involved in it, why would Cebalinus have gone to him in the first place? Of course, there is no reason to assume that Dimnus revealed the names of the conspirators to Cebalinus. Hence, Cebalinus may have thought that Philotas could be trusted.

Then again, if Philotas was a conspirator it is hard to understand why he allowed Cebalinus and his brother to live since either could betray the plot to the king. It seems unlikely that Philotas was aware of the conspiracy, refused to join it, but still allowed it to take its course. He, like his father, may well have been unhappy with Alexander's Asia leanings, or orientalism, but that does not mean he would sit on the fence in this case. If Alexander survived an assassination attempt only to discover that Philotas had been a passive part of it, his days would have been numbered anyway.

The chances are, then, that Philotas was not directly involved in an assassination plot, although he was certainly guilty of not informing Alexander of it. But that does not explain why Alexander accused him of organising it. It is possible that some senior commanders played on Alexander's fears and exploited the opportunity to get rid of Philotas. He was arrogant, disliked, and openly opposed by Craterus, Hephaestion, Perdiccas and even his brother-in-law Coenus. The differing personalities and enmities of Alexander's senior commanders were already showing themselves. They would explode in the aftermath of Alexander's death in 323 as the senior commanders carved up his empire and made war on each other for decades (see Chapter 13).

However, Philotas's grave error, together with his opponents seizing the opportunity to discredit him, does not fully explain the extent of Alexander's action against Parmenion. That Parmenion was involved in this plot is highly doubtful. There are simply no grounds for thinking that he wanted the king dead. Things might be different when he learned of his son's execution of course. He commanded a substantial force, which was obviously loyal to him given its reaction to his murder, and he had easy access to the great treasury of 180,000 talents. Ptolemy tells us that Parmenion 'would now be a dangerous man if he survived after his son had been violently removed. He was held in such great respect by Alexander himself and by all the army, not only the Macedonian, but also that of the Greek mercenaries.'[6] Alexander was not prepared to take any chances.

Why did he take the steps that he did against Philotas and Parmenion? An answer lies in their criticism of Alexander (which the king saw as a personal affront) and the king's ruthlessness. Philotas seems to have expressed concern about Alexander's continued progress and non-Macedonian practices, if the evidence of his mistress at his trial is to be believed. Parmenion, even more significantly, was one of the 'old guard', who had served under Philip and believed in the traditional nature of a Macedonian king. Alexander by now was moving away from that image and showed no signs of stopping. Alexander's men had shown dissatisfaction with him on a number of occasions already, and if Parmenion's criticisms were to gain weight the king would be faced with a serious problem. After all, were Alexander to die, Parmenion and Philotas would take over because of their seniority. The same would be true if Alexander were deposed, for what the Macedonian Assembly could make it could undo. And Parmenion was a senior general who commanded great respect.

Relations between Alexander and Parmenion had been strained for some time. At the start of Alexander's reign Parmenion had been fiercely loyal to the new king, seeing to the death of Attalus in 335 even though he was his father-in-law. The two had had a difference of opinion before the Battle of Granicus in 334, when Parmenion's suggestion to wait was overridden by Alexander. In the same year, when Alexander reached Miletus, Parmenion was keen to do battle with the Persian fleet. Alexander again overruled his wish, given the superior size of the Persian fleet over his own. So far the disagreements had stemmed from military considerations, and probably neither man attached too much importance to them.

Then in 331 a major disagreement took place when Alexander returned to Tyre. Darius sent an embassy offering to surrender all territories west of the Euphrates, to become the friend and ally of the king and to pay 30,000 talents for the return of his family. Parmenion thought the offer too good to refuse, and is alleged to have said that if he were Alexander he would accept the terms. A displeased Alexander replied that if he were Parmenion he would. Alexander may not have answered in this way, but the exchange indicates that Parmenion at least thought the invasion to date had achieved enough. There may also have been concerns over Alexander's attitude towards the succession, for he was still without a legitimate heir. Again, Alexander's decisions to refuse Darius's terms carried the day.

The Battle of Gaugamela in 331 is illuminating. Alexander followed Parmenion's advice about waiting a day for battle so that he could make a full reconnaissance of the Persian camp. However, once the battle was underway Parmenion, in charge of the left flank, found himself outnumbered and sent an urgent request to Alexander for help. The king did not help, but fortunately Parmenion was saved by the news of the Persian rout elsewhere and of Darius's flight. There are several reasons why Alexander did not help Parmenion (see Chapter 8), but perhaps we ought not to discount that with the battle won, as it was by then, Alexander deliberately left Parmenion to his fate. The declining relations between the king and senior general would be solved by his death.

However, Parmenion did not die. The disagreements continued, and Alexander was not one who could handle criticism or disagreement well. In 330, at Persepolis, it would appear that Alexander was keen to destroy the palace but Parmenion urged against this action in case it provoked Persian resentment. Soon after Alexander took steps to isolate Parmenion from his court and the bulk of the Macedonian army proper. While pursuing Darius to Ecbatana Alexander learned that he had already left. He sent Parmenion there, principally to oversee Macedonian control of Media and the safety of the great bullion train. An offshoot of this was that Parmenion was moved out of the limelight. He did not accompany Alexander further east, and there were no plans at that time for him to rejoin the king. The coincidence is too much. Parmenion had been isolated. Alexander's action also isolated Philotas, leaving him vulnerable to his enemies at court, including the powerful Craterus.

Macedonian law dictated that a traitor's family be also executed. Philotas had been condemned for treason, but the removal of his father was not primarily because of legalities. It is very plausible that Alexander implicated Philotas in this conspiracy as a means of getting rid of potential opposition and as a stepping stone against his father. The two of them, especially Parmenion, posed too great a threat to Alexander's plans for the future and how he saw himself. Weight is lent to this by the fact that the other conspirators were relatively minor figures, certainly not in the league of Parmenion or Philotas.

Alexander must be condemned for how and why he acted against Parmenion and Philotas. His action also robbed his army of two highly experienced commanders. With the army so far from home, with the ever-present danger of revolt from the satrapies, and with Bessus still on the loose, Alexander's action was more than ruthless: it was dangerous.

As the dust from the Phrada conspiracy settled, Alexander undertook some military reorganisation. Philotas's position as commander of the Companion Cavalry was split among two commanders, Cleitus the Black and Hephaestion. The choice is significant, for the older Cleitus was one of the Old Guard and the younger Hephaestion (he was only 26) was one

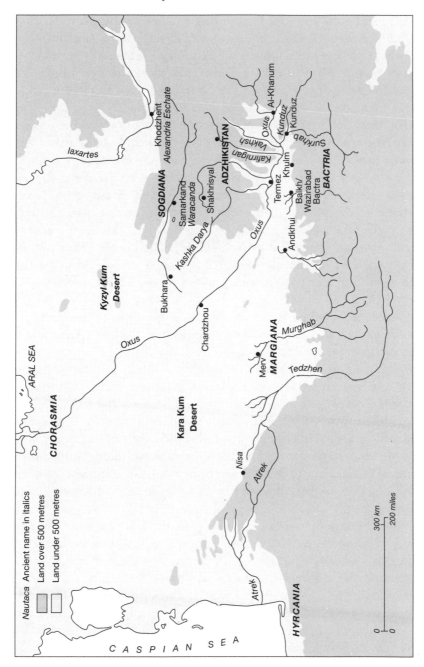

Chorasmia, Margiana, Sogdiana and Bactria
Redrawn from Bosworth, A.B. (1988) *Conquest and Empire: The Reign of
Alexander the Great* (pub Cambridge University Press), Map 7. © Cambridge
University Press 1988, reproduced with permission.

of the 'brat pack', the circle of Alexander's boyhood friends. Alexander had chosen well. Cleitus's promotion would presumably silence any hostility he might feel over Parmenion's murder, and Hephaestion would owe loyalty only to Alexander. Each would also act as a balance to the other: the old and the new. Moreover, the division of command meant that the cavalry would owe allegiance to no single commander.

The king's military restructuring shows that he realised the potential danger from the old guard, and not all of them could be stationed away from the court. Also as part of his reorganisation Alexander took pains to surround himself with his closer friends or relatives. Craterus, Hephaestion, Perdiccas and Coenus between them shared what Parmenion and Philotas had once controlled. The disgraced Demetrius was replaced by Ptolemy, son of Lagus, one of Alexander's boyhood friends. He had been exiled by Philip II for his part in the Pixodarus affair of 337/6. Now, like the others, he received a senior post. Thus, Alexander had moved far from concentrating too much power (and hence army loyalty) in the hands of one man.

Surrounded even more closely now by a group of commanders who owed their elevated and continuing positions to the king, Alexander felt safe enough to track down Bessus.

The army moved south from Drangiana to spend the winter of 330 and early 329 in Ariaspia (Sistan). The number of lakes in this region and fertile soil allowed for the growing of cereal crops, so there were plenty of provisions for the Macedonian army. These days life there is very different, and the area south of Phrada is called the Desert of Death. Alexander accepted the surrender of the people of Ariaspia, along with those of Gedrosia (Makran), over whom he appointed a satrap. In a few more years, he would meet them again in far different circumstances (see Chapter 11).

While in Ariaspia news came that Satibarzanes, supported by 2,000 cavalry and with Bessus's backing, had induced another revolt of Areia. The rain was pouring again for Alexander. Areia's new satrap Arsaces, appointed by Alexander, appears to have done little to quell it. Furthermore, Bessus himself had mobilised troops to foster a revolt from northern Bactria to Medea. Finally, he had expelled Phrataphernes, appointed as satrap of Parthyaea by Alexander, and set up Barzanes. This was a direct flouting of Alexander's authority.

The widespread revolt showed how tenuous the Macedonians' footing in the furthermost reaches of the Persian empire really was. Could Alexander have ever efficiently administered this region? Would the native population have ever accepted Macedonian rule? Alexander was probably asking himself the same questions and coming up with the same answer as we, with the benefit of hindsight, can today. No. However, this did not deter Alexander from continuing to march further east. For the next two years he would clash with some of the toughest opponents to date and be frustrated by revolts and a series of ephemeral alliances. To make matters worse, the Sogdianian noble Spitamenes inflicted a major defeat on part of the Macedonian army, and later, in 328, Alexander would show his darker side when in a drunken fit of rage he murdered Cleitus.

Rather than interrupt his pursuit of Bessus, Alexander ordered three other commanders, Erigyius, Caranus and the Persian Artabazus, to end the revolt in Areia. Phrataphernes was also to invade Areia at the same time. The joint force left immediately, and by spring 329 it had ended the revolt. Erigyius killed Satibarzanes in single combat, chopping off his head and sending it to Alexander. The Macedonian king decided to take no more chances with native satraps. He deposed Arsaces and appointed one of his Companions, Stasanor from Cyprus, as satrap of Areia. Even then, resistance continued. Stasanor had to fight for over a year before he finally captured the deposed Arsaces and established his authority. He was helped by Phrataphernes, who in the meantime had re-established his satrapal position in Parthyaea.

While the Macedonian force was dealing with the revolt of Areia, Alexander took the rest of the army successfully through Arachosia. On the way he founded another city, Alexander in Arachosia, Afghanistan's modern Kandahar. Today in that city the *hakims*, or doctors, trace their heritage to the doctors who accompanied Alexander on his expedition, including Philip the Acarnanian and Critobulus. Alexander's influence continues to live.

Finally, the army reached the modern Kabul. Next lay the formidable mountains of the Hindu Kush, which the Greeks called the Caucasus. They were, so they thought, close to the end of the earth, which Aristotle said could be seen from the tops of the mountains. They were so high that eagles could not fly over them. It was here that Prometheus was chained and tortured by Zeus (he was to be eaten daily by Zeus's eagle) for giving fire to man. Aeschylus's *Prometheus Bound* reveals the extent of his 'crime' and punishment, and the appalling place where Zeus banished him. Beyond the mountains lay Bactria, and Bessus.

Although Bessus's strategy had been to unite Bactria and bring Alexander to battle, he had been let down by the Bactrian nobles who refused to unite under him. That meant his army did not number what he had anticipated. He was forced to retreat north of the Oxus (Amu Darya) River, what is now Uzbekistan and Tadjikistan. There he gambled on support from the Saca peoples. Alexander, on the other hand, wanted to avoid a battle and to capture Bessus with as little trouble as possible. To this end, he sent out word that he was after only Bessus and had no desire to wage war on anyone else. This strategy would pay dividends when he finally crossed this river.

It was mid-winter 330 and the passes of the Hindu Kush were blocked by snow. Alexander could not afford to wait. With the snow still deep in the passes and the temperatures sub zero, he pushed into the mountains, and over the bitter Khawak Pass, a journey that took over a fortnight. The hardship from the snow, cold and winds was tremendous, and during the second week the food ran out. The men were forced to eat the pack animals in order to survive. Since there was no wood to make a fire they had to eat them raw. One source (Arrian) says that they drank the juice from a plant called sylphion (asafoetida) to ensure they did not fall ill from eating raw meat. The plant still grows today and is used as a herbal remedy.

The army survived and made it. The top of the Pass, at a height of 11,000 feet, revealed northern Afghanistan and, beyond, the wide Oxus River, ready and waiting. Perhaps the men did think that they had reached the end of the earth. Then again, Bessus still lay ahead, so the end of the earth beckoned. Would the men have been wondering again when Alexander planned to stop?

Bessus was astounded that Alexander had crossed the mountains during winter. Although he commanded 30,000 Bactrian cavalry he fled across the Oxus, burning every boat that the Macedonian king might use to follow him. However, his flight cost him his Bactrian support.

Alexander's invasion of Bactria had begun. At Drapsaca (Kunduz), the remainder of his army, including the baggage train and siege engines which had been brought across the mountains from Kabul in better weather, reached him. Once again, the army was whole. Alexander appointed Artabazus as satrap, and then he set off in early summer 329 to the north-eastern frontier of the Persian empire,

The 50-mile march across the desert to the Oxus River was terrible in the summer heat. So terrible in fact that Alexander was forced to march at night, using the stars as guide. The men suffered badly from lack of water, which slowed them down considerably. In typical Alexander fashion, when a cup of water was brought to him, he refused it and ordered the man to let his sons drink it. When the army finally reached the river many drank uncontrollably and died.

The king set up camp on the river's banks, not so much because he needed to decide what to do next but to allow his men to recover. In fact, he sent home some of his older Macedonian soldiers, whose age made them unfit for fighting, together with some Thessalian volunteers.

To all he gave a large donative: his generosity never abated. His action may well have been for the benefit of his men, for soon after he held an Assembly and again got them to swear loyalty to the next part of his campaign.

Crossing the Oxus River also posed problems. It was over a half-mile wide, fast-flowing, and Bessus had already burned all the boats. In the end, Alexander used the same tactic as he had at the Danube in 335. He made rafts of skins and grass, and over the course of five days the men crossed the river on these flimsy rafts. The Macedonians were now in Sogdiana, the north-eastern province of the Persian empire, that was bounded by the Oxus and, 350 miles away, the Jaxartes (Syr Darya) rivers.

Shortly after the crossing the Macedonians came across a small walled town in which lived people called the Branchidae. The town is perhaps the modern Talashkan Tepe, on the old road from Termez. They spoke Greek and Persian and their ancestors were priests of the oracle of Apollo at Didyma, close to Miletus. Their pro-Persian sympathies back in the early fifth century had led to their removal by the Great King to this part of the Persian empire. From that time on, so the story went, Apollo never spoke when anyone consulted his oracle at Didyma. Never that is until Alexander's visit in 334 (see Chapter 5). Although the Branchidae surrendered their town to Alexander when he first arrived, Alexander decided to destroy it. The next day the Macedonians killed all of them (they were unarmed), and razed the town to the ground.

His official reason was revenge for the Branchidae's ancestors siding with the Persians, the enemy of the Greeks. He had given the same reason when destroying Thebes in 335 and Xerxes's palace at Persepolis in 330. Given his panhellenic mission and his role as avenger of the Greeks, we should not be surprised at what he did. At the same time, destruction of the town allowed his men to vent their frustration at having to cross the Oxus in such a dangerous and lengthy manner.

Fortunately for the army, Alexander's announcement that he sought only Bessus paid off. Having been unable to unite Bactria under him and reduced to flight with a limited number of men, Bessus's days were numbered. Two Sogdianian nobles, Spitamenes and Dataphernes, captured him and offered him as a sign of their good faith to Alexander. The king needed to be sure of their good intentions. He sent Ptolemy to them:

'At the head of three regiments of the Companion Cavalry and all the horse-javelinmen, and of the infantry, the brigade of Philotas, one regiment of 1,000 shield-bearing guards, all the Agrianians, and half the archers, with orders to make a forced march to Spitamenes and Dataphernes. Ptolemy went as instructed, and completed the ten days' march in four days.

'He arrived at the camp where on the day before the barbarians under Spitamenes had bivouacked. Here Ptolemy learned that Spitamenes and Dataphernes were not firmly resolved about betraying Bessus. He therefore left the infantry behind with orders to follow him, and advanced with the cavalry till he reached a village, where Bessus was with a few soldiers. Spitamenes and his party had already left there, being ashamed to betray Bessus themselves. Ptolemy posted his cavalry around the village, which was enclosed by a wall with gates. He then issued a proclamation to the barbarians in the village, that they would be allowed to depart uninjured if they surrendered Bessus to him. They admitted Ptolemy and his men into the village. Ptolemy then seized Bessus and returned.

'He sent a messenger to ask Alexander how he was to bring Bessus before the king. Alexander ordered him to bind the prisoner naked in a wooden collar, and to lead him like that on the right hand side of the road along which he was about to march with the army.'[7]

Once in Alexander's camp, Bessus was put in chains. He was whipped, and then sent to Bactra (in northern Afghanistan) where his nose and ear lobes were ritually cut off. Finally, a broken man, he was sent to Ecbatana to suffer execution by impalement. The punishment was traditional for someone who usurped the Persian throne, as Bessus had done when he proclaimed himself Artaxerxes IV and started to wear the upright tiara. Alexander proclaimed that he had thus avenged the murderer of Darius III. At the same time, he had rid himself of a very real threat to his own power.

With Bessus out of the way, Alexander marched to the northern boundary of the Persian empire, the River Jaxartes, via the satrapy's capital, Maracanda (Samarkand). This was on the edge of the Kyzl Kum Desert. He followed Aristotle's geographical beliefs, and presumed the Jaxartes to be the upper part of the Tanaïs (Don). The Greeks thought that the Tanaïs was the boundary between Europe and Asia. Alexander subscribed to this view, and believed that the steppe country north of the river was the edge of the inhabited earth. Alexander made a treaty of alliance with the Abii who lived south of the river and the Sacae who lived north, learning from them how extensive the 'uninhabited earth' was. To protect his rear, he established garrisons in various cities. On the south bank of the river, he would also lay the foundations of another city, Alexander Eschate, or Alexander the Farthermost. This is the modern Leninabad.

If Alexander relaxed in Maracanda thinking that he had conquered Bactria and Sogdiana he was sadly mistaken. The first sign came with an attack on his army by 30,000 members of a local tribe, during which he was shot in the leg by an arrow that broke part of his fibula. This attack on the Macedonian army had to be punished. The enemy took refuge in a fortress on top of a hill, which Alexander stormed. Twenty-two thousand died, either in fighting or by throwing themselves off the cliff.

It was the start of the massive revolt of Bactria and Sogdiana.

10

Bactria and Sogdiana

Spitamenes and Dataphernes were behind the revolt. Alexander's forces were massacred in Bactria, the peoples of Bactria and Sogdiana united and from north of the Jaxartes the Sacae (Scythians) mobilised a force. The revolt was the last thing Alexander needed, and he had to act fast before it spread and cost the Macedonians everything. As with Thebes in 335, he determined to make an example of those who defied him; that resistance would be costly.

Alexander suspended the building of Alexander Eschate for the moment and swept against several large fortresses in the Jaxartes region. Their mud-brick defence walls could not withstand the onslaught from the powerful siege engines and they quickly fell to Alexander. The men who were of fighting age in them were killed, and the women and children enslaved. One fortress had stronger defences, however. This was Cyropolis (Kurkath), founded by Cyrus the Great himself in 530. Alexander led a small force that entered the city secretly and opened the doors to the army outside. The Macedonians killed 8,000 there alone. Then at Memaceni Alexander was struck by a stone on his neck, and suffered a throat wound that affected his voice for some time. The army, horrified that the king had been severely injured, razed the city.

As severe as all of these punishments were, they were in keeping with Macedonian and Greek practices from the earlier classical period onwards. We can understand why Alexander reacted with such brutality, given the circumstances of the revolt, especially the murdering of his forces in Bactria.

No sooner had Alexander ended the insurrection in this region than he had to deal with the dual threat of Spitamenes' attack on Maracanda to the south, and an army of the Sacae people taking up position opposite the site of Alexander Eschate. The Sacae's actions, like those of Spitamenes and Dataphernes, showed that they viewed any alliance with Alexander as ephemeral. The king was learning this lesson the hard way, and it would not be until spring 327 that he followed a radical new direction to ensure unity.

Alexander sent a relief force to Maracanda of 60 Companion cavalry, 800 mercenary cavalry, and 1,500 mercenary infantry. He continued the building of Alexander Eschate. He was right to give his new city priority given the immediate threat from the Sacae. Maracanda would be his main base for the next 18 months, but he also needed a forward base on the Jaxartes. In less than three weeks the mud-brick defensive wall, stretching over six miles, was finished. The city was populated by Macedonians who were unfit for military service, as well as Greek mercenaries and some loyal natives from that area. Then Alexander turned to deal with the Sacae. Defeating these would give him the north of Sogdiana.

It was a typically brilliant crossing of the river against odds. The boats at the front of the Macedonian force were equipped with catapults that fired missiles to disrupt the Sacae line. As this line splintered the Macedonian infantry landed safely, followed by the slower-moving cavalry. Alexander knew of the deadly Sacan cavalry's ability to encircle the enemy while firing arrows into its midst, and he had to prevent that at all costs. Deceit would again be the basis of his strategy. He attacked the Sacae line head on with a contingent of his cavalry. As expected, the Sacae cavalry encircled it. Alexander then led a second contingent of cavalry, supported by Agrianians and other infantry, which attacked the Sacan circle and disrupted it. Suddenly outflanked and caught between the pincer movement of two Macedonian cavalry forces, the Sacan cavalry fled.

The battle was over. One thousand of the enemy were killed and 150 captured. On the Macedonian side, 60 cavalry and 100 infantry were killed, and 1,000 wounded. It was a costly win for Alexander, but shortly after the Sacan king sent an embassy seeking mercy and offering submission. Alexander agreed to open negotiations, and as a gesture of his goodwill he released the prisoners from the battle without ransom.

Maracanda was next. As the Macedonian relief force approached Maracanda, Spitamenes fled westwards, in the process gaining reinforcements from the Dahae people to the far west. Instead of letting Spitamenes go, the relief force pursued him, but was then ambushed. The Macedonians were outnumbered and tired, so the cavalry proved ineffectual for once. The infantry was encircled in the deadly Scythian tactic, and cut to pieces by volley after volley of deadly arrows.

Only a handful managed to make their way back to Alexander at the Jaxartes. Spitamenes's victory was a blow to Alexander. It showed that a Macedonian army could be defeated, thus sending out a dangerous signal to those currently in revolt. It also allowed Spitamenes to renew the siege of Maracanda. For now, Alexander ordered that his men were to be told no word about the disaster.

The king wasted no time once he heard of Spitamenes's victory. He marched south at speed with half of his Companion cavalry, the Agrianians and other select infantry. Three days later, he was at Maracanda. Once more Spitamenes fled west. There was no pursuit this time, however. Alexander decided to wreak revenge for his fallen troops, to whom he set up a memorial. For the rest of the summer he plundered and razed the entire valley of Zeravshan for allowing Spitamenes to act as he did and for sheltering his troops. Crops were wasted in a scorched earth policy, and citadels were stormed, followed by the systematic massacre of his opponents.

One hundred and twenty thousand Sogdianians might have died at the hands of the Macedonians, but Spitamenes's victory had sent out a rallying cry to those who defied Macedonian rule. Alexander's action showed what would happen to those who aided – indeed were merely thought to have aided – those who revolted. After his campaign, Alexander moved into Bactria and set up court at Bactra (Balkh) for the winter of 328.

This was an uneasy time for Alexander. He had been forced to cut short negotiations with the Sacae in order to relieve Maracanda and to restore the morale of the army after Spitamenes's victory. As he was quickly learning, the word of a defeated people was not enough, and there was always the danger that the Sacae would mass again. Spitamenes was roaming on the loose, and the whole of Bactria was still in revolt. It was imperative for him to end these two threats, and to this end he reinforced his army by 2,600 cavalry and 19,400 infantry.

Alexander could not afford to spend too much time in Bactria, so as soon as the weather permitted he marched eastwards. His route probably took him along the Oxus valley to Ai Khanoum, which would become the site of another of his cities, Alexandria on the Oxus. There, he split his army, leaving Craterus and three other commanders to garrison Bactria. Not too long after, Spitamenes, supported by soldiers from Sogdiana and a force of Massagetae, attacked a fort in Bactria. Craterus marched at full speed to its rescue. He defeated Spitamenes, but the enemy was able to escape. Nonetheless, it was some redress for what Spitamenes had inflicted on the Macedonians a short time before.

In Sogdiana Alexander again split his army, this time into four contingents. The first was under the joint command of Coenus and Artabazus, and the others under the sole commands of Hephaestion, Ptolemy and Perdiccas. They were to reduce different parts of Sogdiana. During this campaign Hephaestion, on Alexander's orders, founded six new cities.

Alexander intended them to be secure bases for his troops in that region, but each had a citadel in case of attack. The troops in them would serve to keep the area pacified; the pattern to Alexander's foundations continued.

Alexander himself pressed on through Tadjikistan to the eastern part of Sogdiana, where he successfully besieged several citadels in the summer of 328.[1] One of these was a rock fortress under the command of Ariamazes, where many rebels and families had taken refuge. Set high on top of sheer rocks, the defensible nature of this fortress offered no hope for an attacking force. Those in the fortress jeered at Alexander and said he would need winged soldiers to take them. That gave the king an idea.

The king called for volunteers to climb the cliff face that lay to the rear of the defenders, for it was not guarded. He offered a reward of 12 talents to the first man that reached the summit. This huge amount well reflects the Herculean labour and especially the danger that lay in this climb. Three hundred men volunteered. They drove tent pegs into the hard snow and during the night climb 30 fell to their deaths. Eventually some, then the remainder, made their way to the top. Alexander proclaimed that he had indeed found his winged soldiers, and when the commander Ariamazes realised that the Macedonians encircled him he surrendered. Alexander spared the people's lives, but he scattered them among his new cities to work in the fields.

With the summer campaigning season of 328 drawing to an end, and satisfied with his successes, Alexander returned to Maracanda. While there, he formally announced his intention of invading India. India or 'Indike' at this time was the land of the Indus and its tributaries, what today is Pakistan and Kashmir. For how long Alexander had this plan in mind is unknown. Some of the Indian rulers had already approached him seeking his support in disputes with each other and in plans to expand their own territories. These appeals must have had an effect on him, as did the lure of India itself.

Also of note during Alexander's stay at Maracanda was the proposal by the King of the Sacae that his daughter marry Alexander and that children of leading Sacae families marry his Companions. Alexander declined both offers. However, he was still able to negotiate a treaty with the Sacae that kept them on the far side of the Jaxartes, and so no longer a threat to him. It is interesting to note that at Susa in 324 he and 91 members of his court married Persian women. The reason at that time was simple pragmatics, but the seed for the intermarriages may well have been sown at Maracanda.

There also came the welcome news that Phrataphernes had secured Parthyaea and Stasanor had reimposed Macedonian influence in Areia. Alexander's western flank was now secure again.

As something of a change from all the recent campaigning Alexander and some of his men went to a safari park in Basista and took part in a massive wild animal hunt. Apparently 4,000 animals were killed, including a lion allegedly killed by the king himself. However, a more odious killing was soon to happen back in Maracanda: Alexander's drunken murder of Cleitus.[2]

A thanksgiving sacrifice to the Dioscuri turned into a drinking party, held in the palace of Maracanda late that summer. The Macedonians enjoyed such gatherings, where they could drink huge amounts of neat wine. Women were not permitted to attend, and apart from the king's omnipresent seven-man bodyguard no one was armed at them. At this particular party flatterers at the court tried to outdo each other in their praise of Alexander but at the expense of Philip. As more and more wine flowed, the praise grew more sycophantic, and some compared Alexander's birth to that of Heracles. The downplaying of Philip's achievements became more pronounced, and some said that Alexander alone was responsible for all Macedonian successes.

Alexander himself joined in the criticisms of Philip, and even went so far as to say that he was responsible for the victory at the Battle of Chaeronea in 338 and not his father. A song was sung that blamed the commanders of the force that Spitamenes had defeated and killed at Maracanda for its failure. Alexander laughed as he heard it and encouraged the man to sing it again.

At some point Cleitus, son of Dropides, known as the Black, spoke up angrily. He was a senior general, who had been co-commander of the Companion Cavalry since Philotas's execution in 330. He was also to be the new Satrap of Bactria. Like Parmenion and Philotas, Cleitus disliked the king's growing orientalism. Alcohol loosened his tongue. He spoke the thoughts of the older Macedonians present who were angry at the king's put downs of his father, and at the song about their fallen comrades which they thought was in bad taste. This he followed by criticising Alexander's divine pretensions and his Asian policy. To make matters worse, he finished off with a eulogy to Philip, and boasted that Alexander owed Cleitus his life because of his quick thinking at Granicus when Spithridates was about to kill him (see Chapter 5).

Alexander did not want to hear this sort of thing. Furious, he shouted, apparently in Macedonian, for his hypaspists (who were positioned outside the palace) to take Cleitus. His call in Macedonian presumably indicated that he wanted his men to react immediately – in other words, they did not think as fast in Greek. He also bounded forward to fight Cleitus himself, but his bodyguard held him back. In the meantime, Cleitus was bundled out of the hall and taken outside, apparently by Ptolemy. At that point, with the danger over, Alexander's bodyguard presumably released him and dusted him down. Then, for some reason, Cleitus, who could not control himself, returned and faced Alexander. A shouting match ensued, and a furious Alexander grabbed a long pike and ran Cleitus through. He died on the spot.

Alexander is said to have instantly regretted his murderous deed, probably because Cleitus was unarmed. The king tried to take his own life with the same pike, but his bodyguard prevented him. In remorse, he stayed in isolation in his tent for several days refusing food and water. Finally, the philosopher Anaxagoras persuaded him to leave by arguing that Cleitus' fate was part of a divine plan, and that Alexander could do no wrong because he was king. The king agreed. So great was the relief of his men that they condemned Cleitus for his words (regardless of their veracity) and even voted not to bury him. There was no other fallout from Alexander's murderous action.

In Alexander's response to Cleitus's taunts, we see a man who drank too much and whose reason, like that of most drunks, gave way to emotion. There is nothing to suggest that Alexander thought Cleitus was about to assassinate him; he could not, in any case, for he was unarmed. In fact, relations between the two men were generally good. Cleitus had known Alexander since he was a baby, for his sister Hellanice had been one of Alexander's nurses. The king had recently made him Artabazus's successor as satrap of Bactria, and as co-commander of the Companion Cavalry with Hephaestion Cleitus was held in great trust.

However, he was one of the old guard, like Parmenion, and he had criticised Alexander's Asian plans. More importantly, he had lauded Philip over Alexander. That is significant, for it was only when he did so that Alexander reacted as he did. There is no question that Cleitus crossed the line, and insubordination could not be tolerated. However, in a sober mood it is unlikely that Alexander would have put him to death. Then again, given Parmenion's fate, it is perhaps not too great a jump to imagine that Cleitus would never have redeemed himself, and that before long Alexander would engineer the downfall of another critic.

Cleitus's drunken praise of Philip was a serious miscalculation on his part. Alexander, out to distance himself as far as he could from the exploits of his father, could not tolerate such an appreciation at his own expense. Cleitus ought to have known that; perhaps he did, and his better judgement was clouded by an angry drunken mood. What the affair did show was the need for everyone to be on guard so as not to anger the king and suffer the same fate. The rift between the old guard and the new men, those who were the boyhood friends of Alexander, was growing, and the king was doing nothing to appease the older generation. The daily situation for both court and army was deteriorating. What would Alexander do next?

What Alexander did do next was to deal with Spitamenes. Craterus had been making good ground against rebel leaders, and Alexander some time previously had sent out Coenus to attack Spitamenes's nomad allies. As Alexander prepared to leave Maracanda, Coenus was given reinforcements and ordered to oversee operations from the base there. Alexander himself moved south to Nautaca (Uzunkir), in central Sogdiana, making that his base of operations for the winter.

In the north, Coenus had gained ground and in the winter of 328/7 he defeated Spitamenes and his army of Bactrians, Sogdianians, and Massagetae. Spitamenes lost 800 cavalry to the Macedonians' 25, and his Bactrian and Sogdianian support deserted to Coenus. Spitamenes fled once again, but for the last time. Shortly later he was killed by the Massagetae and beheaded. As a good faith gesture, they sent his head to Alexander. Soon after, the other chief rebel Dataphernes was handed over to Alexander by the Dahae.

The king himself had also been busy. In early 328/7 he moved against another rock fortress, used as a refuge by the local ruler Sisimithres. It lay on the far side of a deep chasm. The king decided to bridge the ravine, himself directing operations by day, and Leonnatus, Ptolemy and Perdiccas by night. Protected from enemy arrows by large wooden screens, the soldiers climbed down the banks of the ravine, and drove wooden stakes into its sides. On top of these they laid a foundation of wooden struts, and piled soil on top. The wooden bridge was completed, and Alexander prepared to trundle his siege engines into position. The sight proved too much. Before the Macedonians crossed their bridge, those inside the fortress surrendered. Alexander spared them, and reinstated Sisimithres as ruler of the area.

Thanks to Alexander's own operations and the mopping-up ones of his generals elsewhere, the threat to Macedonian rule in Bactria and Sogdiana was over.

The Macedonian king had almost bitten off more than he could chew. It had been a long, hard-fought campaign for the Macedonians, stretching over two years from the time that Bessus had inspired revolt against Alexander. The tenacity and fighting superiority of the Macedonian army must be acknowledged. Apart from Spitamenes's victory over the relief force sent to Maracanda, the army had been singularly successful against some of the toughest foes it had ever faced and in a region that was unknown and always hostile. The drunken murder of Cleitus was unquestionably a low point, but Alexander's leadership must be lauded. At no time did his army doubt him, and the campaign again proved his military genius. It was a pity that he was not just a general, though, but also a king. Kings ought not to murder senior staff in fits of drunken rage.

Alexander spent about two months of the winter making administrative and other arrangements before moving south to Bactra to prepare for his march into India. In an effort to prevent further revolt, he left the Satrap of Bactria with a large force of 10,000 infantry and 3,500 cavalry. He also exploited the presence of the thousands of people he had settled into his new cities. Alexander hoped that their presence would keep rebellion at bay. As a means of ensuring goodwill, or rather loyalty regardless of true feeling, he incorporated a large number of native cavalry into his army.

Finally, in early spring 327, while in Bactria, Alexander married for the first time. His bride was a Bactrian princess, Roxane, the daughter of a previous opponent, Oxyartes. She was reputedly the most beautiful girl in all Asia, and he fell in love with her at first sight, according to reports. They married soon after, though whether this affected his relationship with the pregnant Barsine is unknown. At the ceremony, Alexander and Roxane's father shared a loaf of bread, as was the Macedonian custom, which the king cut with his sword.[3]

Why did he marry now? He could just as easily have lived with her as he had with Barsine since 332. It may well be that in reaching the extreme easternmost limits of the Persian empire Alexander now believed he had truly fulfilled the panhellenic mandate of the League of Corinth. He could now stop, marry and start thinking about heirs. He might also have seen his marriage to a Bactrian instead of a Greek as a means of uniting the different cultures together under his one leadership.

These explanations seem unlikely, or at least are not the real reason for the marriage. Alexander had already announced his intention of advancing into India well before he met Roxane, so he clearly did not intend to stop after Bactria. In any case, the panhellenic nature of the mission had disappeared into something more Macedonian and more personal after Persepolis. It is puzzling why he married Roxane and not a Persian noblewoman. He could have had a choice of potential brides, for the royal princesses, taken after Issus, were still dutifully waiting for him (and learning Greek).

More likely is that in marrying Roxane Alexander was taking a leaf out of his father's book. Of Philip's seven marriages, the first six were for political and diplomatic reasons as Philip established a series of alliances. Alexander's campaign in Bactria and Sogdiana had shown him that the native rulers saw any peace negotiations as ephemeral and seized the first chance to revolt. Spitamenes' victory had cost him dearly in reputation and manpower, and had rallied the opposition. Alexander could not allow that to happen again. However, his treatment of Roxane had earned him the support of her father Oxyartes, and the inter-racial marriage would cement Alexander's rule in the satrapies far more so than any military conquest. So too would any children from that marriage, for unlike Heracles (the son of Barsine) they would be legitimate.

Thus, his reasons for marriage, as in everything, were pragmatic: the liaison underscored his rule over these areas and attempted to placate the natives. At the same time, Philip's ghost again appeared. Alexander had left his father behind as far as exploits went, but he still could not escape the examples he had set and policy he had followed. In this case, it was the political and military advantage of marriage.

The marriage to Roxane did not sit well with his men. For one thing, any children from it would not be full-blood Macedonian. Alexander seems to have forgotten Attalus's prayer of a decade earlier, when Philip married Cleopatra, that Macedonia might finally have a legitimate heir (see Chapter 3). More importantly, perhaps, was that Alexander was marrying someone from a conquered race, and the men may have thought this was wrong. In marrying Roxane, then, Alexander was causing further upset among his men, and setting in motion the confusion and havoc that would attend the aftermath of his death in 323.

Bactria would also be the setting for a further attempt by the king to promote his personal divinity. It would also be the setting for another conspiracy, one that Alexander exploited to get rid of Callisthenes who had just defied him.

The subjects of the Great King when coming into his presence prostrated themselves before him. They did this by either slightly bowing and at the same time blowing him a kiss or lying flat before him. The act was called *proskynesis*, and by it the people showed their subservience to the Great King. It may also have acknowledged his divine status, but this is more controversial. The Greeks derided this custom because they felt it impinged on personal freedom; it was something that slaves should do. Moreover, they thought the custom was sacrilegious. It was tantamount to worship, and they only worshipped gods or dead heroes. Even the posture was unacceptable. A Greek worshipped before a statue by standing up, with hands raised towards heaven.

Alexander's Persian subjects now prostrated themselves before him as their king. On one occasion, a Persian stumbled and almost fell over as he started to lie down. Alexander's men, one of whom was Leonnatus, a royal bodyguard, laughed at the scene. Their mockery angered and insulted the Persians, and it also had the same effect on Alexander. He publicly berated Leonnatus (at least), but later forgave him.

Why did Alexander try to introduce *proskynesis* at his court? The answer is that he wanted his own men to perform it before him. This was a radical move on his part, given the connotations of the act for the Greeks. It is possible that his intention was foreshadowed by Anaxarchus the philosopher, who had to sell the idea to the courtiers. He argued that Alexander had now eclipsed the deeds of Heracles and Dionysus. Therefore, since he was going to be worshipped when he was dead, why not worship him now. Some members of Alexander's court were in agreement, but not all, Callisthenes for one.

At a banquet:

'Alexander drank from a gold goblet to the health of the circle of guests, and handed it first to those with whom he had organised the ceremony of prostration. The first who drank from the goblet rose up and performed the act of prostration, and received a kiss from him. This ceremony proceeded from one to another in due order. But when it was Callisthenes's turn to make the toast, he rose up and drank from the goblet, and drew near, wishing to kiss the king without performing the act of prostration. Alexander was at the time talking to Hephaestion, and so he did not observe whether Callisthenes performed the ceremony completely or not. But when Callisthenes was approaching to kiss him, Demetrius, son of Pythonax, one of the Companions, said that he was doing so without having prostrated himself. The king would not permit him to kiss him, whereupon the philosopher said: "I'll go away the poorer by a kiss".'[4]

Callisthenes's stand was not an extreme one, and in fact if Demetrius had not said anything Alexander would not have known anything. Nonetheless, Callisthenes's defiance and then departure, against Alexander's wishes, seems to have encouraged others who were against *proskynesis* to defy Alexander as well. The king was forced to abandon his plan. Callisthenes's opposition would, however, cost him his life.

The second event at Bactria that casts a dim light over Alexander was the Pages' Conspiracy. The Royal Pages were youths who were Alexander's closest attendants. They had full access to the king and some stood by his bed while he slept. During a hunt, one of them, Hermolaus, killed a boar. Killing animals in hunts was part of the course, except that Alexander had this particular boar in his sights. He was not pleased that Hermolaus beat him to it, for the Macedonian king had the right of killing the quarry first. Perhaps Hermolaus had overstepped his bounds in a fit of youthful zeal, but Alexander had him publicly caned and seized his horse (as was the Macedonian custom).

Hermolaus was not content with merely licking his wounds. He persuaded at least four of the Pages to help him to assassinate the king one night while he slept. The conspiracy had more than a reasonable chance of success given the Pages' access to Alexander. No one else would be present in his tent to protect him, and he would be asleep. The plot did not succeed, and our sources give two explanations.

On the night in question, Alexander, who had been partying, decided to continue drinking rather than go to bed. He drank until dawn, and so he unknowingly foiled the plot. The second explanation involved a Syrian prophetess:

'At first she was an object of fun to Alexander and his courtiers. But when all that she said in her prophecies came true, he no longer treated her with neglect. She was allowed to have free access to him both by night and day, and she often took her stand near him even when he was asleep.'[5]

Thus, Alexander trusted her completely. On the night in question as Alexander was leaving the party, 'she met him, being under the god's inspiration at the time, and urged him to return and drink all night.' Alexander trusted her vision, and returned to the party, thus foiling the plot.

The veracity of this second account can be questioned. If the woman had told Alexander why she was worried for his life, we would expect him to have acted immediately against the conspirators rather than heading back to the party. What is at the heart of both explanations is Alexander's drinking instead of retiring for the night. For once, then, alcohol saved his life.

The day after, one of the Pages, Epimenes, told his lover about the conspiracy. The lover then told Epimenes's brother, who reported it to Ptolemy immediately. Given what had happened to Philotas for keeping quiet about a plot, Ptolemy wasted no time in informing the king. The conspirators were arrested and, despite their young age, were brutally tortured. They confessed, and all were executed by stoning. Their execution was preceded by a trial before the Macedonian Assembly, but this was probably a show trial to satisfy legalities. One source (Curtius) has Hermolaus and Alexander delivering lengthy speeches. These are invention to allow Curtius a vehicle to expound on freedom and tyranny for his own Roman audience. Those accused probably did not even have a chance to speak.

We can understand that Hermolaus wanted revenge for the humiliation he had suffered. Yet regicide was a major crime. Why would the other Pages allow Hermolaus to persuade them to murder their king? Alexander had not punished them. Moreover, their identities would soon be known since the assassination was to take place when only they stood over the sleeping king.

This leaves a political motivation for the conspiracy, which may have involved Callisthenes.[6] He was responsible for the Pages' instruction at court, and there is a story (whose authenticity is dubious) that when Hermolaus asked him how he might become the most famous of all

Callisthenes told him he had the kill the most famous man. Moreover, he had led the opposition to Alexander over *proskynesis*, and the army as a whole had serious reservations about Alexander's kingship. Indeed, the most recent wave of dissatisfaction may have started with his marriage to Roxane, and so Callisthenes may have exploited Hermolaus's upset.

However, some sources say that the Pages did not name Callisthenes as the instigator or even a co-conspirator when tortured, while others say the reverse. Nonetheless, after the trial of the Pages, Callisthenes too was accused of treason. There are various reports as to his end: he was subjected to the rack and then hanged, he was kept in chains and later died from natural causes (obesity is one explanation), or he died from sickness. The sources' inconsistency on his death and on his involvement in the conspiracy was even noted by contemporary writers.[7]

The whole affair is murky, but there is no doubt that the conspiracy had been a real threat to Alexander, far more so than that involving (allegedly) Philotas. As with the Philotas affair, we can see more than paranoia on the part of a king suspecting his court of intriguing against him. Once Alexander was crossed redemption was out of the question. Callisthenes's opposition was not trivial for he had forced Alexander to abandon his plan of introducing *proskynesis* at his court. That had made the king look bad in front of his men, not to mention the personal insult that he could not handle. Alexander was far angrier with him than with those who laughed at the stumbling Persian. Moreover, his anger persisted against him for far longer than against the others who had mocked the custom. These he had reprimanded and punished on the spot. Whether Callisthenes was implicated in the plot was immaterial. The moment he resisted the king's will he was a dead man. All Alexander needed was a scenario to justify his removal, and the Pages' Conspiracy gave him that.

We should also not discount the possible influence of the other philosopher at Alexander's camp, Anaxarchus. The two men had different philosophies and different lifestyles, plus Anaxarchus had supported Alexander's attempt at *proskynesis*. There differences may well have led to rivalries, and Anaxarchus, who had the king's ear, seized the opportunity afforded by the conspiracy to eliminate Callisthenes.[8] The court was not a safe place to be, and at its dangerous heart was the king himself.

Alexander could finally turn to what the Greeks called India, whose people were known collectively as the Indi and were famed for their physical toughness and fighting ability. They carried very long bows and swords, and both infantry and cavalry attacked with javelins:

'The Indians are not all armed in the same way; but their infantry have a bow equal in length to the man who carries it. Placing this down to the ground and stepping against it with the left foot, they discharge the arrow, drawing the string far back. Their arrows are little less than three cubits long; and nothing can withstand one shot by an Indian archer, neither shield nor breast-plate nor anything else that is strong. They carry on their left arms targets of raw oxhide, narrower than the men who carry them, but not much shorter in length. Others have javelins instead of arrows. All wear a sword that is broad, and not less than three cubits in length. When the battle is at close quarters, a thing that very rarely happens between Indians, they bring this sword down upon the opponent with both hands, in order that the blow may be a mighty one.'[9]

Alexander's men were certainly going to have their work cut out for them once they invaded.

Alexander may have had several motives for the invasion. As far as his panhellenic campaign was concerned he had no need to go to India for Persia had little, if any, influence there at that time. Those who lived in the Kabul Valley had sent a force to assist Darius at Gaugamela, so conceivably Alexander had a pretext for invasion. Presumably the rulers who had approached him the previous summer had whetted his appetite to explore as well. He may have wanted to extend his empire to the Southern (Indian) Ocean (which he thought was close to Punjab), following the exploits of a previous Great King, Darius I. According to Arrian, Alexander was supposed to have said that if he subdued India he would control all Asia.

There was a mythical element too, one that would especially appeal to his divine pretensions, and that was to follow in the footsteps of Heracles and Dionysus. Dionysus with his panthers, grapes and ivy, had travelled from India to become a god in Greece, and early on in his campaign Alexander seized the chance to outshine Heracles. Finally, there was his *pothos*, which played as important a reason as any of the others. It would cost him dearly.

I I

India

For Alexander and his contemporaries India was the land of the Indus and its tributaries. Aristotle thought it was merely a small promontory that extended into the Southern (Indian) Ocean. By this point in his march Alexander would have known this was not so from the locals he encountered and used as interpreters.[1]

The following ancient sources show that the Greeks had some knowledge of the geography and climate of India. They also had some knowledge of the Indians themselves, though accuracy was mixed with fable. It is important to bear in mind that generally most Greeks knew very little about India as a place as well as the history and customs of its people. We can thus understand all the more the lure for Alexander who was intent on exploring fresh lands:

'Aristobulus says that only the mountains and their foothills have both rain and snow, but that the plains are free from rain and snow. They are inundated only when the rivers rise. The mountains have snow in the winter time, and at the beginning of spring time the rains also set in and increase more and more, and at the time of the Etesian winds they pour unceasingly and violently from the clouds, both day and night, until the rising of Arcturus. Therefore, the rivers are filled from both the snows and the rains, and they water the plains.'[2]

'All the Indians wear their hair long and dye it to a sable or saffron colour. Their particular luxury is jewels. They make no display at funerals. Besides, as has been made known in the works of Kings Juba and Archelaus, the dress is as varied as the people's customs. Some dress in linen robes, others in woollen ones; some are nude, others cover their private parts only and several are just girded with flexible bark fibres. Some tribes are so tall that they clear an elephant with as easy a leap as they would a horse. Many do not kill an animal nor eat meat; most of them subsist on fish alone and depend on the sea for food. There are some who kill their parents and nearest kin just as they would victims of sacrifice, before age or disease reduce them to nothing. Then they banquet on the insides of the dead. This is not considered a crime there, but an act of piety. There are even those who on

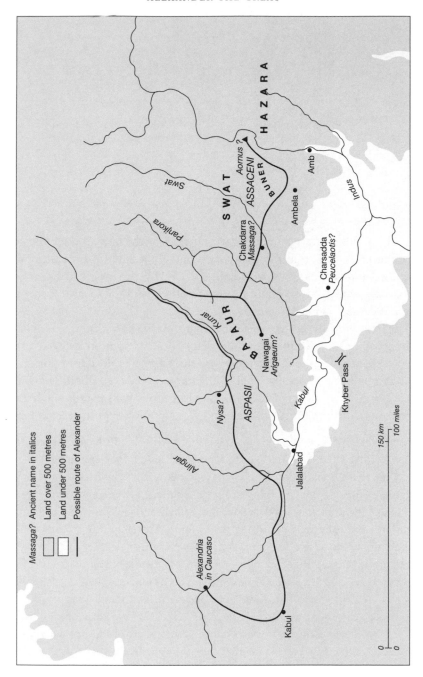

The Kabul Valley
Redrawn from Bosworth, A.B. (1988) *Conquest and Empire: The Reign of Alexander the Great* (pub Cambridge University Press), Map 8. © Cambridge University Press 1988, reproduced with permission.

falling sick withdraw into hidden places far from other people and wait for death with equanimity.'[3]

It is hard to imagine a man leaping with ease over an elephant. The account is clearly wrong here, as are those sources that talk about the tribe of men who had the heads of dogs or the tribe whose feet faced backwards. But such descriptions give us a fascinating insight into how the Greeks imagined Indians, no different from our stories about little green men on Mars.

Indian women, who apparently could give birth in their seventh year and were considered old at 40 (at least those of the Mandi), were very chaste to a point:

'The Indians do not think it disgraceful for them to prostitute themselves for an elephant, and to the women it even seems an honour that their beauty should appear equal in value to an elephant. They marry, neither giving nor receiving any dowry, but the fathers bring forward the girls who are of marriageable age and station them in a public place for the man who wins the prize for wrestling.'[4]

The value attached to the elephant as a working animal and as an integral part of the army is thus seen.

The Macedonian army marched towards the plain of the Indus down the valley of the Cophen (Kabul River), and it was there that Alexander split it in two. Both halves were to invade India by different routes. Hephaestion and Perdiccas were given command of one half of the army and all of the mercenaries. They were ordered to secure the main road into India, through the Khyber Pass, and to deal with any resistance as it occurred.

They faced very little, apart from the prince of Peucelaotis who stood fast in his capital of Charsadda. After 30 days, he was killed and an Indian appointed as governor of the capital. The army then marched relatively quickly to the Indus. Hephaestion bridged the river, having already constructed a number of boats from local timber. He was supported with food sent by the native prince Taxiles, ruler of Taxila, who had earlier made diplomatic contact with Alexander.

Alexander led the other half of the army, which included the hypaspists and valuable Agrianians, and marched through the Bajaur and Swat regions, which were north of the river. He was heading towards the northwest frontier of Pakistan. He probably expected to face more opposition than Hephaestion and Perdiccas, and for the rest of 327 and early 326 this turned out to be the case. Although he did not know it at this time, his route would also allow him to build on his divine aspirations and to succeed where Heracles had allegedly failed.

If the natives thought that Alexander was merely on an information-gathering adventure, they were soon mistaken. After he crossed the River

Choes they sought refuge in various fortresses. Alexander attacked the first one and was wounded by an arrow in the shoulder. The next day it was stormed. Many of the inhabitants fled, but those that did not were murdered. As a result, the nearby city of Andaca surrendered immediately. Those who defied Alexander in the Persian empire learned the cost the hard way, and now the Indians were learning the cost of resistance in similar fashion.

As Alexander continued his march into the Kunar Valley and beyond into Banjaur, in early 326, the natives fled before him into the mountains. Some were able to make good their escape, taking refuge in the great mountain fortress of Aornus (Pir Sar, the 'peak of the holy man'). Others were hunted down, though no massacre followed. As he had done in Sogdiana to consolidate his control, Alexander followed his military subjugation with founding a new city.

A short time before Alexander reached the Kunar Valley a delegation of 30 men came from a city called Nysa to plead for mercy. Their grounds were that they were descended from those who had travelled with Dionysus through the region, and Nysa was the name of Dionysus's nurse. Alexander was delighted when he saw ivy growing there, Dionysus's symbol. The plant was actually scindapsos, but it was close enough to ivy, and that was all that mattered. When he found out that their local god (Indra or Shiva) was the equivalent of Dionysus, he held a near-orgy there, a Bacchic revel that Dionysus himself would have enjoyed. During this he and his followers crowned themselves with ivy, and ran through the forest glades yelling wildly. He granted the city its autonomy, and 300 of Nysa's cavalry served with him for almost a year. At the same time, its ruler was subject to the king's satrap of the region, and he took as hostages the ruler's son and grandsons. Zeus's son might be travelling in the footsteps of his divine relatives, but he also needed to make sure that Macedonian power would not be challenged.

There was still more fighting to face. In the Swat Valley lived the Assaceni. Their army numbered about 30,000 infantry and 2,000 cavalry, a number bolstered by mercenaries, as well as 30 elephants. As Alexander invaded their kingdom they fled to various strongholds throughout the valley. One of these, Massaga, at the northern end of the valley, was especially important, and there at least 30,000 Assaceni, supported by a force of 7,000 mercenaries, resisted him. Alexander brought his siege towers to bear on its mud-brick and stone walls. It took four days before the walls were breached, during which time many of the defenders were killed. The widow of the dead commander sent an embassy to Alexander to plea for terms.

The king agreed to show leniency to the native population as long as Massaga surrendered immediately and the mercenaries joined the Macedonian army. The defenders agreed. However, as the mercenaries prepared to leave the fortress Alexander gave orders for them to be surrounded and massacred. Alexander's action cannot be justified, and as the mercenaries fought to their death they continually accused him of breaking his own terms of surrender.

He was mistaken if he thought that in making this example other strongholds holding out against him in the valley would surrender. If anything, Alexander's action sent the message that acceptance of any terms he dictated did not guarantee safety. Hence, with nothing to lose, the Assaceni resisted even more stoutly. For example, Coenus's attempt to take Bazira (Bir Kot) failed, as did that of another Macedonian force to take Ora (Udegram). The army's failure was something that Alexander had to reverse before word got out, and so he moved his entire force against Ora. It fell almost immediately, and Bazira was next. Now, the people fled to the formidable mountain fortress of Aornus (Pir Sar), to which inhabitants from the Kunar Valley had earlier sought refuge.

They could not have picked a worse place as far as Alexander's personal desire to outdo his ancestors went.

Aornus was connected with the Indian deity Krishna, whose counterpart in Greek mythology was Heracles. Whether the move came from Alexander himself or from one of his generals, the story was put out that during his Twelve Labours Heracles had twice tried to take Aornus but failed. Alexander now had the chance to outdo his divine ancestor, and he seized it with both hands. His *pothos*, his personal desire, may have been as important a factor as the strategic in his determination to take the place. Hephaestion and Perdiccas had probably reached the Indus by now, but control of the entire Cophen Valley was essential in Alexander's communications route from Asia to India.

To besiege Aornus would be no easy task given its rocky, steep terrain, its height of over 10,000 feet, and the abundance of natural resources on its flat top. Alexander left garrisons in Massaga, Ora and Bazira, while Craterus was headquartered at Ecbolima, the town closest to Aornus. He was to collect and store grain for a potentially protracted siege. As it turned out, this was unnecessary. Local guides took Alexander, together with some of the phalanx troops and light infantry, up to a high position on a ridge. This was over the 800-feet Burimar–Kandao ravine that led to the citadel of the rock fortress. Once established there, Alexander ordered the building of a bridge over the ravine that would reach to the defenders and on which the siege engines would stand.

To get his army up there had been a considerable feat given the narrow, winding tracks, but to bring the siege engines too was a labour worthy of Heracles. The whole process took four days, and when completed so filled the defenders with dread that they opened negotiations with Alexander. Their only escape now was down the steep slopes of Aornus.

This diplomatic initiative was a ploy to distract Alexander's attention while the defenders escaped by night. Unfortunately for them, the king had deployed scouts to warn him of any enemy withdrawal. When he heard the news, Alexander and 700 of his men simply climbed from the ridge to the rock fortress and, led by the king himself, attacked the enemy from the rear. Thus, Aornus fell to Alexander fairly quickly and easily. He had succeeded where even Heracles had failed. He built altars to Nike and Athena in celebration, parts of which exist today in the walls of the small mosque on top of Pir Sar.

Precise numbers are not known, but certainly many of the defenders would have been killed as the Macedonians attacked from the rear. As a result, the Assaceni's resistance throughout the valley collapsed. Many of the fighting stock fled across the Indus to join forces with Abisares, Prince of Hazara, in Kashmir. Alexander did not pursue them, but instead rounded up their abandoned elephants, and incorporated them into their army. He was now free to march to the Indus and so join the other half of the Macedonian army under Hephaestion and Perdiccas. Within a year though the Assaceni revolted, which showed that the Indians too would seize the first chance to oust the Macedonian presence.

Probably around Ohind (Udabhandapura) Alexander joined the other half of his troops and crossed the Indus. The army now numbered around 80,000 men with perhaps as many as 30,000 followers and hangers-on. It was now spring 326, less than a year since Alexander had invaded India. His rate of advance had been astonishing. The vast country, inhospitable conditions, and constant defiance of the natives, had been no match for him. There would still be plenty to face, however.

The reunion was a happy one, and both it and the crossing were celebrated with sacrifices and athletic games. Taxiles, the prince of that area, who had earlier sent provisions to Hephaestion, personally came to him with gifts. For his loyalty, his ruling power was reconfirmed, although he was made subject to a Macedonian satrap. He escorted Alexander to the capital, Taxila (Takshicila), about 20 miles north-west of modern Islamabad. This was the largest city between the Indus and Hydaspes rivers. There, the Macedonians enjoyed the exotic delights of a civilisation unknown to them, and in return it soaked up their own culture. For half a millennium after Alexander, Taxila was a prominent centre for Greek culture in India.

The Macedonians were especially impressed by the local Brahman sages. They were a fanatical religious sect who lived an ascetic life. Alexander even persuaded one of them, Calanus, to accompany him when

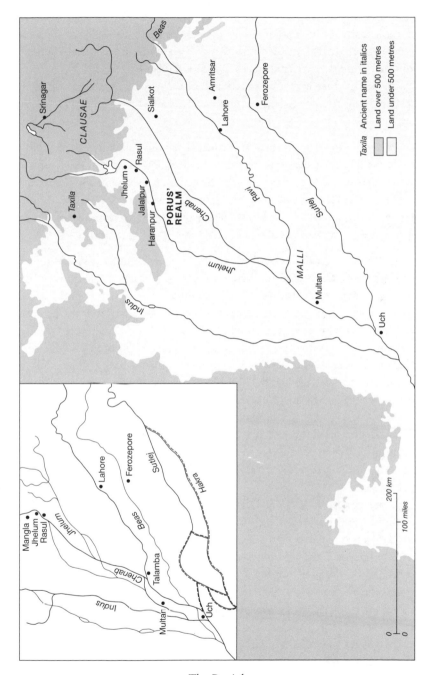

The Punjab
Redrawn from Bosworth, A.B. (1988) *Conquest and Empire: The Reign of Alexander the Great* (pub Cambridge University Press), Map 9. © Cambridge University Press 1988, reproduced with permission.

he left Taxila. He may have relied on him for advice, for the Brahmans were politically active and acted as advisers to the various kings.[5] Calanus stayed with the army until the return to Persepolis in mid-324, when he committed suicide by ritual burning (see Chapter 12).

Some of the customs of the natives here, however, shocked them. For example, what impoverished fathers had to do in order to marry off their daughters:

'Those who are too poor to marry off their daughters take them to the market-place in the flower of their youth to the sound of both trumpets and drums (the same instruments used to signal the call to battle), thus assembling a crowd. To any man who comes forward they first expose her rear parts up to the shoulders and then her front parts. If she pleases him, and at the same time allows herself to be persuaded, on approved terms, he marries her.'[6]

Not that the invaders could judge. In Greece a man normally married in his early thirties while his bride was only 12 or 13. Moreover, mar-riages were arranged, and the bride might not see her husband until the day of the wedding. As can be seen from the extract, at least at Taxila even the poorest of girls had to agree to the choice of husband.

Several rulers from the surrounding regions surrendered to Alexander, including Abisares. However, the games and sacrifices that followed Alexander's arrival at Taxila were marred by the activities of one of Taxiles's enemies, the neighbouring prince Porus. He ruled a large area of Punjab between the rivers Hydaspes (Jhelum) and Acesines (Chenab), and commanded a substantial army. He had sent no envoys to Alexander at Taxila, a sign that he did not recognise Alexander's authority. To make matters worse, he levied an army to prevent Alexander's crossing of the Hydaspes.

Leaving behind a Macedonian garrison in Taxila, Alexander took his army and the boats from the Indus crossing to the Hydaspes river. His route lay south towards the Great Salt Range. At the top of the Nandana Pass the Macedonians would gaze upon the Hydaspes, beyond it the rivers of Punjab, and then beyond that the Ganges. Here, 'every year they bury an old woman condemned to death near the ridge called Therogonus. As soon as she is buried, a swarm of reptiles creep out of the ridge's crest and eats up those of the dumb animals that fly around.'[7] From the topography and the stories they must have felt that they were – finally – reaching the end of the world.

Reality struck as they came down to the river, and on its opposite bank saw Porus's army of 4,000 cavalry, 300 chariots, 30,000 infantry, and a massive 200 elephants. Their own army was easily twice that of Porus, but even so another battle lay ahead.

The Hydaspes was a wide river, with a number of small islands in midstream. It was already starting to swell from the melting snow of the Himalayas, so Alexander faced a difficult crossing. On top of that, it was now May, and in June the monsoon rains started and lasted until September. For Alexander, the battle with Porus was less of a problem than fording the river in these dangerous conditions or waiting so long that the monsoons would force him to stay where he was.

Rather than cross immediately, Alexander decided to lull his enemy into a false sense of security. He set up a base camp and ordered the dismantling of the vessels from the Indus crossing. Large amounts of grain were to be procured from the fertile surrounding lands. To Porus, Alexander's army was apparently arranging to ride out the oncoming monsoon weather and to wait for the river to subside – until September it seemed. However, Alexander wanted to keep Porus's army guessing and tired. Therefore, he made dummy attempts at crossing the river, usually stopping at the islands in its middle. These diversions forced Porus to have his army continuously deployed, and frustrated.

The king had no intention of waiting for the monsoon rains to pass. While engaged in his diversionary strategy, he was secretly readying boats at a headland of the Salt Range that came down to the river but was hidden by thick woods. This would be his strike camp. Opposite was an island that would aid his fleet as it crossed. Craterus, heading a large number of cavalry and infantry, stayed at the base camp, while Meleager, Attalus and Gorgias commanded the mercenaries and other infantry and cavalry which were ranged along the riverside. These forces would continue with Alexander's strategy of distracting Porus's attention. At his secret strike camp, the king had assembled a relatively small force of perhaps 6,000 infantry and 5,000 cavalry, mostly Macedonians along with the Bactrian and Saca cavalry. Once on the opposite bank, they would force Porus to meet them, thereby allowing Craterus and the other troops to follow in some degree of safety.[8]

Alexander decided to take his strike force across the river under cover of darkness. A late spring thunderstorm a little before dawn provided even more cover, and he and his men were past the midstream island before the enemy spotted them. Then luck abandoned Alexander for a while. Past the island was another channel of the Hydaspes that caught the Macedonians by surprise. They had no small difficulty in crossing it, and by now dawn was breaking so they had lost their cover of darkness.

If we can believe one tradition, as the men struggled to cross the river Alexander cried out: 'O Athenians, can you possibly believe what perils I am undergoing to win glory in your eyes?'[9] The saying is not likely to ring true, for Athens had not suffered at the hands of the Indians, and in any case the panhellenic motive for the war on Persia was the last thing in Alexander's mind at this time. The story was added later, perhaps at Alexander's insistence, to complement his legend.

Fortunately, the Indian army was not quick enough to attack them as they landed on the opposite bank. A force of 120 of the Indians' peculiarly large six-man chariots and 2,000 cavalry led by one of Porus's sons was the first to arrive. Alexander's cavalry quickly and easily defeated the Indian cavalry, which lost about 400 of its number before fleeing. In the meantime, the mud from the rains bogged down the chariots that had stayed too close to the river bank.

The battle was little more than a skirmish, but some of the survivors who fled back to Porus mistakenly told him that Alexander and the main Macedonian army had crossed. Porus immediately led his entire army to face Alexander, leaving only a small number of elephants and troops to hinder Craterus's crossing. On a sandy plain he set up his battle line of infantry, ten-men deep and over a mile long, with the war elephants stationed every 50 feet. Each flank was protected by a contingent of 150 chariots with 2,000 cavalry behind. Porus was close to six feet six inches tall, so he was clearly visible on his chariot. He expected his elephants to win him success, for the Macedonian horses would not attack the elephants head on, and the large animals would trample the infantry to death.

Against anyone else, Porus's strategy would probably have worked. Alexander, however, was not just anyone else, and part of his military genius was his ability to adapt. He had encountered elephants before, and he knew their weaknesses as well as their strengths. Accordingly, he drew up his battle line. He led the largest contingent of cavalry and faced Porus's left wing, while Coenus, with 1,000 cavalry, faced the Indian right. The infantry was between both cavalry flanks (Fig. 5).

Alexander attacked the Indian left flank with such ferocity that it gave way, and in order to bolster it Porus sent reinforcements from his right. In the meantime, Coenus's charge of the right flank had caused disruption, but instead of pressing home his advantage he suddenly wheeled, and the Indian cavalry found itself attacked on two fronts. Alexander had ordered Coenus to execute this manoeuvre, thus foxing Porus into thinking that he would keep his attention only on the Indian right. In an effort to escape, the riders turned their horses into the line of infantry and elephants, causing no small degree of confusion and disruption. Then Alexander ordered his infantry to attack the Indians. The long sarissas did their deadly work so effectively that Porus perhaps had to order his elephants to begin their attack a little earlier than planned.

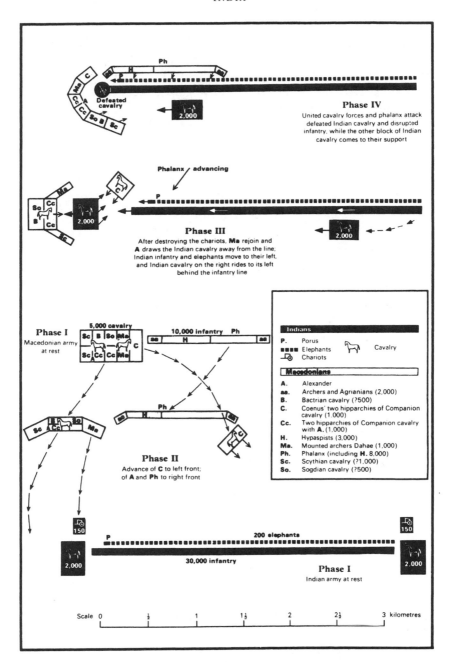

Figure 5. Battle of Hydaspes: Indian and Macedonian battle lines.
From N.G.L. Hammond, *The Genius of Alexander the Great* (1997), p. 165

The Macedonians were ready. As the charging elephants bore down on them, the phalanx split to avoid them and to open up a passage for them to travel through. As they did so, the men used their sarissas to dislodge the mahouts, and with no riders the elephants began to go out of control. The sarissas were then turned on the elephants themselves, blinding them and wounding their undersides, perhaps also cutting off or slashing their genitalia in the process. Horrifically wounded, they stampeded back to their own line, killing many of the Indians under their feet.

While this was going on, the Macedonian cavalry had encircled the Indians, and was attacking them from the rear. Surrounded on all sides, the Indian cavalry was all but annihilated, and the elephants were captured. With the danger from the elephants over, the phalanx regrouped and attacked the Indian infantry. Some of them managed to escape, but they were hunted down and killed by Craterus' troops and the mercenaries under Meleager, Attalus and Gorgias. These had crossed safely while the battle was being fought.

The Battle of the Hydaspes was a brilliant victory for Alexander. His army lost about 800 infantry and 300 cavalry, whereas as many as two-thirds of Porus's men were killed in the battle or in the subsequent pursuit. Against the numerically superior and superbly drilled Macedonian army Porus's army stood little chance. His only hope of victory lay with the elephants, but Alexander had built into his strategy the means of using them against the Indians. Porus himself, wounded but alive, refused to surrender and faced the Macedonian king as defiantly as before the battle. His bearing and his heroism impressed Alexander enough to reconfirm his power. Moreover, he gave him additional territories east of the Hydaspes. As might be expected, though, Porus became a vassal of the Macedonian king.

Alexander celebrated his victory with athletic games where he had crossed, and the founding of two new cities, each on an opposite side of the Hydaspes. Both were on main lines of communication and were for the defence of the frontier. Thus, they were not impulse foundations set up by Alexander merely to celebrate his victory. One, appropriately named Nicaea ('Victory City'), was on the site of the battle, and the other was on the site of his base camp. This was to be called Bucephala in honour of his horse Bucephalus, who had died shortly after the battle.

Philip had given this horse to Alexander when he was about 15, in 341. Bucephalus had fought valiantly in almost all of Alexander's battles since then:

'It was a noteworthy characteristic of this horse that when he was armed and equipped for battle, he would never allow himself to be mounted by any other than the king. It is also related that Alexander in the war against India mounted that horse and performed valorous deeds, but had driven him with disregard of his own safety too far into the enemies' ranks. The horse had suffered deep wounds in his neck and side from the weapons hurled from everyone's hands at Alexander. Though dying and almost exhausted from loss of blood, he yet carried the king as swiftly as he could away from the enemy's midst. When he had taken him out of range of the weapons, the horse at once fell, and satisfied with having saved his master breathed his last, with sighs of relief that were almost human.'[10]

Old age as well as battle wounds had finally taken their toll. Clearly Alexander doted on him, and that gives us an interesting insight into the man. He loved his own horse, and yet could kill those men he had known for years without hesitation.

At some point afterwards, Alexander's mint at Babylon issued special commemorative coins. These were the tetradrachms, which depicted an Indian bowman with the characteristic body-length bow on the obverse and an elephant on the reverse. Also the decadrachms, which on the obverse depicted Alexander on Bucephalus attacking two Indians on an elephant with his sarissa, and on the reverse a standing Alexander, with a diadem, holding a pike in his left hand and thunderbolt in his right, being crowned by Nike with an ivy wreath of victory.

Coins circulated widely in the ancient world, and these were minted for propaganda reasons.[11] They magnified the extent of Alexander's victory, and they contributed to the legend that we have today. Alexander's victory over Porus was elevated to become his victory over India.

Leaving Craterus to keep an eye on Porus and the garrison in Taxila, Alexander campaigned against the Glausae. They lived in the rich timber-producing country of the north in Kashmir. There were perhaps half a million of these people living in 37 villages in the region, but they surrendered without a fight. Alexander added their land to Porus's territory. He himself had no need of their land, but he did have a reason for their timber. It would be used to build a fleet for his journey to the Southern Ocean in later 326, a plan that was evidently in his mind at the time of his stay in Taxila.

Alexander had believed that the Indus flowed into the Nile because of the similarity of the flora and fauna, but the local Indians had dispelled that idea by telling him that the Indus flowed into the Ocean. This was the Southern or Indian Ocean, and Alexander resolved to march to it and sail on it. If he had declared this intention in Pella he would surely have been met with derision given the vast distances and unknown terrain. However, the young king (he was, after all, only 30, and had been king only ten years) had already travelled further than anyone before him. Hence, his audacious desire to see the Southern Ocean probably raised few eyebrows in his camp.

The Battle of Hydaspes was the high point in Alexander's campaign in India. The next few weeks were spent in both resting the troops and reducing Porus's enemies west of the Acesines river. As a vassal to the Macedonian king, Porus's enemies became those of Macedon. The Acesines was now swollen with the onslaught of the monsoon rains, and a number of Macedonians drowned in the crossing. The losses soured the victory at the Hydaspes.

The most formidable opponent in this period was a cousin of Porus, who was also called Porus. Cousin Porus had surrendered to Alexander before the Battle of Hydaspes, but when Alexander did not punish his namesake cousin and enemy but in fact elevated his power, he fled across the Hydraortes (Ravi) River with an army. Alexander set off after him, having ordered his vassal Porus to levy an army, and leaving Coenus at the Acesines. In ordinary conditions, a campaign such as this would not have been an especially arduous one. However, the weather had fast deteriorated because of the monsoon rains. The non-stop torrential downpours created havoc when it came to river crossings, sieges and the general movement of troops.

The lands of Porus the treacherous cousin were easily seized, and Coenus, Craterus and Hephaestion stayed in them to ensure Macedonian control. Alexander crossed the Hydraortes and besieged the town of Sangala (near Lahore), in which Indians were resisting him. He was reinforced by a contingent of troops and elephants headed by Porus the vassal, and prepared to bring his tried and tested siege engines to bear against Sangala's brick walls. These turned out to be unnecessary, for after a series of frontal assaults over three days the city fell.

The Macedonians, perhaps unduly influenced by depression from the continuous rains, slaughtered almost everyone and razed the town to the ground. Seventeen thousand were killed and 70,000 captured that day. Those Indians living in nearby cities fled for safety, but they were not allowed to escape. In fast pursuit the Macedonians bore down on those too sick or exhausted to keep up with the rest, and massacred them. In gratitude, Alexander ceded this region to his vassal Porus, whose growth of power despite his original enmity towards Alexander was astonishing. The territory that Porus ruled was said to have more than 2,000 cities. The population must have been several million.

Despite the terrible weather conditions of the monsoons, Alexander pushed his army on further. At the second last river of Punjab, the Hyphasis (Beas), matters came to a head in a way that he could not have expected. There seems little doubt that he intended to cross this river, believing that he would find the end of Asia. He was also probably curious to see the Ganges, the greatest river in India, since he would have heard of it by now from the locals who were with him.

The Macedonians were none too keen at the prospect of more fighting, this time against the wealthy people of the Nanda dynasty. Their capital Pataliputra was at the confluence of the Son and Ganges, by modern Patna. This city alone had a population of 400,000, with riches that beckoned as seductively as Babylon. Never mind the end of Asia or the Ganges: the prospect of further fighting against unknown opponents led the army to have other ideas. Alexander the Great was about to face his first mutiny.

Seventy days of marching through demoralising monsoon rains, during which time the army had continued to face resistance, had taken their toll. It is important to try to imagine how the men must have fared and felt. Day after day, week after week, in fact for ten weeks, they had marched in drenching rain, their clothes and bodies permanently soaked. Dysentery would have been prevalent, perhaps malaria too. Snakes, especially pythons and cobras, were a constant hazard, and the bite of a cobra was deadly. And always there was the rain. Alexander shared their hardships, no doubt about that, but Alexander's hardships were brought about by his own desires to reach the end of Asia. As such, he could handle them better than his men for that reason.

When the Macedonians reached the Hyphasis River, they must have been, we can imagine, exhausted and totally sick of being constantly wet and the burdens this brought. At the Hyphasis Alexander would have found out that, in fact, the end of Asia did not lie just across the river. What did was more opposition. The men had had enough.

The king was aware of their mood, and he called his senior commanders to him. For once, neither his appeals nor authority had any effect on them. After what must have been an uncomfortable silence, Coenus voiced the opinion of those men under him, but in reality of the whole army. Enough was enough: it was time to return to Greece and enjoy the fruits of the new Macedonian empire. Coenus had fought side by side with Alexander in some of his most bitter battles, and so his was a voice that the king needed to listen to carefully. But no. A furious Alexander broke up the meeting. He called another the next day, but met with the same response. This time, he withdrew to his tent, like his hero Achilles in the last year of the Trojan War, and stayed there for three days. He was hoping that such an act of obvious disappointment with his men would produce the desired effect. It did not.

Alexander must have been in despair, and he may have decided on a novel plan to save face. After his period of sulking in his tent, he took the auspices the following morning for the river crossing. As king, this was one of his daily duties. This time, he declared, the auspices were unfavorable. To the army's joy, he proclaimed that the gods themselves had decided that the Macedonians had marched far enough east and thus had to return home. It was a climbdown for Alexander, but he made it plain that it had been the result of not the army's opposition but the gods' decision.[12]

The king had been spectacularly successful to date. In order to reinforce this he ordered the building of 12 huge stone altars, each about 80 feet high. Each one was dedicated to one of the 12 Olympian gods as a thanks offering for all of his successes. There was no altar to Alexander, whose belief in his own divinity was great now (see Chapter 14), but that would have been too much. These altars marked the eastern boundary of his empire, just as those he erected on the Hellespont marked his western.

Although no one ventured to replace Alexander, the army's reaction should be termed a mutiny.[13] The men refused to obey their king's order to cross the Hyphasis. They refused to be swayed by his appeals of greater glory and riches to be gained by marching further east. And they forced him to abandon his plans, and to begin what they thought would be the long march home. That was a vote of no confidence in their king and leader, which can only be called a mutiny. Although Alexander used the excuse of unfavourable omens to disguise the turn around at the Hyphasis River, all there would know that the real reason was that the army did not want to go further.

Alexander, as we know, did not take any opposition lightly, especially from those close to him. He must have been furious that his dream of further conquest had been thwarted, and only a few days after the mutiny Coenus, its protagonist, was found dead. There is no evidence that the king was involved in his death, and one source says he died of disease. However, the coincidence of Coenus's sudden demise so soon after his role in the mutiny is too much. For one thing, what was this disease that was supposed to have killed Coeneus, and why were no others in Alexander's camp affected by it? Coenus was also the son-in-law of Parmenion, whose clashes with Alexander had led to his death (and that of his son Philotas) some time before (see Chapter 9). Coenus's defiance may well have brought back to Alexander memories of his father-in-law.

The death of another successful opponent of Alexander may be brought in here. Not long after he had forced Alexander to abandon his attempt to introduce *proskynesis* at Bactra in spring 327, Callisthenes was killed (see Chapter 10). Would Coenus, whose display of opposition was even more spectacular and far-reaching in that it caused Alexander to abandon his plans to march further eastward, have escaped unscathed? When we think of Alexander's reaction to Callisthenes, we find it hard not to see his hand at work in the death of Coenus. Those at Alexander's court would have made a connection between Coenus's demise and the king – and what happened to those who defied him.[14]

Coenus received a magnificent funeral, but we would not expect anything less of Alexander if he were attempting to cover up his role in Coenus's demise. Craterus, a traditionalist as fervent as Parmenion and Philotas, may also have fallen out of royal favour. He would shortly be sent to Carmania with a number of veteran soldiers, thus distancing him from the king and his court.

By late September 326 the army was back at the Hydaspes, and based itself at Bucephala and Nicaea. At the latter an artificial harbour was built and Alexander assembled a new fleet, much of which was built from scratch. When finished it numbered between 800 and 2,000 vessels. Alexander had also received reinforcements from the Greek mainland, including 6,000 cavalry and 30,000 infantry, of whom 7,000 were mercenaries, as well as armour and medical equipment.

The new fleet was not meant to be a war fleet but transport for the men, horses and food. Alexander might have been thwarted in his bid to cross the Hyphasis, but he was determined to conquer Southern India (Pakistan today) and to travel to the Southern (Indian) Ocean. His army could be transported a lot faster by river, and Alexander now laid the plans for this next venture. As commander of the new fleet Alexander appointed his boyhood friend, Nearchus of Crete, the former satrap of Lycia and Pamphylia. Onesicritus of Astypalaea, the helmsman of the royal flagship, was made second in command.

Finally, in November, the time came for embarkation. The departure was celebrated in splendid fashion. On the evening before, musical and athletic games were held, and sacrifices to various gods, including those of the river (Poseidon, Amphitrite and the Nereids), were performed. On the actual day, Alexander performed more sacrifices, including to the Hydaspes, and then from his flagship another round, this time including Ammon and Heracles. Finally, a bugle rent the air, and the fleet set sail. The scene was perhaps not too distant from today when a fleet sets out from its harbour as crowds of spectators gathered to watch it go. Hephaestion and Craterus with two contingents of troops had left some time before. Hephaestion led the larger (which included the 200 elephants) down the river's left bank and Craterus the other on its right. They joined the fleet at a prearranged place further down the river.

The fleet made good time, but by the junction of the Hydaspes and Acesines it ran into trouble with the fast-flowing water, and a number of boats and men were lost. While Alexander attended to these there was some inconsequential warfare with neighbouring tribes. That would change as the fleet continued its journey to lower Punjab. There, Alexander faced a possible combination of the most warlike of peoples, the Sudracae (Ksudrakas) and Malli (Malavas). These two tribes outnumbered the Macedonians, so Alexander had to act fast. His plan was to stop them from joining together, and to achieve this he decided to reduce the Malli.

At the Acesines River, the king split his army into several groups. He took 6,500 infantry and 2,000 cavalry including half of the Companion Cavalry, the hypaspists and the Agrianians, and marched at speed over the desert to the Hydraortes to attack the Malli from the north. He marched 50 miles in a day and a night. Nearchus and the fleet sailed south from the Acesines to the borders of the Malli. Craterus and Philip son of Machatas (satrap of northern India) marched with a contingent of troops and the elephants down the river's right bank. Hephaestion was to march down the left bank five days ahead of Alexander's troops, and Ptolemy was to follow three days behind Alexander to mop up Mallian survivors and escapees.

Alexander's strategy was devastatingly effective. The Mallian towns west of the Hydraortes fell quickly to the Macedonians, who, following Alexander's order of no prisoners, massacred the inhabitants. Eventually, the Malli staked everything in one last-ditch defence. They barricaded themselves in the citadel area of the strongest city of that region, perhaps Multan. Alexander stormed the city, which fell to him with ease, and then turned to the citadel.

For some reason the assault on the citadel was lacklustre, perhaps because Alexander's men were simply tired from the constant fighting and sieges of recent months. This forced Alexander to set a personal example. In an effort to spur on his men he climbed a scaling ladder to the battlements. Unfortunately, his action had too much of the desired effect. Others climbed up with him, but in an effort to prove their worth, not to mention protect their king, the hypaspists stormed up the ladders in such great numbers that they broke them. Alexander and perhaps only three other men, Peucestas, Leonnatus and Abreas, were suddenly on their own at the top of the citadel wall, and with no hope of immediate reinforcement.

Alexander's seer Demophon had advised the king to delay his siege, but he had rejected the advice. Now, that decision almost cost him his life. Without a second thought, Alexander jumped down into the citadel and faced the enemy by himself. The others followed him, but in the fierce fighting Abreas was killed by an arrow. Alexander was cornered against a fig tree, and then an arrow (apparently three feet long) hit him in the chest. It penetrated his armour and seems to have lodged in his right lung, for 'air was breathed out from the wound together with his blood'.[15]

Somehow Peucestas managed to hold the Shield of Achilles from Troy over the king and protected his body while the Macedonians outside stormed the walls and opened the citadel gate. Their frenzy when Alexander was cut off from them on the battlements was increased when they saw him covered in blood and lying still on the ground. Thinking their king dead, they went on an orgy of murder, and slaughtered the entire enemy. Alexander was bleeding badly, for the arrow 'went in at his breast and came out of his neck',[16] but Critobulus of Cos cut it out of him and sewed up the hole. He saved Alexander's life in the nick of time.

There is some controversy as to the identity and number of those fighting with Alexander when he jumped into the enemy's midst. However, the king's heroism at the Malli town was beyond doubt. The reaction of the men is telling. If Alexander had died, who would have succeeded to lead the army home? There was no heir at that time, and the aftermath of Alexander's death, when his generals fought a series of wars against each other that lasted for decades, showed there was no one undisputed leader. The men were far from home, and presumably the conquered territories would have revolted once news of the king's death was known. In that scenario, would the army have been able to march home successfully? How much more fighting would it have faced? And, without Alexander, how many defeats?

That these questions and others were in the men's minds is shown by Alexander's action when he was transported by boat to the base camp at the confluence of the Hydraortes and Acesines to recover fully. There, all the Macedonian forces reunited and the army was whole again. Despite his injury, he appeared before his men, and even climbed on his horse to show how fit he was. They were euphoric, and crowned him with many different, local flowers. Nonetheless, Alexander had suffered the most serious wound of his life, and it was some time before he recovered.

It may have been now, or a short while later, perhaps June 325, that Alexander sent Craterus with about 9,000 infantry and cavalry and the whole of the elephant corps back to Carmania, and then to Persis. His route took him through Arachosia and Drangiana and, apart from some native unrest that was easily crushed, the march was uneventful.

Alexander's reason was that these men were too old or unfit for military activity, and also that Craterus was to reassert Macedonian influence if need be in the areas through which he passed. However, the men may also have included those who had criticised Alexander's continued advance. He was still determined to reach the Southern Ocean, and even while he recuperated the size of the fleet was increased. He could not afford another Hyphasis situation, and the easiest way to offset opposition was to get rid of it. He also had a much more mobile army, now that the veteran and unfit soldiers had left, to use in his campaigning further south.

Meanwhile, as Alexander had intended from his systematic slaughter of the Malli, the Sudracae and remaining Malli formally surrendered to him. Their lands were made part of the vast northern India satrapy of Philip, son of Machatas, and a new city was founded, Alexandria in Opiene. This was to have a dockyard, like several other of Alexander's foundations, showing that the king was intent on using the excellent river systems for transport and especially trade, something the Indians had never properly exploited.

Shortly after, Alexander led his men south to the confluence of the Acesines and Indus, receiving the submission of the peoples he encountered along the way. He was now at the border of northern and southern India, and there he made Peithon, son of Agenor, satrap of all the lands south to the Southern Ocean.

One of the nearby princes, Musicanus, who was said to rule over the richest kingdom of the Indus Valley, did not surrender to Alexander. Not surprisingly, Alexander could not allow this disregard. He grouped together a force, and sailed downstream at such speed that he arrived at Musicanus's lands before Musicanus heard that he had left! In no small panic he immediately surrendered, and gave Alexander all manner of gifts and, more importantly, all his elephants. The king allowed Musicanus to remain ruler of his princedom, and spent some time with him at his capital. However, it received a Macedonian garrison in order to ensure Musicanus's continued loyalty, and Musicanus became another of Alexander's vassals.

Further campaigning followed, this time against Musicanus's neighbours, all of which was successful. These included a revolt by tribes west of the Indus, who were led by Sambus. They were influenced by the Brahman sages in their towns, for 'the Brahmans take part in affairs of state and attend the kings as advisers'.[17] Religion and politics did not mix well; the same is still true. Their defiance was futile and earned terrible reprisals as the Macedonian army destroyed these towns. Alexander allowed his troops to keep all of the spoils, and the native death toll was put as high as 80,000.

Meanwhile Musicanus proved as fickle as Porus's cousin the previous year. Despite the Macedonian garrison in his capital, his Brahman advisers persuaded him to declare against Alexander. The king was not in a good mood, and he sent Peithon against him. There were no second chances, and when Peithon captured Musicanus he crucified not only him but also the Brahmans who had pushed for revolt. The Indians' reaction to Alexander's rule proves that they saw it as merely ephemeral, whereas he continued to believe that defeated in battle (or siege) meant conquered. Many years later, in the second century AD, the military writer Polyaenus (4.3.30) believed that Alexander's actions persuaded the Indians to accept his rule willingly. This is nonsense.

At least Alexander's present harsh action ended opposition to him as he continued his march south to the Southern Ocean. For example, the ruler of Patalene, the land of the Indus delta, submitted himself and his territory to Alexander long before the king arrived there. Thus, it was without incident that in about July 325 Alexander and his army reached Patala, where he encamped at its capital. The exact location is unknown, but Patala could well be Hyderabad in southern Pakistan.

From there Alexander planned an exploration by land and by sea of the Makran coast of the Indian Ocean, over 1,000 miles long. Thus, a little under two years after he had invaded India, Alexander had achieved his aim of reaching the Southern Ocean. It was his intention to have a fleet sail along the unknown coastline as far as the Persian Gulf under the command of Nearchus. This was to be a voyage of exploration that would also settle an important question: was this Southern Ocean an inland sea like the Mediterranean or an open sea that encircled all the lands of the world, as Aristotle believed. The fleet was composed of lighter, faster slips such as the triaconter, an open boat with 15 oars on each side. It would have the advantage of moving faster, and such ships could land on open beaches. The disadvantage was that the ships could not carry much food and water, hence Alexander's plan of marching along the coast at the same time so that he could gather provisions for the fleet.

It would be necessary to find the best navigable route to the Ocean for the fleet, which meant exploring the main arms of the Indus. Hephaestion was left in command at Patala while Alexander set off down the western arm. He was hit by bad weather that destroyed several of his lighter ships, forcing him back. Another attempt met with better luck, and Alexander sailed out well into the Ocean. He sacrificed bulls to Poseidon, god of the sea, together with gold cups as a thanks offering. Given the hazards of the weather, especially the gales, and the unknown topography, it was prudent to keep the god of the sea on side. He also landed on a small island and set up altars to Ocean and Earth. The altars are significant, for they marked the southern boundary of the Asian part of his new empire, just as those on the Hyphasis marked the eastern and those on the Hellespont his western.

After his venture down the western arm, Alexander returned to Patala and sailed down the eastern arm of the Indus. He successfully sailed the length of this river and then out into the Ocean, leaving his land troops by a large saline lake. This, he decided, would not only be the best route for his men, but also the lake could be turned into another harbour. He gave orders for the construction of dockyards and a fort for a garrison. By now it was late July or early August 325. The south-west monsoons had begun, and they lasted for three months. Nearchus and the fleet could not safely sail during this time, and so all the Macedonians returned to Patala.

The best-laid plans, however. Alexander left Patala before the fleet was due to sail as planned. Nearchus departed before the monsoons had subsided, however, and he sailed down the western, not eastern, arm of the Indus. This was a radical change from Alexander's plan, but one that Nearchus was forced to make because of native unrest. The Indians had not welcomed the Macedonians with open arms, and had continually defied them. The actions of Porus's cousin and of Musicanus show not so much that the natives were fickle but that they saw any alliance with Alexander as ephemeral. He was an invader, and invaders were not tolerated.

While Alexander was at Patala, the local Indians had constantly harried his men while they dug wells for water in the desert. Nearchus may well have left when he did to escape attack. He took the different route because the Indians may have overrun the second harbour at the Indus mouth, and he did not want to place the fleet in danger. His early departure cost him time, though, for he was marooned on an island off the coast for over three weeks (where he and his men ate oysters for the first time since they had left Greece) until the monsoons subsided. However, at least the fleet was safe, and it could begin its great exploratory mission.

The native unrest that faced Nearchus was in fact the start of a revolt of the areas of India that Alexander had conquered. Once again he had confused defeated in battle with conquered. The revolt was led by his vassal Porus, who clearly and unsurprisingly showed where his true loyalty lay. There was a reason why the Great Kings of Persia had not tried to annex India and turn it into satrapy, and Alexander had failed to see it. Or rather, he thought he could accomplish what they never did. However, other things were now on his mind.

The king marched north from Patala with anything up to 30,00 men and a baggage train that included the partners and children of his men. His soldiers, as could only be expected, had met women of various races during their march, and many had established de facto relationships of several years. The baggage train was placed under Hephaestion's command, to follow Alexander at its slower pace. The army reached the River Arabis (Hab) without incident. There, Alexander attacked the Oreitae, and followed that up with an invasion of their lands. The wells that his men had previously dug in the desert had aided the army considerably in its march, and the king ordered more to be dug along the coast. His plan

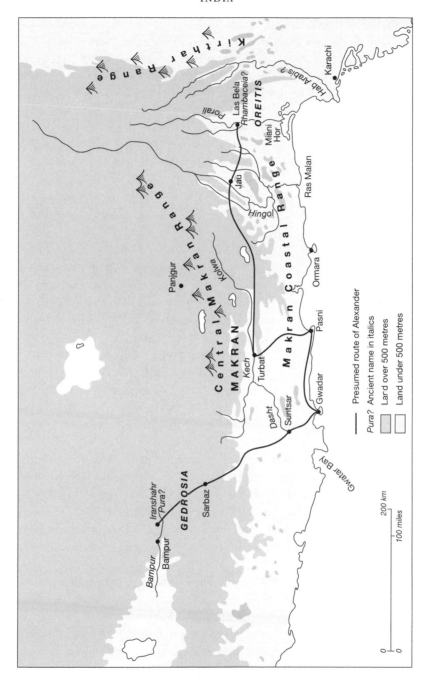

Las Bela and the Makran
Redrawn from Bosworth, A.B. (1988) *Conquest and Empire: The Reign of Alexander the Great* (pub Cambridge University Press), Map 10. © Cambridge University Press 1988, reproduced with permission.

was that they would furnish water for Nearchus's fleet as it sailed along, given that the lighter ships could not carry much food and water.

The invasion of this region in what is now around Las Bela in Baluchistan was fast and effective, with only minor skirmishes. This was in spite of the fact that it was the monsoon season. The most important village, Rhambaceia, was earmarked by Alexander as another new Alexandria, and Hephaestion, who arrived after Alexander had subdued the people, was put in charge of the process. During their resistance the Oreitae had tried to block the passes into the Makran, and had received some support from their neighbours to the west, the Gedrosians. The latter probably expected that Alexander would come after them next, but they did not have any actual contact with the Macedonian army at this time. That would come later.

Alexander appointed Apollophanes as satrap of the region, supported by a force of Agrianians, archers and mercenary infantry and cavalry under Leonnatus. His job was to ensure the area remained loyal to Alexander and to arrange provisions for Nearchus's fleet as it sailed along the coast. In about October Alexander left his new Alexandria bound for Carmania and the Persian Gulf to the west. Leonnatus would serve the king well. Almost immediately, he was faced with an uprising of the Oreitae who managed to defeat the Macedonian troops under him. He came back quickly, and in a full-scale battle killed at least 6,000 of them. This ended the resistance, and Leonnatus then gathered ten days' supply of corn to provision the fleet under Nearchus when it arrived off the coast in November.

Perhaps at the oasis of Turbat, Alexander decided to turn south to Pasni, about 80 miles away, on the coast. His aim would be to provision Nearchus when he arrived at that part of the coast and to dig wells for him so that he would have access to water. The plan failed. On the march south the men became so famished and thirsty in the gravel desert that they ate most of the food meant for the fleet. Alexander was forced to turn back.

He had learned a valuable lesson. The needs of the army that was with him were more important than the needs of the distant fleet. Despite his intention to provision the fleet as it sailed along the coast, his route took him inland. Nearchus was thus left to fend for himself. Alexander needed to keep his army battle-ready, but that readiness and fitness would be tested to the utmost in the terrain through which he was about to embark.

Alexander's march west would take him through the notorious Gedrosian Desert. Those who had previously tried to cross it, Semiramis, Queen of Assyria, and Cyrus the Great of Persia had failed. Semiramis emerged with only 20 men of her army, and Cyrus with only seven. This reason might have spurred Alexander to take this route in an effort to succeed where others had so dismally failed. For the eastern part of his march in Gedrosia, he had been able to use the crops that were growing there because of the monsoon season. Further west would be a different story.

For a week the men marched west from Pasni along the coast to Gwadar, before heading north to rejoin the inland road. Then it took them 60 days of hard marching with very little food through the Dashtiari Plain and north of the Bampur river to reach Pura (perhaps modern Iranshahr), the capital of Gedrosia.

The march was a terrible one for the entire Macedonian army and the baggage train that accompanied it, as a contemporary source reveals:[18]

'The scorching heat and lack of water destroyed a great part of the army, and especially the pack animals. Most perished from thirst and some of them even from the depth and heat of the sand, because it had been thoroughly scorched by the sun. They encountered lofty ridges of deep sand, not compact and hardened, but such as received those who stepped upon it just as if they were stepping into mud, or rather onto untrodden snow. At the same time the horses and mules suffered still more, both in going up and coming down the hills, from the unevenness of the road as well as from its instability. The length of the marches between the stages also greatly demoralised the army; for the lack of water often compelled them to make marches of unusual length. When they travelled by night on a journey that was necessary to complete, and at daybreak came to water, they suffered no hardship at all. But if, while still on the march because of the length of the route, they were caught by the heat, then they did indeed suffer hardships from the blazing sun, and were at the same time oppressed by unquenchable thirst.

'The soldiers killed many of the beasts of burden of their own accord. When provisions were lacking, they came together, and slaughtered most of the horses and mules. They ate the flesh of these, and said that they had died of thirst or from the heat. There was no one to divulge the real truth behind their actions because of the men's distress and that all alike were implicated in the same offence. What was being done had not escaped Alexander's notice, but he saw that the best cure for the present state of affairs was to pretend to be ignorant of it, rather than to allow it to happen when he knew.

'The consequence was that it was no longer easy to convey the soldiers who were suffering from disease, or those who were left behind on the roads because of the heat. This was partly from the lack of the animals and partly because the men themselves were smashing the wagons to pieces. They were not able to draw them because of the depth of the sand, and this forced them in the first stages to go not by the shortest routes but by those that were easiest for the wagons. Thus some were left behind along the roads from sickness, others from fatigue or the effects of the heat, or from not being able to survive the drought. There was no one either to lead them or to remain and tend them in their sickness. For the expedition was being made with great urgency, and the care of individual persons was necessarily neglected in the zeal displayed for the safety of the army as a whole. As they generally made the marches by night, some of the men were also overcome by sleep on the road. Afterwards, when they woke up again, those who still had strength followed the tracks of the army; but only a few out of many overtook the main body in safety. Most of them perished in the sand, like men going off course at sea.

'Another calamity also afflicted the army, which greatly distressed men, horses and beasts of burden. The country of the Gedrosians is supplied with rain by the periodical winds, just like that of the Indians; not the plains of Gedrosia, but only the mountains where the clouds are carried by the wind and dissolved into rain without passing beyond the mountains' summits. On one occasion the army bivouacked near a small brook that was a winter torrent for the sake of its water. At about the second watch of the night the rains in the mountains that had fallen unperceived by the soldiers suddenly swelled the brook that flowed there. The flood advanced with so great a rush as to kill most of the wives and children of the men who followed the army, and to sweep away all the royal baggage as well as all the beasts of burden that still lived. The soldiers, after great exertions, were hardly able to save themselves together with their weapons, many of which they lost forever. When, after enduring the burning heat and thirst, they came upon an abundance of water, many of them died from drinking it to excess as they were unable to check their appetite for it.'[19]

It was not just the rank and file that suffered terribly from thirst, but Alexander as well. During the march he performed a selfless act that makes us understand why his army stayed so fiercely loyal to him for so long – and the extent to which things must have deteriorated for them to question him, or lose confidence in him, as at the Hyphasis:

'They were far on the journey, and Alexander himself, though oppressed with thirst, was nevertheless with great pain and difficulty leading the army on foot, so that his soldiers also, as is usual in such a case, might more patiently bear their hardships by the equalization of the distress. At this time some of the light-armed soldiers left the army in search of water. They found some collected in a shallow cleft, a small and mean spring. Collecting this water with difficulty, they came with all speed to Alexander, as if they were bringing him a great present. As soon as they approached the king, they poured the water into a helmet and carried it to him. He took it, and praising the men who brought it, immediately poured it upon the ground in full view of all. As a result of this action, the entire army was reinvigorated to so great a degree that anyone would have imagined that the water poured away by Alexander had furnished a drink to every man.'[20]

Despite acts such as these, Alexander knew in advance the problems that would face him on the march through the Gedrosian Desert. There is no doubt that he was guilty of a major logistical blunder. The searing heat (35°C/95°F even at night) with the men in full armour should have been taken into more account. The baggage train of women and children should have been sent by another route to escape the rigours of the terrain. Regardless of the actual numbers lost, the discontent, even fury, of the men must have been great because of the hardships and losses suffered. His motives too would only have added fuel to the fire. If he had wanted to take the coastal route to provision Nearchus's fleet, then he had been absolutely unsuccessful. If he had marched inland merely to eclipse his predecessors who had failed, Semiramis and Cyrus, then he had been absolutely successful. But at what cost?

During the march, Alexander sent urgent requests for food to Stasanor, satrap of Drangiana in the north, which had surrendered in 329. When the men finally arrived at Pura, exhausted and starving, they found that he had responded quickly to Alexander's request. Additional food, sent by fast camels, was waiting for them. After only a few days to recover, however, Alexander ordered the army to make ready for departure. Grumbling, the men obeyed him. They were soon marching west through the Jaz Murian into the Halil Rud Valley, the borders of Carmania. There, more provisions from Stasanor were waiting for them.

It was now about January 324, and the horrors of the march through the Gedrosian Desert were fast becoming memories, and India was already a long way behind. The men could look forward to a return to Greece through friendlier lands, and they were probably far better disposed to Alexander than in a long time. Unknown to them, their king had already set his sights on another campaign, Arabia. And also unknown to them, he had less than two years to live.

12

'We'll Say Goodbye in Babylon'

In Carmania Craterus and the veterans met up with Alexander, and the natives gave them much food and wine. The Macedonians made up for the conditions of the Gedrosian Desert in their consumption of wine. For seven days, the army marched west through Carmania in a state of total intoxication. Alexander dressed as Dionysus and was pulled on a platform above his carriage by eight horses, all the time dancing and drinking. Some of his Companions were with him. The rest, as well as the senior members of his staff, were pulled on platforms behind him. The men with their womenfolk and other hangers-on marched behind, or rather staggered, because everyone drank continuously. When they were not drinking, they were playing music, singing or having sex. Recovery time after the wild drunken romp through Carmania must have been considerable, but who could blame them after the horrors of their desert march?

When Alexander reached Pura he would have heard of various insurrections that were relatively small-scale. More serious was the behaviour of about 14 of his 23 satraps and governors. While Alexander was away campaigning in Central Asia and India, they led extortionate and in some cases despotic lives. They probably thought that Alexander would never return. They could not have been more wrong. Now, the king decided to embark on a series of purges, which were not directed solely against the high-level officials.

In almost one fluid movement, Apollophanes, satrap of Oreitis, was deposed and Astaspes, satrap of Carmania, was executed. Cleander and Sitalces, who had brought 6,000 men from Ecbatana to join Alexander, were next. Their maladministration in Media was enough for their condemnation, but they were also accused of misconduct on the march, including the rape of virgins and other local women. Alexander's investigation confirmed this, and 600 troops were also put to death.

The message was clear: any misconduct would be treated in the harshest way possible. At the same time, the Bacchic revelry through Carmania, and these executions, for Cleander was the commander at Ecbatana who killed the popular Parmenion in 330, may have had another purpose. After the rigours of the desert march, it was imperative for Alexander to get back into the men's good books.

Alexander followed his executions with an extraordinary resolution. He sent letters to all his satraps and generals in Asia ordering them to disband their mercenary armies immediately. During his absence in the east, some satraps had been building up their armies with mercenaries. If Alexander were to die, then they would be in a position to vie for power. The Dissolution Decree, as it is commonly called, may well have been an attempt to limit the satraps' power. It may also have as its genesis the need for more mercenaries. Alexander's order would thus kill two birds with one stone. It would diminish the power of any satraps tempted to overstep their authority and it would replenish mercenary numbers in the main army with the king.

Many unemployed mercenaries did make the journey to Alexander, but a large number of them did not. Thousands roamed the empire as bandits and robber bands, plundering native towns and villages in an effort to survive. Many more joined the services of the influential Athenian general Leosthenes, who transported at least 50,000 to the mercenary base at Taenarum on the southern tip of the Peloponnese. At Taenarum was now a ready army for anyone who had the money to hire it. Alexander's move did limit the power of ambitious satraps or over-mighty generals. However, it created a dangerous political and military problem that forced the king to issue another wide-ranging directive from Susa (see below).

Another target for punishment as Alexander continued his march west was the imperial treasurer, Harpalus. He was one of Alexander's boyhood friends who had been elevated to great power. He had fled once before, shortly before the Battle of Issus, perhaps out of fear, perhaps because of embezzlement, but the king had recalled him (see Chapter 6). As soon as Alexander had moved into India, Harpalus was up to his old tricks again. He lived in luxurious style at his headquarters in Babylon, where he indulged himself in sexual liaisons with local women and embezzled money without a second thought. He imported a vast amount of fish from the Red Sea, and enjoyed the pleasures of two Athenian mistresses, who did not come cheap.

A corrupt administrator was one thing, but Harpalus potentially was more than that. He may have minted his own coinage at the Babylon mint, and:

'After the death of Pythionice, Harpalus sent for Glycera to come to him from Athens. When she came, she lived in the palace at Tarsus, and was honoured with royal honours by the people, and was called queen. An edict was issued forbidding anyone to give Harpalus a crown without at the same time giving Glycera one. And at Rhossus, he went so far as to erect a bronze statue of her by the side of his own statue and that of Alexander.'[1]

Alexander was a long way away, and Harpalus did not expect him to return. Now, if Glycera were a queen, and Pythionice had a temple to her, and Harpalus had his own coins, what did that make him? Was he really thinking he was a king and never expected to see Alexander again? Perhaps. One of his centres of control was Ecbatana, and both he and Cleander came from Elimiotis. There may have been a connection between the two men that the returning Alexander saw as politically dangerous. The bottom line is that he had more than exceeded his authority. He would have to pay.

Given Cleander's fate it is no surprise that Harpalus took to his heels again. In winter 324, with a force of 6,000 mercenaries, 5,000 talents of stolen money and 30 warships, he fled again, this time to seek asylum in Athens. He had received Athenian citizenship for sending corn to the city (presumably on the urging of his Athenian mistresses) during a famine that lasted from 330 to about 326. That, together with its anti-Macedonian history and power, made Athens the logical place to go. He may have wanted to incite a revolt against Macedon by the Greeks, spearheaded by Athens, which he considered was the only option to ensure his safety.

At this time, Alexander would not have known that Athens was Harpalus's destination. He may not have seen any danger from his flight. The king continued his march west, and by mid-winter reached Salmus, the capital of Carmania, where he set up residence in the royal palace. This was about five days' march from the coast, where the principal harbour was called Harmozeia (near the modern Bandar Abbas). At Salmus, games and musical events were held to celebrate the Macedonians' victories over the Indians and safe passage through the Gedrosian Desert. The irony of the latter would not have been lost on the men.

The joyous and of course drunken occasion was suddenly marred when Nearchus and only a few of those who had sailed with him appeared before the king. The men were so dishevelled and in such poor condition that Alexander did not recognise his boyhood friends at first. He thought that the men were the only survivors from the fleet, and so asked Nearchus how the ships and men had been lost. He thought wrong. Nearchus and just a handful of men had come to report that after a four-month journey the fleet had arrived safely, and had anchored at Harmozeia. The king is said to have broken down at the news and wept for joy. He immediately ordered another round of sacrifices, in gratitude for the safe passage of his fleet, to Zeus the Saviour, Apollo, Poseidon,

Heracles and the other gods of the sea.

The fleet had travelled over 1,000 miles in 60 days. The journey had lasted from late October 325 to January 324, and only one ship was lost. Nearchus had plenty to tell, from description of the coastline, to super-size crabs, the coastal people called the 'fish-eaters' and meetings with whales:

'There are monsters measuring one half of a stade in length and whose breadth is proportionate to their length. They say that these have such power that often when they exhale through their nostrils they spout up the wave of the sea to such a degree that the ignorant and inexperienced think they are bellows.'[2]

The sail west from Indus to Oreitis had been uneventful and supplies had been reasonably plentiful. In part, this was due to the provisions that Leonnatus had prepared for them. Once past Oreitis it was a different story, and the sailors had to make do with fish and dates. This caused them to lay waste any towns along the desert coast they came across for what little food there was, regardless of the hardships caused to the natives. The point of the expedition, to explore and to map the coastline, must have seemed of little significance to them as they fought off hunger and ate the same miserable food day after day. Finally, the fleet came to the coast of Carmania. There, arable crops, fruits and vines, could be had. It had been an epic voyage and, as Alexander had ordered, Neachus had explored every inch of the coast, recording the fertile and barren areas, water supplies, the inhabitants and safe anchorages. After Alexander's death, Arrian published a version of Nearchus's stirring voyage called the *Indica*.[3]

Nearchus had shown that, albeit with hardship, a fleet could sail along an unknown coastline without receiving supplies from a land army. That would be a turning point for Alexander's future expansionist plans, including his next venture, the invasion of Arabia. Did he know anything but conquest? Apparently not. His Arabian plan showed that he had no intention of returning to Pella yet. That of course raises the question, which must also have been in the minds of his people: what or where would he turn to after Arabia? One place was Carthage in North Africa (see Chapter 13).

Just as Nearchus was starting to get his land legs back, Alexander ordered him to explore the coast between Carmania and Susa. This he did, and eventually he reached the Euphrates.

Alexander prepared to leave Salmus to march directly to Pasargadae. He took a small contingent of men and their route lay first north and then east. Hephaestion with the bulk of the army and the elephants followed a coastal route to Persepolis. Alexander had appointed Phrasaortes satrap of Persis. He died a natural death, and Orxines assumed the position.

Persis may have been the most important satrapy in the Persian empire because of its ceremonial significance, probably shown by Alexander's burning of the palace at Persepolis the last time he was there. Orxines had in effect seized power, and both he and his action were unacceptable to Alexander. Perhaps it was because he was related to Cyrus, and had commanded Persian troops against the Macedonians at Gaugamela. Alexander needed to deal with the situation.

Orxines met Alexander in the plain of Pasargadae. He bent over backwards to greet him with respect and gave him lavish gifts, but Alexander was not swayed. At some point during what was a short stay, the king visited the tomb of Cyrus the Great, the founder of the Persian empire. He had died in battle in Scythia in about 530, and his tomb was revered and protected by Magi. Alexander ordered it opened, only to discover that it had been looted. The skeletal remains of Cyrus lay in pieces on the floor where they had been sacrilegiously thrown. The Magi were immediately tortured, but released when it became clear they had no idea what had happened. Alexander ordered Aristobulus to see to the repair of the tomb to be repaired and reburial of Cyrus, together with suitable grave goods.

Soon after, Alexander marched south to Persepolis. The desecration of Cyrus's tomb gave him the pretext he needed to remove Orxines. Alexander's favourite eunuch and lover Bagoas accused Orxines of an inability to rule effectively, of temple desecration and of arbitrary executions of his people. These charges were without foundation, but Bagoas's scheming and influence engineered Orxines's crucifixion without a trial. The king then appointed Peucestas as satrap. He had shielded the king as he lay terribly injured during the attack on the Malli (see Chapter 11). Peucestas seems to be the only one of Alexander's Macedonian satraps who learnt Persian, and Alexander also encouraged him to dress in Persian style. This endeared himself to the native population of the 'heart of Asia', as the king no doubt intended. This was a satrapy that *had* to stay loyal to Macedonia.

Hephaestion and his men arrived at Persepolis without incident. At Pasargadae the Brahman sage Calanus, now in his seventies, had fallen ill and decided to be burnt to death. Nothing could change his mind, and Alexander granted his wish. A large pyre was built by the burnt ruins of the palace at Persepolis. He rode to it on a royal horse from Nesaea, home of the horses used by the Achaemenids. He bade farewell to the Macedonians, but to Alexander apparently said, 'We'll say goodbye in Babylon.' This was an ominous prediction of Alexander's death there in June 323.

The Brahmans, as was their custom, 'when the pyre has been made ready, they stand motionless, resting in front of it. Then they climb on top and there they sit, smouldering away in a dignified manner, never budging an inch.'[4] When the fire was lit, 'the trumpets sounded, as per Alexander's order, and the whole army shouted the war-cry as was its custom when advancing to battle. The elephants also chimed in with their shrill and warlike cry, in honour of Calanus.'[5] Calanus sat still and unflinching as the flames flared up around him, and then consumed him.

Alexander ordered games as well as a musical recital of his praises in his honour. These included a drinking contest, something that had become commonplace by now. In this one, 'the prize for the winner was a talent, for the second-best thirty minas, for the third ten minas. Of those who drank the wine, thirty-five died immediately of a chill, and six others soon after in their tents. The man who drank the most and was the victor drank twelve quarts and received the talent. But he lived only four days more; he was called Champion.'[6] An unfortunate name, as events turned out.

From Persepolis Alexander marched 24 days along the Royal Road to Susa, where he arrived in late March 324. There he was joined by Peucestas, his satrap of Persis, and more importantly reunited with Nearchus. The fleet had managed to reach the mouth of the Euphrates. However, Nearchus had been forced to keep mostly to the open sea because of the treacherous coastline and tides. He was unable to give the sorts of details that he had from his previous voyage. Still, he had returned safely, and the king ordered a fresh round of games and sacrifices. Moreover, he bestowed a gold crown on Nearchus for his entire voyage, one on Leonnatus for his victory the previous year over the Oreitae and one on Peucestas for rescuing him at Malli town.

In Susa Alexander issued a royal directive commonly called the Exiles Decree.[7] This measure called for the return of all Greek exiles to their native cities excluding those under a curse (in other words, murderers) and the Thebans. Antipater was ordered to use force against any city that refused to receive its exiles back. We know so much about the wording of the decree because Diodorus quotes it for us:

'King Alexander to the exiles from the Greek cities. We have not been the cause of your exile, but, apart from those of you who are under a curse, we shall be the cause of your return to your own native cities. We have written to Antipater about this so that if any cities are not willing to restore you, he may force them.'[8]

The Exiles Decree perhaps grew out of Alexander's Dissolution Decree issued at Pura. It appears that when the satraps disbanded their mercenary armies thousands of mercenaries remained in Asia. Diodorus tell us vividly that all Asia was overrun with ex-mercenaries who were plundering native towns.[9] Thus they seemed to be roaming the empire as bandits. Their presence was a major source of concern for Alexander, given that they were so easily available to the highest bidder. Therefore, he decided that the simplest way to solve the problem was to send them home.

Not all of the exiles who were subject of this decree would have been mercenaries of course, but Alexander probably thought that a measure sending only ex-mercenaries home would have caused resentment with non-combatant exiles, so it was easier to issue the one blanket measure. He probably thought that those who had been exiled from their cities would prefer to return to them. It was to be proclaimed by Alexander's royal messenger Nicanor of Stagira at the Olympic Games of August 324. News leaked out in advance, for 20,000 exiles had already gathered there before his arrival.

The decree rode roughshod over the autonomy of the Greek states. It showed the power that Alexander wielded. He made no pretence of going through the constitutional League of Corinth, as he had done after Thebes's revolt in 335, for example. It affected almost all of the Greek states, not least because Greece was still recovering from a famine, and the return of thousands of exiles would add to economic instability. Some were affected more personally than others. The Athenians, for example, had seized the island of Samos in 365. After the Battle of Chaeronea Philip II had allowed them to keep the island, but now under the decree they would have to return it to its native owners. Nationalistic pride was hurt.

The Greeks sent embassies to Alexander to appeal against the decree, and he heard them when he reached Babylon (see Chapter 13). Alexander's action threatened the peace and stability that Greece had enjoyed for a decade, and to make matters worse Harpalus was now in Athens, trying to incite the Greeks to revolt. The Exiles Decree and Harpalus's flight now mesh together, and give an insight into the Greek attitude to the Macedonian hegemony (see Chapter 13).

When Harpalus reached Athens, Demosthenes, still Athens' most influential politician, persuaded the Athenians not to admit him. Harpalus went to the mercenary base at Taenarum, where he left most of his force. He returned to Athens as a suppliant, bringing with him a substantial amount of money (700 talents). To have denied refuge to a suppliant who was a citizen was unthinkable to the Greeks. The Athenians had no choice but to admit him. Thanks to Demosthenes's influence (again), the Athenians decided to imprison Harpalus, impound his money and send an embassy to the king to ask what was to be done with him. Demosthenes's course of action led to a split with the more militant anti-Macedonian politician Hyperides, who was anxious to seize the chance to revolt.

In the same summer a satirical play called the *Agen* was performed at Alexander's court. The title denotes a leader, and so it may have been in celebration of Alexander. In it, Harpalus and Pythionice were abused, and her temple is described as that of a whore. References were also made to his bribing Athenian statesmen. Relations between Alexander and the Athenians were obviously now tense, but at least they were playing safe by imprisoning the fugitive treasurer. For now, nothing happened.

After Harpalus's arrest Demosthenes travelled to Olympia to discuss the Exiles Decree with Nicanor. Shortly after he returned to Athens Harpalus escaped (or, more likely, was forced to flee by Demosthenes). Given the tension between Athens and Alexander over Harpalus, it was prudent to get him out of the city. Moreover, it would bolster the chances of success of the Athenian embassy to the king over the Exiles Decree. That was Demosthenes's strategy, but it would soon backfire on him.

Back in Susa, Alexander enforced a mass marriage on 91 members of his staff and court and he also married again. In part, this grew out of his promise to arrange the marriages of the Persian royal princesses, captured when Darius fled after Issus, when he returned to Susa. They were still there, and still unmarried. During his absence they had learned Greek as he had ordered. In a ceremony lasting five days, most of which time was spent on games, dramatic plays and general festivities, the mass marriage with Asian (Persian, Median and Bactrian) noblewomen took place.

Alexander constructed a special area, in which were built 92 bridal chambers, one for each couple. The opulence and extravagance of the ceremony are well recorded by Chares of Mytilene, a member of Alexander's court:

'There was a house built that was able to contain a hundred couches; and in it every couch was adorned with wedding paraphernalia to the value of twenty minas, and was made of silver itself, but his own bed had golden feet. And he also invited to his banquet all his own private friends, and those he arranged opposite himself and the other bridegrooms, and his forces that belonged to the army and navy, and all the ambassadors which were present, and all the other strangers who were staying at his court. And the apartment was furnished in the most costly and splendid manner, with sumptuous garments and cloths, and beneath them were other cloths of purple, scarlet and gold.

'And, for the sake of solidity, pillars supported the tent, each twenty cubits long, plated all over with gold and silver, and inlaid with precious stones. All around these were spread costly curtains embroidered with gold figures of animals, and they had gold and silver curtain-rods. And the circumference of the court was four stades. The banquet took place, beginning at the sound of a trumpet, at that marriage feast, and on other occasions when the king offered a solemn sacrifice, so that all the army knew it. This marriage feast lasted five days. A great number both of barbarians and Greeks brought contributions to it, as did some of the Indian tribes too.'[10]

We then have a list of various conjurors, rhapsodes, harp-players, flute-players, and tragic and comic actors who performed at the wedding. So much money was spent in gifts to the bridegrooms that, Chares goes on to say, 'the crowns sent by the ambassadors and by other people amounted in value to fifteen thousand talents'.

The ceremony followed the Persian custom, in which the bridegroom kissed the bride, and the king gave each couple a dowry. He himself took two wives, one was Stateira, the eldest daughter of Darius III, and the other was Parysatis, the youngest daughter of Darius's predecessor, Artaxerxes III Ochus. An offshoot of the wedding was Alexander's conversion of the de facto relationships of 10,000 of his men with Asian women into official marriages. As wedding presents, he paid off all of these men's debts.

Why did Alexander order this set of marriages and on such a large scale? There was a belief that he was trying to bring about a brotherhood of mankind, such as was later propounded by the Stoic philosopher, Zeno. Alexander, now all-powerful, could unite all men together in a common race. This was a 'policy' that can be seen also in his integration of foreigners into his army and administration and his *proskynesis* attempt. This is quite wrong, for there was no such policy and Alexander had no intention of any such union of the races.[11]

For one thing, while he did integrate some foreigners into his army and administration, his motive in both cases was pragmatic. In the case of the army, he needed specialist troops such as mounted archers and for these he had to turn to the Iranians. He needed locals also in his administration because of their linguistic expertise and knowledge. The ultimate goal was the smooth running of his administration. He had taken the Persian satrapal system and made changes to it that best suited the Macedonian empire, especially in the spheres of local government and finance. He probably could have done more as far as imperial administration went, but he was too preoccupied with fighting. Asians may have been satraps, but when that happened a Macedonian was always in charge of the army and the treasury. Policy, not idealism, then.

The same is true for the Susa mass marriage. No Macedonian or Greek women were brought out from the mainland to marry Persian noblemen. This we should expect if Alexander wanted a real union of the races. The reason for the Susa marriages is that Alexander could not afford Asian noblewomen to marry their own races, and so provide the potential for revolt. Alexander could not afford another Bessus once he left for Arabia. The easternmost satrapies and India were a lost cause, but Alexander had to maintain control of Persia otherwise his empire was nothing. A mixed marriage with Macedonians would severely hinder, if not prevent, revolt.

This is shown by the localisation of his policy only to Asia. No attempt was made to encourage inter-racial marriages in Macedonia. In fact, when Alexander sent his veterans home from Opis a few months later the men had to leave behind their Asian wives and children. The mass marriage was symbolic, but the symbolism was that the conquerors had married the conquered. A new ruling group was coming into being. Europe and Asia were part of Alexander's new Kingdom of Asia, with the Macedonians firmly in control and Greek as the official language. It is important to note that Alexander never learned Persian.

Alexander forced these inter-racial marriages on his men, and they were clearly far from happy with the arrangement. Even today, the mass marriage raises much emotional bitterness among the native people (see Chapter 15). After Alexander's death the following year, only Seleucus stayed married to his wife, Apame, daughter of Spitamenes of Bactria. The rest divorced their wives. This was not just because they had to accept Alexander's choices. It was one thing to live with an Asian woman in a de facto relationship, but, for a Macedonian noble at any rate, quite another to marry one. Alexander seems to have forgotten what lay behind Attalus' taunt when his father married Cleopatra, of Macedonian blood.

The lesson from Alexander's failed *proskynesis* attempt in 327 had also not been learned, for his oriental leanings had not diminished over the past few years. They were also about to cause another army mutiny.

In spring 324 the army left Susa. It followed the course of the Tigris River north into Mesopotamia, and reached Opis in mid-summer. By now, Alexander was making clear his intention of further campaigning, in particular an invasion of Arabia. There are several reasons why he had his eyes set on Arabia. The land was very fertile, and he wanted to establish colonies on the fertile islands of Tylus (Bahrain) and Icarus (Falaika). Arabian spices were legendary, so much so that the king probably saw the trading benefits from them. He did make it a primary objective to secure the trade centre of Gerrha, on the coast opposite Tylus. That would give him control of the highly lucrative spice trade with Arabia Felix. He may even have wanted to control all of the spice lands as far as Yemen.

Then there is the personal reason. The Arabs had not recognised Alexander's power or even sent a diplomatic mission to him. Indeed, they were 'the only barbarians of this region that had not sent an embassy to him or done anything as befits their position and showed respect to him'.[12] This neglect was taken personally, thus conforming to a pattern. The Arabs needed to be punished and Arabia conquered. It would not be easy, but Nearchus's journey had shown him that a fleet could operate independent of a land army. That would allow a two-pronged attack. Alexander's destination was Babylon. This was the most logical place for his headquarters before the expedition, for the Euphrates flowed into Arabia. Babylon was fast becoming his preferred capital, in any case, but where did that leave Pella? And, for that matter, his people back home?

Alexander's divine pretensions also play a role. The Arabs worshipped only Uranus and Dionysus, and Alexander decided to conquer Arabia so as to be worshipped as a third god (see Chapter 14).

If Alexander did intend to reap the economic benefits of the spice trade, then the Arabian invasion was going to take quite some time. Pella, already a distant memory, was fading even faster. The army could not have welcomed his new plan with glee. At Opis, he called an Assembly and announced that all of his veteran and unfit soldiers, several thousand in fact, were to be honourably discharged and sent home. For some reason, those to be discharged as well as those who were to stay reacted against the announcement. They told Alexander that he should discharge all of them, and, more sarcastically, that he should continue his campaign with his father Ammon.

Alexander ordered the hypaspists to seize 13 of the most vocal protesters, who were executed for mutiny on the spot. He then publicly berated the remainder. His speech is preserved in Arrian, but cannot be accepted as authentic. In it, he praised the exploits of his father Philip and how he had made Macedonia a superpower in the ancient world. This was followed by what Alexander had done to extend the Macedonian empire and to bring the men even more glory and reputation. He accused them of disloyalty, of ingratitude and he finished off by telling them to go home if they wanted as he would replace them with Asians. The men remained unmoved. As at the Hyphasis, Alexander walked in disgust away from them, this time into the palace. Although their defiance was not on the same level as that at the Hyphasis, the men did refuse to follow Alexander's orders. For the second time in his reign, Alexander faced a mutiny.

The king remained in the palace for two days, but this time no manipulation of the omens and involvement of the gods could resolve the clash. On the third day, as the men refused to budge, Alexander decided to live up to his promise. He called selected Persians to him, and began transferring Macedonian commands to them. This he followed by transferring Macedonian titles to the Persian units including the Foot Companions and Companion Cavalry. He built on his method of addressing the Persians as his 'Kinsmen' by announcing that only they had the right to kiss him. All of this did the trick. His men threw down their arms in front of the palace, and in great consternation begged for forgiveness. Alexander came out and forgave them, significantly saying that everyone was his kinsman. The men wept for joy at Alexander's mercy, and the mutiny was over.

Alexander had averted the threat to him by playing on the hatred between Macedonians and Asians. However, he needed both, and thus a united army, for his invasion of Arabia. Therefore, when the reconciliation with his men ended, he ordered the preparation of a magnificent banquet, attended by over 9,000 invited people. Alexander sat at the head of the table. On either side of him were Macedonians, then Greeks, then, fanning out, Persians and other races. During it, he stood and prayed, says Arrian, for 'various blessings and especially that the Macedonians and Persians should enjoy harmony as partners in government'.[13] No one could be in any more doubt that a Kingdom of Asia, with Alexander ruling as king over subjects of different races and ethnic backgrounds, now existed.

Like his *proskynesis* attempt or the mass marriage at Susa, the banquet, and especially the symbolism of Alexander's prayer, has been seen as part of an attempt to create a unity of mankind. Again, this is not the case. When incidents like this occur, they are not part of any policy but are simply incidents, which can so easily be misconstrued. Alexander had played on the hatred between the Macedonians and the Persians in ending the mutiny. Further, the seating arrangement at the banquet is significant. The Macedonians were seated closest to him, thus emphasising their racial superiority and power. Finally, we would expect a prayer to future concord between the races. Alexander had just faced down a mutiny. Dissension in the ranks was the last thing he needed given his future plans. He also needed harmony among the different races to keep his new empire together, to help to govern it, as Arrian said.

The men's reaction to Alexander's discharge order is odd at first sight. The mocking reference to Ammon more than suggests that they had had enough of their king's divine aspirations. Alexander, as a god on earth, had shown the vulnerability of a mortal at the siege of Malli, when he almost died, and less than divine planning in the march across the Gedrosian Desert. The men's remark was akin in tone to ones that Greeks would contemptuously make in 323 when they were discussing divine honours for Alexander (see Chapter 13). Demosthenes said that 'Alexander could be the son of Zeus and of Poseidon if he wanted to be'.[14] He was echoed by the Spartan king Damis: 'We concede to Alexander that, if he so wishes, he may be called a god.'[15]

The men were also unhappy with their king's continuing oriental practices, which included his manner of dress and enjoyment of oriental luxuries. These were all alien to Macedonian ways, but then Alexander was more like an oriental potentate than a Macedonian warrior king by now.

Moreover, he had been bringing an increasing number of Asians into his army (though not integrating them into existing Macedonian units).

These included the youths whom he had ordered to be trained in Macedonian fashion in Lydia, Lycia, Syria, Egypt and the north-east satrapies. The last in particular caused the greatest worry. They were called the *Epigonoi* and numbered 30,000. Now, aged 20, the training was over and they joined him at Susa. Their number and skills showed the Macedonians that they were first-rate soldiers. More than that, their very name was a source of concern: *Epigonoi*, The Successors. They were replacements for at least some of Alexander's current army, to fight with him in his new campaigns.

Alexander was losing touch with the rank and file of his army, and they now distrusted him and his motives. The projected invasion of Arabia, and hence more fighting in yet more unknown territory, did not help. The Arabs were not as heavily armed or well drilled as the Macedonian army, but there would still be battles to be fought. Then came the announcement at Opis. It was the straw that broke the camel's back given the implications of sending home tried and tested Macedonian soldiers.

After the banquet of reconciliation Alexander's original plan to discharge his veterans and those unfit for service went ahead. He agreed to pay each man the regular daily rate of pay until he reached Macedonia, plus a bonus of one talent. The men had to leave behind their Asian wives and children. The boys were to be brought up in Macedonian fashion, and would be allowed to return to their fathers when the training was completed. The wives, presumably, were divorced or abandoned. Craterus, aided by Polyperchon and Cleitus the White, was selected to lead 10,000 infantry and 1,500 cavalry back to Macedonia. En route, he was to stop in Cilicia and spend the winter there, attending to the troop preparations for the Arabian campaign. When he reached Macedonia, Antipater, now 73, would leave to bring 10,000 reinforcements to Alexander.

Craterus's selection, as before, may have been to get rid of him since he was one of the old guard. Alexander's boyhood friend Hephaestion, who as *chiliarch* was second only to the king in the Macedonian hierarchy, had openly argued with Craterus a number of times. Their disputes had centred on Alexander, his adoption of Persian practices, his divine pretensions, his abandonment of what a Macedonian king was all about. Alexander could not afford criticism levelled from one so powerful as Craterus – as had been the case with Parmenion and Philotas.

There is even the possibility that Craterus was sent to replace Antipater, given that relations between him and Olympias, the king's mother, had been deteriorating for years. Olympias had actually left Macedonia and returned to her homeland Epirus. From there, she sent a barrage of letters complaining about Antipater to her son. Her daughter Cleopatra, who was in Macedonia, did the same. The effect of the letters on Alexander is unknown, but Antipater was one of the old guard, and there were very few of them left by now.

The evidence that Craterus was sent west to replace Antipater is only circumstantial. Indeed, if Alexander had wanted to remove a critical Craterus from the court, it seems odd that he would send him home. Alexander had only stayed there for two years as king before leaving for Asia, and his people did not really know him as king. All they heard were the worrying stories from those who did return home of his drunken rages, his paranoia, his orientalism, even his belief that he was a son of Zeus. These were the sorts of things that Craterus criticised. It does not seem a wise move to send him home to replace Antipater, for Craterus would assume deputy leadership of the League of Corinth and hence control Greece.

On the other hand, Antipater did not welcome with open arms Alexander's directive to bring him troops. Instead of going to the king himself he sent his son Cassander, who said that Antipater was hard-pressed for men because of the various demands for reinforcements over the years. He may also have been concerned about the number of mercenaries returning to Greece, who posed a danger to the stability of the Macedonian hegemony. Alexander was far from happy at Antipater's action. However, Antipater may well have thought it prudent, with Craterus still in Cilicia, and the number of mercenaries growing at Taenarum, to remain on native soil to keep an eye on things. He was also in his seventies, and would not have relished the long trip.

For the moment Alexander did nothing as far as Antipater was concerned, but prepared his army to march to Ecbatana. The march was leisurely and there were plenty of drinking parties and stops along the way. In the autumn of 324 they arrived in Ecbatana, where the satrap of Media entertained Alexander in lavish style. The king was also greeted by various embassies from the Greek states, whose sycophancy showed itself in the number of crowns and honorary decrees showered on him. It did not hurt the courtiers to praise Alexander and to write in praise of him either. The story goes that Pyrro wrote a poem in his honour and a delighted Alexander paid him 10,000 gold coins.

During a sacrifice to Dionysus in Ecbatana, as the wine flowed in its usual abundance, the contemporary Ephippus tells us:

'There were some arrogant proclamations made, more insolent than even Persian arrogance was used to say. As different people were saying different things, and proposing to give Alexander large presents, which they called crowns, one of the keepers of his armoury went beyond all the previous sycophancy. He had previously arranged the matter with Alexander, and he ordered the herald to proclaim that "Gorgus, the keeper of the armoury, presents Alexander, the son of

Ammon, with three thousand pieces of gold. He will also present him, when he lays siege to Athens, with ten thousand complete suits of armour, the same number of catapults, and all weapons required for the war".'[16]

Harpalus's flight to Athens was evidently still a hot topic at the Macedonian court. If Gorgus's announcement is true, then Alexander may have contemplated war against the city. No such attack took place, for news came of Harpalus's flight from Athens. That let the city off the hook for the moment. Harpalus went to Crete where he was murdered: a fitting end.

The parties and drinking contests did not stop. During one of them, in October, Hephaestion fell ill. Alexander had known Hephaestion since boyhood, and he was his closest friend and confidant. For his loyalty he was well rewarded: he had been made *chiliarch*, hence second in command of the Kingdom of Asia, and Commander of the Royal Hipparchy of the Companion Cavalry. Seven days later, despite the best efforts of his doctor, Glaucias, he died.

Alexander was inconsolable for days, just like Achilles when Patroclus was killed and, like Achilles, he cut off his hair. He ordered the immediate crucifixion of Glaucias, and senior members at court were quick to pay their respects to Hephaestion in case Alexander decided to vent his grief on them. For three days he stayed by the corpse of his friend and refused to eat. The whole empire was to be in mourning, funeral games involving 3,000 competitors were held, and Alexander sent an embassy to Zeus Ammon at Siwah to endorse his wish for a hero cult of Hephaestion. A hero cult was in recognition of someone's achievements during his lifetime. It did not amount to divinity, so Hephaestion became a demigod to Alexander's god on earth. Then Hephaestion was cremated and the ashes were taken to Babylon. There, an enormous funerary monument was to be built of brick and decorated with five friezes. It would stand over 200 feet high and cost 10,000 talents. Alexander himself would supervise its building when he got to Babylon. In the aftermath of the king's death, it was abandoned.

The honours that were heaped on Hephaestion and the extent of Alexander's mourning were extreme. Then again, Hephaestion had been his closest friend, and he had known him from their youth. Alexander must have been feeling increasingly isolated over the past few years. He had faced criticism, mutiny and conspiracy. Perhaps also Harpalus's recent flight had an effect. Harpalus too had been a friend since childhood, but he had proved to be utterly different in character and in loyalty from Hephaestion. Alexander now faced an emotional void: who was there left to trust? That might explain why he decided not to replace Hephaestion with a *chiliarch* and a Commander of the Royal Hipparchy.

This was the period though when Perdiccas came to prominence. He became Alexander's right-hand man, and so the second most powerful man in the empire.

That winter, before he left Ecbatana for Babylon, Alexander waged a 40-day campaign against the Cossaeans of the Zagros mountains that border Media. They controlled communications routes and had a long history of receiving passage money from those that travelled between Ecbatana and Babylon. The king decided that they did not deserve their independence. He had waged a similar campaign against the Uxians in the winter of 331 who also demanded payment for passage (see Chapter 8). In their case, they were blocking his route, and he had no choice. That was not the case with the Cossaeans. As Plutarch says, he may well have ordered the campaign as a deliberate distraction from his grief over Hephaestion's death.[17] There was no major fighting of any sort, and when several of the Cossaean tribes were starved into surrender he ended the operation. They did not remain subservient, and Alexander's death gave them the opportunity to reassert their independence.

In early 323, the army reached Babylon. Arabia beckoned. But Alexander now had only a few months to live.

13

Death and Disorder

As Alexander crossed the Tigris in early 323, a group of local Chaldaean philosophers met him. The story goes that they took him aside from his Companions and urged him to abandon his march:

'For they said that the god Belus had given them an oracular declaration that his arrival in Babylon at that time would not be for his own good. But he answered their speech with a line from the poet Euripides to this effect: "He is the best prophet that guesses well." But the Chaldaeans said: "O king, do not at any rate enter the city looking west nor leading the army in that direction, but rather go right around towards the east."'[1]

Alexander seems to have taken this advice to heart, for he detoured to the north and approached the city from the east. The boggy terrain though made this impossible, so he was forced to enter from the west after all. Ominously, the same source as above says that this was inevitable, for the god 'was leading him to the place where, once he entered, he was fated soon to die'.

This would not be the only time that Alexander was warned that his end was near in Babylon. Some time later he had apparently gone in search of a drink and left the royal throne empty. His Companions accompanied him, and so only the eunuchs standing around the throne were left behind. A man whose name is not known but is described as being 'of obscure condition' walked through the line of eunuchs and sat down on the throne. Persian law dictated that the eunuchs could not touch the man. Instead:

' [They] rent their clothes and beat their breasts and faces as if due to a great evil. When Alexander was told this, he ordered the man who had sat upon his throne to be tortured in order to discover whether he had done this according to a plan as part of a conspiracy. But the man confessed nothing, except that it came into his mind at the time to act as he did. Even more for this reason the seers explained that the event boded no good to him.'[2]

The man was put to death, but Alexander's days were numbered.

Calanus's ominous farewell at Persepolis (see Chapter 12) was probably sending shivers down the king's spine.

Why the Chaldaean philosophers tried to keep Alexander from Babylon is unknown. It is unlikely that they genuinely had the conqueror's best interests at heart. They may have hoped that if he did not enter Babylon he would turn his attention to rebuilding Egasila, and hence concocted their story to this end. When Alexander had first gone to Babylon after the Battle of Issus in 331, the local priests had hoped that he would rebuild the great temple complex of Egasila (see Chapter 8). Their hopes were dashed. If the Babylonians wanted to rebuild, then that was fine with him as long as they used their own money and labour. Evidently, they had not done so by the time of his return. Alexander himself suspected this was their reason for the warning.

Another reason may have been anxiety about the cult attached to Hephaestion. This would run counter to their religious beliefs but evidence of the cult would be seen every day in the huge monument to him. News of his Arabian campaign would be well known by now. That would mean demands on the city, as well as exploitation of its resources, all reasons for keeping him at bay. More likely, though, is that the Babylonians did not want Alexander in Babylon on any long-term basis, especially if he were thinking of making Babylon the capital of his new empire. In 331, he had been joyfully welcomed because he had brought the end of oppressive Persian rule. Since then, they had been forced to endure Harpalus's corrupt and extortionate practices, and had come to realise that they had swapped the devil for the deep blue sea. If the hidden agenda was to keep Alexander out of Babylon, it failed.

In November 331 Alexander had left Babylon for Susa. He had not wanted to devote time then to any reconstruction projects. In 323, things were different. As the king dealt almost daily with a steady stream of embassies, he set about rebuilding Egasila and planning Hephaestion's funerary tower. The former was no doubt meant to appease the people for the core of the king's activity was the preparation of his campaign to Arabia. This greatly affected the people of Babylon.

The fleet for the Arabian expedition was slowly being assembled. The ships that had sailed under Nearchus from the Persian Gulf up the Euphrates had joined the king, and others from the Mediterranean coast had begun to arrive. More were built using cedar wood from Babylonia. If the Babylonians had feared that Alexander would ruthlessly exploit their natural resources, they were right. He also ordered the building of a vast harbour at Babylon to hold 1,000 warships, and next to it dockyards. The massive dredging project must have thrown the city into no small disarray. Miccalus of Clazomenae was given 500 talents and sent to

Phoenicia and Syria to hire experienced crews. Alexander organised competitions on the Euphrates between the various ships and between the rowers and helmsmen with crowns for the victors. This was not so much for mere sport but to ensure that his crews would be prepared to deal with anything they met.

Alexander also blocked some canals and widened others on the Euphrates, and built a new dam. His aim was to help the fleet's passage and at the same time that of the army by diverting some of the river's floodwaters away from the surrounding marshes on the Arabian border. While his men were busy with these projects, he sailed down the main draining canal, the Pallacotta, to the Arabian lakes. There he established another (and last) Alexandria. It would be the stepping stone for his two-pronged invasion of Arabia: by land across the Arabian marshes and by water down the Euphrates.

During one of his voyages, he sailed through marshes that had tombs of the Assyrian kings in them:

'[He] was himself steering the trireme, when a strong gust of wind fell on his broad-brimmed Macedonian hat, and the band that encircled it. The hat, being rather heavy, fell into the water. However, the band was carried along by the wind, and was caught by one of the reeds growing near the tomb of one of the ancient kings. This incident itself was an omen of what was about to occur, as was the fact that one of the sailors swam off towards the band and snatched it from the reed. But he did not carry it in his hands because it would get wet while he was swimming. He therefore put it around his own head and brought it to the king. Most of the biographers of Alexander say that the king gave him a talent as a reward for his zeal. Then he ordered his head to be cut off; as the prophets had explained the omen to the effect that he should not allow the head that had worn the royal head band to be safe. However, Aristobulus says that the man received a talent and a scourging for putting the band around his head.'[3]

Doing a good deed for Alexander was not without its dire consequences.

While Alexander was in Babylon embassies came to him from widely different geographical areas including the Greek mainland, Thrace, Illyria, Scythia, Carthage, Spain and even Rome. Those from many of the Greek states were almost solely concerned with appeals over the Exiles Decree as it affected them. The embassies from elsewhere came with their own problems. Some, such as those from Scythia and Thrace, were probably trying to explain recent defiant actions and crave his indulgence. In 326 Alexander's general in Thrace, Zopyrion, was forced to invade Scythia but had been soundly defeated in battle at the River Borysthenes. His failure was followed by a revolt of Thrace led by Seuthes, who proclaimed his independence. Alexander was not one to take defiance lightly, hence these embassies.

Other embassies went to Alexander in the hope of making terms. The Carthaginians in particular were on perilous ground. News of Alexander's plans to invade Arabia would have reached the western Mediterranean, and after Arabia the king seems to have set his eyes on the entire Mediterranean coast. During the siege of Tyre in 332 a Carthaginian embassy had sympathised with the Tyrians' plight but had not offered military help (see Chapter 6). Alexander captured the delegation and was not impressed with its stance. Although he allowed it to leave, it took home the message that the king would deal with Carthage at a future time. Alexander had a long memory, and now that time had come. Given Alexander's unprecedented conquests, the Carthaginians would see him as a real threat. We can imagine the stress felt by their ambassadors at Babylon.

Why the Romans sent an embassy to Alexander is at first sight puzzling, and not every ancient writer says this happened. At this time, Rome was still establishing itself as a power in Italy. It had defeated the Etruscans, and annexed their lands (Latium, 'the cradle of Rome'), and from 326 it was involved in a war against the Samnites to its south-east. The Romans were probably not seeking Alexander's help in their war, and in any case he was unlikely to send help to the western Mediterranean when he needed all of his army for Arabia. The answer might have something to do with the Etruscan embassy to Alexander. Etruscan piracy in the Adriatic was a cause of concern to the Athenians. They had complained formally to the *Hegemon* of the League of Corinth, and Alexander let it be known that he was displeased with Etruscan activity. That probably accounts for the Etruscan embassy to Babylon, and the Romans may have felt it prudent to send one as well since they had subjugated the Etruscans. After all, if Alexander were successful in Arabia (and his track record did not indicate otherwise), his future plans would bring him into contact with Rome.

The Roman embassy is interesting as an example of later propaganda. According to one tradition, Alexander, 'when he met their embassy, predicted something of the future power of Rome when he saw the men's clothing, their love of labour and their devotion to freedom'.[4] Later writers added this forecast of Rome's future greatness to show Alexander's powers of prophecy, a divine talent. The historical Alexander thus slipped further into the king of legend.

Alexander arranged the embassies in Babylon in a fixed order of business. He first heard those who had come on religious affairs, and then those who brought him gifts as evidence of their submission or acceptance of his orders. Next were those with disputes involving their neighbours, and then those on private missions. Lastly, he heard those embassies protesting the Exiles Decree. That he placed the Exiles Decree last might indicate his dissatisfaction that his directive was being challenged. More plausibly, however, is that he realised the issue was a complex one and that the many embassies would take up a great deal of time. It made more sense to dispense with issues that would take less time first, before turning to the business of the Exiles Decree that affected most Greek states.

Many, if not all, of Greek embassies came to Alexander wearing gold crowns and bringing gold crowns, as one would to honour a god. This was in keeping with the fact that the Greeks were discussing his divinity. Some island states had worshipped him as a god since 334, so the extension of divine worship to the mainland seemed a logical progression. One source refers to 'the instructions sent from Alexander that they should pass a formal vote deifying him'.[5] Whether Alexander issued an order to the mainland Greeks that they recognise him as a god is possible but unlikely.[6] The Exiles Decree was already causing enough damage, and the *proskynesis* attempt proved the reaction to worshipping a living god.

Did the embassies really come to honour him for bringing stability to the Greek world, the overthrow of the Persian empire and the stimulation of trade to Asia, for example?[7] Hardly. The Greeks had a more cynical – and understandable – motive for their actions.

Alexander's order that the whole empire should mourn Hephaestion's death can be linked to the Greeks' reaction to the Exiles Decree. If Alexander had elevated Hephaestion to demigod status, then that could only mean he saw himself as a god. If the Greeks did the same, then perhaps their appeals against the decree would be successful. Some states even instituted their own heroic cult of Hephaestion. That was hardly out of respect for Hephaestion but to pander all the more to the king.

In Athens, Demosthenes had refused to use Harpalus's men and money in a revolt against Alexander, and he had also refused to accept Alexander's divinity. After he returned to Athens from meeting Nicanor at Olympia, he changed his tune. Nicanor himself could not alter the terms of the Exiles Decree. However, he would have been able to expand on Alexander's reasons for it, and advise on what might be attractive to him in any appeal against it. Back in Athens, Demosthenes arranged for Harpalus's escape and called for recognition of Alexander's divinity. His strategy was a bold and finely spun one. If the embassy took the news that the Athenians were no longer sheltering Harpalus and that they recognised Alexander as divine, then he would grant their request not to have the exiles return and to keep Samos. Demades, another politician, hit the nail on the head with his remark that the Athenians were so concerned about heaven that they stood to lose the earth. In other words, what did it matter to call Alexander a god if he let them keep Samos?

Harpalus's escape unexpectedly caused uproar in the city. Accusations were made against Demosthenes and others that they had taken bribes from him – bribes against the state, in fact, which meant treason. When only half of Harpalus's 700 talents were found on the Acropolis, things looked grim for Demosthenes. On his proposal, the Areopagus, an age-old body in the constitution, began an enquiry into the matter. Demosthenes even offered to submit to the death penalty if it found him guilty, and issued a challenge to the people to present it with proof of the accusation. The enquiry would last six months.

All of the Greeks' appeals against the Exiles Decree were unsuccessful. When the Athenian embassy returned to Athens after its long journey to and from Babylon the Areopagus found Demosthenes guilty. Significantly it cited no evidence, but only the names of those suspected of receiving a bribe, together with the amounts supposedly taken. Demosthenes issued a challenge to the Areopagus to produce evidence, but it could not. Even so, he was brought to trial, in about March 323, found guilty and condemned. He fled into exile, and did not return to Athens until Alexander was dead.

Demosthenes's guilt or innocence cannot be fully resolved, and here is not the place to discuss it.[8] He may well have taken money from Harpalus, not as a bribe but to use in the city's administration. However, his trial was clearly political. The prosecution speeches[9] rested on the premise that the Areopagus's reputation alone should be sufficient for accepting its report against Demosthenes. However, others indicted in the affair, against whom likewise no proof was offered, were acquitted.

The coincidence of the Areopagus's report on its enquiry coming at about the same time as the embassy delivered the news that Alexander had rejected the Athenians' pleas over the Exiles Decree is too much. Demosthenes's strategy had failed, and in the defence speech at his trial he pleaded that he was being sacrificed to please the king. Why? The plausible answer is that the Athenians were preparing a second attempt to resist the Exiles Decree. This time an embassy would take the news that the principal opponent of Alexander and of his father had been found guilty of misconduct (and that he had fled the city). After all, Alexander had asked for Demosthenes before, in 335 (see Chapter 4), and Demosthenes had continued his anti-Macedonian stance in political life. There was no need to resort to this desperate action for Alexander soon died.

The Exiles Decree also died with Alexander, as did any acknowledgement of his divinity. Only one state, Tegea in the Peloponnese, received back its exiles. The document that sets out the terms on which they returned exists today.[10] It is long, complicated and covers every conceivable factor that might affect the harmony between those who stayed and those who returned as exiles. Of particular concern was the return of property seized from exiles and religious debts. Any dispute was to be submitted to a foreign court, from Mantinea, within 60 days, and after that to a civic court in Tegea. The decree ends with an oath of reconciliation:

'I swear by Zeus, by Athena, by Apollo, by Poseidon that I shall be well disposed towards the returned exiles whom it was decided by the city to receive back. I shall not bear a grievance against any of them for whatever he may have plotted, from the day on which I swore the oath, and I shall not defy the safety of the returned exiles.'

It is also clear from the opening that it is a revised version of one originally submitted to Alexander: 'The edict is to be inscribed in accordance with those terms corrected by the city that were objected to in the edict.' This shows that the original terms for return were unacceptable to the king. It is unlikely that Alexander was personally concerned with the politics and stability of one small state (or every state, with the possible exception of Athens). The Tegeans' decree was probably handled by one of his staff. However, its detailed content shows Alexander's concern to ensure stability on the mainland.

In May 323 the invasion force was ready: Arabia would soon be Alexander's. The king must have felt the same stirrings of excitement as in spring 334 when he crossed the Hellespont. Who knew what great deeds would be performed and what spectacular stories there would be to tell? His men had to have shared his feelings to a very large extent. Alexander now had an army that was loyal to him. Those who had previously defied him or criticised him had either come over to his way of thinking or had been purged. In fact, Alexander's army was now a mixture of Macedonian and Asian. Peucestas had brought to Babylon 20,000 Persian infantry, who were now incorporated into the Macedonian phalanx. In the first three ranks and rear rank were Macedonians armed with their sarissas, and between them the Persian soldiers armed with bows and javelins. Admittedly, Alexander had decided that this arrangement was to alter once Antipater and the 10,000 Macedonians from the mainland reached him, but for now the men's worst fears at Opis had been realised.

In the end, there was no invasion. A month later, on 10 June 323, aged 32 years and 8 months, Alexander was dead.

The circumstances surrounding Alexander's death are as controversial as his life. In late May the embassy to the Oracle of Zeus Ammon at Siwah returned with news that the god endorsed Alexander's plan for a hero cult of Hephaestion. The king was delighted, and celebrated the news with a huge feast, which included the usual copious quantities of wine. At some point in the wee small hours when Alexander ought to have staggered off to his bed, Medeius of Larisa (in Thessaly) invited him to another drinking party. There, 'he pledged the health of everyone at the dinner, there being twenty altogether, and he accepted the same number of toasts from everyone'.[11] After a final toast, Alexander was reputed to have drunk a pitcher of undiluted wine in one hit, and compelled the others to do so. The king was used to drinking, of course, but this pitcher was a particularly big one and held 12 pints. After he had drained it the king collapsed. The doctors could do nothing, and Alexander died.

One tradition has it that after his collapse Alexander's body suffered a series of spasms, consistent with being poisoned. It was apparently believed because in Athens Demosthenes proposed that the alleged poisoner, Antipater's son Iollas, receive the highest state honours. However, this explanation was probably put out after Alexander died by Olympias as part of her struggle with Antipater.

The king's *Royal Diaries* (*Ephemerides*), which recorded the events of each day and were kept by his secretary Eumenes of Cardia, gave a different story.[12] Its authenticity is in doubt, and in all likelihood it was not something that covered the entire length of the reign but just the last few days. Also, it was not a diary in any official sense, but one written by Eumenes shortly after Alexander's death, probably to rebut the belief that the king was poisoned. Arrian and Plutarch followed its account of Alexander's death, and so we move back to the death as being due to natural causes.

According to the *Ephemerides*, Alexander had the drinking party with Medeius, but on the 18th of the Macedonian month Daesius (end of May) he contracted a fever and slept the whole day. The day after he spent playing dice with Medeius, bathed, sacrificed and then went to bed, but still with a fever. He was able to continue his duties, including the daily religious sacrifices on behalf of the state, as well as discuss his future campaign and even vacant posts in the army. On the 20th and 21st he listened to Nearchus' account of his voyage, but the fever became worse. He ordered his bed to be moved next to his bath so that he could bathe with more ease. Alexander's daily bathing is what we should expect from someone who was feverish in the heat of an Iraqi summer.

By the 24th Daesius the fever intensified and he was confined to his bed. This did not stop him performing the state sacrifices, as was his duty, although he had to be carried outside in his bed to do so. His voice then failed him. On the 26th Daesius his men's anxiety gave way to panic, and they thought him dead. They 'came with loud shouts to the doors of the palace, and threatened his companions until all opposition was broken down; and when the doors had been thrown open to them, without cloak or armour, one by one, they all filed slowly past the couch' on which he lay. Alexander could not speak, but was apparently still conscious. He was able to raise his head a little and indicate that he recognised his men with his eyes. Then he lapsed into a brief coma and died in the evening of the 28th Daesius.

Alexander's death can be ascribed to malaria or even acute alcoholic pancreatitis. The latter is no surprise given his excessive drinking habits. His resistance was probably weakened by his lifestyle, as well as by all the illnesses and wounds he had suffered – especially the chest wound at Malli. The true cause of his death will probably never be known.[13] However, it is not surprising, given the legend he already was, that even his death is shrouded in mystery and controversy.

With him died his future plans, which the Macedonian Assembly officially cancelled. These were outlined in his alleged will that was read out to the army by Perdiccas. They included the invasion of Arabia, the conquest of the entire Mediterranean basin, the circumnavigation of Africa, the building of a memorial to his father to rival the greatest pyramid, an enormous temple to Athena at Troy and the transpopulation of people from Asia to Europe and vice versa.[14] We can well understand the reaction of the Assembly to the very last one.

Had Alexander lived, who knows how successful he would have been. He probably would have conquered Arabia, and Nearchus may well have sailed around much of Africa. However, Alexander's success in any campaigns in the western Mediterranean, especially against Carthage, is less predictable. In any case, how far would his new army have let him advance before it too might have had enough and forced his return to Macedonia?

The news that this seemingly superhuman king was dead was greeted with blank disbelief at first. In Athens, the story goes, Demades said that if he were really dead the whole world would smell his corpse. But Alexander really was dead, and the Greek states, with the exception of the Boeotian and the Euboean Leagues, revolted against Macedon. The League of Corinth was dead too. Hyperides, who had come to the fore in Athenian politics after Demosthenes's disgrace in the Harpalus affair, used the remains of Harpalus's money to hire mercenaries from Taenarum. While Alexander was alive, rebellion was out of the question. Alexander dead – and the bulk of his army so far away in Babylon – was quite another matter.

The Greek revolt against Macedon is commonly called the Lamian War, and it broke out probably in September 323. Under his own auspices, Demosthenes toured the various states marshalling support against Antipater. On the motion of his cousin Demon, he was officially pardoned and returned to Athens, the people turning out in force to greet him. At first the war went in the Greeks' favour. Under the Athenian general Leosthenes they defeated Antipater in battle close to Thermopylae, and it was with no small difficulty that he escaped and fled for refuge in the town of Lamia. There he was besieged for the winter.

Then the Greeks' luck ran out. In one attempt to take Lamia Leosthenes was killed, and Leonnatus's arrival with Macedonian reinforcements allowed Antipater to escape back to Macedonia and regroup. In summer 322, the Macedonian admiral Cleitus destroyed the powerful Greek fleet, thus establishing Macedonian superiority at sea. That allowed Craterus and 13,000 troops a safe crossing from Cilicia to Macedonia. The writing was now on the wall for the Greeks, and Antipater defeated them at the decisive Battle of Crannon (in central Thessaly) in August 322. Antipater's army consisted of 48,000 soldiers including 5,000 cavalry, and that of the Greeks 25,000 soldiers and 3,500 cavalry. The Greeks lost over 500 men and the Macedonians 130.

The Lamian War was over. Athens suffered the indignity of having an oligarchy enforced on it, and a Macedonian garrison. Antipater also enforced a wealth requirement of 2,000 drachmas for citizenship, as a result of which as many as 12,000 citizens may have been disfranchised leaving only 9,000 actual citizens in the city. Hyperides and Demosthenes were condemned to death, and fled into exile. Demosthenes committed suicide rather than suffer capture by Macedonian pursuers, but Hyperides was captured and executed. Thus was the inglorious end to Athens' proud history and democracy.

Antipater's punishment was severe but understandable. He could not afford another revolt, especially since a power struggle was raging between Alexander's successors. Alexander left behind no undisputed successor (a major factor in the Greeks' decision to revolt). Roxane was still pregnant when he died, and the only other male candidate was his half-brother, the youthful but apparently incompetent Philip Arrhidaeus, son of Philip II.

As Alexander lay dying, 'his Companions asked him to whom he left his kingdom, and he replied, "To the best" '.[15] Alexander gave his signet ring to Perdiccas, perhaps designating him as his heir, but this action did not mean anything to the Greeks. Nor did it mean anything to the other generals, who wanted their own share of power. Arrhidaeus (then about 35 years old) was proclaimed Philip III, and when Roxane gave birth to a boy (Alexander) in August, he became Alexander IV. This was a dual kingship. However, there was no real loyalty to them, and both were used as pawns by Alexander's successors. They were eventually killed, Philip III in 317, and Alexander IV in 311. Heracles, Alexander's son by Barsine, was living in Pergamum when his father died, and he was completely ignored.

The successors' power struggles lasted until 301. In the wars of those two decades, the whole empire was involved and most of the generals were killed. Alexander's empire was split apart, carved into what would become the great empires of the Hellenistic period: Antigonid Greece, Ptolemaic Egypt and, the greatest of all, Seleucid Syria (with its capital at Babylon). The one empire was gone, which was now split between east and west, and so too was a stable Macedonian dynasty. How different was Alexander's legacy from that of his father.

Alexander's body was embalmed, and considerable time was spent building a magnificent funeral wagon to transport it back to Aegae, burial place of the Macedonian kings. It never arrived. Ptolemy, who had seized Egypt in 323, kidnapped it. Alexander might have given his signet ring to Perdiccas, but Ptolemy now had the king's body. It is perhaps Ptolemy who first coined the title 'Great' to describe Alexander, an epithet that has stayed with him to today. Alexander's body was first taken to Memphis, and then to Alexandria, where it was buried. The tomb has not yet been found. What a find that would be.

14

Man and God

Question: 'How can a man become a god?' *Answer*: 'By doing something a man cannot do.'[1]

This question was one of several that Alexander asked of several Indian philosophers, who were reputed for their terse answers, in an effort to catch them out. Other questions included which are the more numerous, the living or the dead (answer: the living, for the dead no longer exist); which is the most cunning of animals (answer: the one not yet discovered by man); and how can a man make himself most beloved (answer: if he has supreme power but does not inspire fear). The question about how a man might become a god is the one that best explains Alexander's motives for what he did – and thus how he saw himself:

'Alexander used to wear sacred clothes at his parties. Sometimes he would wear the purple robe, and cloven sandals, and horns of Ammon, as if he had been the god. Sometimes he would imitate Artemis, whose dress he often wore while driving in his chariot; having on also a Persian robe, but displaying above his shoulders the bow and javelin of the goddess. Sometimes also he would appear as Hermes; at other times, and almost every day, he would wear a purple cloak, and a tunic shot with white, and a cap that had a royal diadem attached to it. And when he was in private with his friends he wore the sandals of Hermes, and the petasus on his head, and held the caduceus in his hand. Often also he wore a lion's skin, and carried a club, like Heracles .... And Alexander used to have the floor sprinkled with exquisite perfumes and with fragrant wine; and myrrh was burnt before him, and other kinds of incense.'[2]

Ephippus, the contemporary writer who describes the above, makes it plain that Alexander went beyond merely dressing up as a god in disguise. He is describing a scene towards the end of Alexander's reign. Incense was burned in his presence, and he goes on to talk of a reverential silence in Alexander's presence. Both show that there was a cult to him at his court. By the end of his reign, then, he was worshipped, and while alive. By tracking the significant events in the development of Alexander's divine pretensions throughout his reign, we see a pattern to how his vision of himself changed, and why.[3]

Philip was deified on his death, and Alexander could reasonably be expected to follow in this 'tradition'. However, he sought divine honours for himself while still alive. Was he making a break with tradition or had his father been deified at the end of his reign, while still alive?[4] The day after his daughter's wedding to the King of Epirus at Aegae in 336, Philip held games and dramatic contests to celebrate the event (see Chapter 2). The day began with a religious procession into the theatre where the people had already gathered to watch the events. The royal procession entered the theatre carrying statues of the 12 Olympian gods, and a statue of Philip that was on a par with the others in terms of size and adornment. On the same day, Philip was assassinated.

Philip's statue is interesting, for to have it carried in this procession and next to the statues of the gods may have indicated that he saw himself as divine. He had certainly done more for his state than any other Macedonian king, and he was going to continue to do more as his plans to invade Asia revealed. Had he done enough though to be a god on earth? Ephesus had erected a statue of Philip II in its temple when the advance force under Parmenion invaded Asia in 336. In Eresus (on the island of Lesbos) there was an Altar to Zeus Philippios. Here, though, the link is with Zeus's role as Philip's protector, not with Philip's being seen as Zeus by the people.[5] Was Alexander trying to build on the lead of Ephesus and to exploit the association at Eresus?

Philip's divine leanings are overshadowed by those of his son. However, a common factor in both cases would be the reaction of the people. Worship of a living man was considered blasphemy. At the end of the fifth century, the Spartan general Brasidas was revered as a hero in Amphipolis. However, he was dead by then, and a hero cult was not the same as a divine one. It made the dead man merely a demigod. Yet in the same period it appears that the Spartan Lysander was worshipped as a god while alive on the island of Samos, and he had a festival in his honour. Dion of Syracuse a little later may also have been worshipped as a god by his people while alive.

The explanation for the apotheosis of these living men is unknown. However, Samos was not the Greek mainland, and Syracuse was on Sicily in the western Mediterranean, somewhat alien to the Greeks of the eastern Mediterranean. Moreover, Lysander and Dion certainly did not set a trend, for there were no other men revered in this way (that we know of) until the late fourth century, with Alexander. If anything, the worship of the living Lysander *stopped* what might have become a trend for several decades.

In Philip's case, what happened at Ephesus (again, not on the mainland but in Asia Minor) seems to have been an anomaly; a knee-jerk reaction by the people that showed more their distaste of Persian rule and the hope that this would end. Also, it is made plain that the people are not bestowing divine honours on him, merely placing his statue in the temple as a thanks offering. At Eresus (on an island, and well away from the orthodoxy of the mainland) he is connected with a local cult, not worshipped alone.

Philip may well have *wanted* to become divine, and his planned invasion of Persia may have been the stepping stone to that. Then again, if he had sought divine honours at the end of his reign, we would expect the reaction of the people to be far different from the adulation in which they clearly held him. His reign showed that he knew how to read people and how to handle them in order to achieve his objectives (see Chapter 2). He had given his own people a feeling of nationalistic pride and he had established a unity that Macedonia had never had before. At the core of all of this was the army. He never lost touch with the rank and file of his army (as Alexander would do), and he was, to put it bluntly, too savvy to do something that would risk everything.

It is unlikely that the appearance of his statue in the theatre of Aegae that day meant that he was divine. More probably, it reflected his glory as a great king and his piety. It is important to remember that when he fought in the Sacred War he did so as the Saviour of Delphi, the Liberator of Apollo. He and his men wore white wreaths in their hair in the battles against the Phocians to show they were fighting for Apollo. The Sacred War was the turning point for the formal expansion of Philip's power in Greece. His intervention in it led to its end in 346 and the liberation of Delphi. After it, Macedonia was granted a seat on the hallowed Amphictyonic Council, a religious body charged with maintaining the Oracle of Apollo at Delphi, but one which also had much political influence in Greece. He was also elected President of the Pythian Games for 346.

Philip continued to advance into Greece and eventually defeated the Greeks at the Battle of Chaeronea in 338. That gave him control of Greece, and the League of Corinth gave him the legal means to enforce and ensure Macedonian rule. Yet what happened in 346 set up Philip's future moves. In 346, in less than 15 years after being acclaimed king, the 'barbarian' had come from nowhere to great prominence in terms of his power in Greece and in Greek religious events. His statue next to those of the gods in the procession emphasised this, and thus his piety. Perhaps also the white cloak he wore to the theatre that day evoked the white wreath he wore when fighting for Apollo in the Sacred War.

As has been said (see Chapter 3), Alexander's admiration of his father changed to resentment, especially in the last two years of his father's reign. The young heir was eager for glory himself. He had his nose (and aspirations) put out of joint when Philip told him he intended to leave him behind as regent while he campaigned against the Persians. Whether Alexander had a hand in Philip's murder or not, he pushed ahead with his father's plan to invade Asia once he became king. But he did not just want to conquer like his father. He wanted to do more, to establish an absolute monarchy and to be worshipped as a god while alive. That would propel him far ahead of his father.

Alexander's boyhood had been normal or as normal as that of the heir to the Macedonian throne could be. However, once he left Macedonia things were quite different, and he took on a very different persona. This was part of his policy to eclipse his father of course. The divine element increased dramatically when Alexander was in Asia. It really began with the story of the Oracle of Apollo at Didyma that had been silent since the Persian Wars of the early fifth century (see Chapter 5). When Alexander arrived at Didyma in autumn 334, Apollo suddenly found his voice, and started speaking again. Perhaps not at this time, but when the king was in Egypt the following year, he proclaimed that Alexander was born of Zeus.

Before Didyma, Alexander's dealings with gods and dead heroes had been for pious reasons and for the good of his mission. At Elaeus, for example, he sacrificed at the tomb of Protesilaus, and then as he crossed the Hellespont to Poseidon and the Nereids. These sacrifices combined political symbolism with heroic symbolism (see Chapter 4). So too did his sacrifice at Achilles's tomb, and to the Trojan Athena and Priam, in the Temple to Athena, at Troy. Didyma, however, was different. He had actually detoured somewhat to go there after the siege of Miletus and before pressing on to Halicarnassus. It seems clear, then, that he wanted to use Apollo's silence and his breaking of it to his own advantage.

His visit had done something that Philip never did: it had brought an oracle back to life. It showed his piety – and his power. That power was confirmed by Zeus himself (apparently) when Alexander severed the Gordian knot at Gordium in spring 333 (see Chapter 5). A violent thunderstorm happened that night as Zeus greeted the man who would rule Asia. Alexander sacrificed to him the next morning. The gods, then, were on the side of Macedonia in the invasion of Asia, and the future blossomed rosy for Alexander. As the king, he could look forward to great conquests, to great wealth and to the expansion of the Macedonian empire. All of that would give him the great reputation that he desperately needed. By now he had defeated the Persians at Granicus and Issus, after which battle Darius fled, controlled all of Asia Minor, the Levant and Egypt, and marched further than Philip had ever done.

Then he went to Egypt, and that changed everything (see Chapter 7). At Siwah, in 331, Alexander the man would become also Alexander the god. Siwah is thus the real turning point in his quest for divine status.[6] Alexander was probably not crowned Pharaoh, but by virtue of his control of the country he assumed all the titles and powers. That meant he was a god on earth, and worshipped by his Egyptian subjects. He was also only 24 years old. It is not a surprise that everything he had so far done (and would do) went to his head. After all, he was only human, and it was easy to become deluded.

Like Philip, Alexander could trace his ancestry back to Zeus and Heracles. His own people and those of Asia worshipped both, sometimes in other forms (for example, at Tyre Heracles was Melqart). But now the Egyptians were worshipping Alexander. And now, I suggest, the Didyma visit was exploited for another, more ominous, reason. At some point after Alexander arrived in Egypt came the 'news', manufactured by the king, that Apollo at Didyma had said that he was a son of Zeus. On top of this were the stories, which I suggest were put out by Alexander, or at least had his official sanction, at this time about the divine nature of his birth. Artemis had delivered him and his real father was Zeus, who had appeared as an incarnation of a snake and impregnated Olympias (see Chapter 3). Alexander was setting himself up as divine even from the day he had been born. He had begun to see himself not merely as a descendant of Zeus, but as a son.

However, Zeus's greeting at Gordium did not mean the future ruler of Asia was his son. That explains why Alexander visited the Oracle of Zeus Ammon in Siwah in 331. Apollo at Didyma had told him he was Zeus's son, now Alexander needed to hear that from Zeus himself. With Didyma 'on line', it was necessary to go to Siwah. It is significant that Alexander wanted to go there. There was a temple to Zeus Ammon at Aphytis in the Chalcidice, not so far from Macedonia itself. Alexander certainly knew about it and most likely visited it. After all, his ancestor Heracles had done so, and there was the story that he had been conceived by a snake that had sex with Olympias – a snake that was the incarnation of Zeus Ammon himself (see Chapter 3). There were plenty of reasons for going to Zeus Ammon. As a boy, he would simply have worshipped at his shrine. In 332, with two defeats of the Persian army under his belt and Egypt subjected, he was a very different person.

We do not know what the priest of Zeus told Alexander at Siwah as the king met him in private and we have only his word for what happened. Not that it matters in the end. It is significant that we hear from a contemporary source that he went there to learn 'his own origin more certainly, or at least that he might be able to say that he had learned it'.[7] In other words, it did not really matter what the priest told him. Alexander believed he was Zeus's son, and that was what he told everyone. From that time, he referred to himself as son of Zeus, not descendant of Zeus.

One event that stands out in Alexander's promotion of his personal divinity is *proskynesis*. At Bactria in 327 he tried to make everyone at his court perform this Asian custom of prostration before him. When Callisthenes refused, and the majority of his court seems to have followed suit, Alexander had to abandon the plan (see Chapter 10).

Why did Alexander want to introduce *proskynesis* at his court? He may have wanted to establish a common social protocol between Greeks and Asians so that all would greet him in the same way. He did now rule over several races of people, who all had their different customs and beliefs. He called himself Lord of Asia, thus establishing a common form of address. Therefore it made sense to have a common custom for his subjects to greet him. However, the Greeks disliked this custom, principally because they saw it as blasphemous. It implied worship of a living man, and they only worshipped gods or dead heroes. Alexander was brought up to believe in the traditional gods, and traditional worship. He must have known that his men would react in this way, and that they would resent and resist it. Anaxarchus's argument (if indeed he did say this), that since Alexander was going to be worshipped when he was dead, he may as well be worshipped while alive, was hardly a convincing one.

The only explanation that makes sense is that Alexander now thought of himself a god. Thus, *proskynesis* was a logical vehicle for all of his subjects to recognise his divine status in public. His action shows that he had lost touch with his men, for he was well aware of the religious connotations associated with the act. It shows that he had also lost touch with the religious beliefs on which he had been raised. Alexander had performed great deeds, and he would have been deified on his death, as his father had been. For Alexander, however, that was not enough now. Certainly, he would not eclipse Philip if he stayed a 'mere mortal'. He had already taken that extra step, and believed himself divine. Siwah had 'proved' that to him. He was prepared to ignore his men's religious orthodoxy. The army followed him into battle and into new lands. Now it needed to follow a new lead. The Asians already performed *proskynesis* before him, so too should the Greeks and Macedonians. Alexander was now man and god.

Callisthenes was later implicated in the Conspiracy of the Pages and executed. Indeed, those who disagreed with Alexander's policies and the way that he viewed himself, men such as Philotas, Parmenion,

Callisthenes, Cleitus and perhaps Craterus, were either killed or sent far away from court. That did not mean that Alexander the man and god came to be accepted. When the army mutinied at Opis in 324, the men sarcastically told him to continue his campaign with his father Ammon (see Chapter 12). Alexander's mortality had shown itself every time he had been wounded. In particular, he had almost died of a fever after his swim in the river Cydnus and of loss of blood after his chest wound against the Malli. Gods are supposed to be immortal. It is a sign of Alexander's megalomania and then belief in his own godhead that he never seems to have recognised the implications of his wounds.

Of course, there is a difference between divine pretensions and actually thinking of oneself as a god. Did Alexander really think he was a god, or was he just a megalomaniac, exploiting ruler cult for the political advantages it offered? In 324 the Greeks of the mainland were discussing divine honours for him, and they sent embassies to him that wore gold crowns and brought him gold crowns.[8] These actions were what one did to honour a god. But that does not mean they believed he was a god. Indeed, they did not believe this, as Demosthenes's contemptuous 'Alexander can be the son of Zeus and of Poseidon if he wants to be'[9] proves. What they did was all part of a diplomatic policy to get Alexander to rescind the Exiles Decree (see Chapters 12 and 13). Nor is there any evidence that Alexander issued a directive ordering the mainland Greeks to worship him. Some island states had worshipped him since 334, but these were few and far between. They were doing so as a mark of gratitude, no different from Ephesus and Philip II. The Greeks were simply pandering to Alexander, and we get the impression he would have known this.

However, there are two indications towards the end of Alexander's reign that showed megalomania had given way to his belief that he actually was a god. The first is one of his motives for invading Arabia (see Chapter 12). He had several, including trade and further conquest, but a contemporary source reveals the following. The Arabs worshipped only two gods, Uranus and Dionysus:

'The former because he is himself visible and has in himself the stars of heaven, especially the sun, from which comes the greatest and most evident benefit to all mankind. The latter on account of the fame he won by his expedition to India. Therefore he thought himself quite worthy to be considered by the Arabs as a third god, since he had performed deeds by no means inferior to those of Dionysus.'[10]

Second, and more important, is the heroic cult to Hephaestion. When he died in 324, the king heaped many honours on him and requested a heroic cult for his dead friend from Zeus Ammon (see Chapter 12). In May 323 Zeus agreed. The cult meant that Hephaestion was now a demigod, as Alexander intended. However, if he were a demigod, that made Alexander a god on earth. Hephaestion was not the king's equal, and Alexander could not elevate his friend to the same divine level as himself. That meant he must have seen himself as a living god if he arranged for Hephaestion to be a demigod.

As his reign progressed, Alexander came to think of himself as a god. This is shown especially by the *proskynesis* incident at Bactria, his relationship to the dead Hephaestion, his decision to conquer Arabia in order to be worshipped as a third god, Ephippus's account with which we started this chapter, and even by his coinage, especially after Issus (see Chapter 6). Alexander was worshipped by the Egyptians, he wanted to be worshipped by the Arabs, and attempts such as *proskynesis* showed that he wanted to be worshipped by his own people. At no time did he shirk his duties as king, which included the daily sacrifices on behalf of the state, but now he was sacrificing for his state to equals, not as a mortal king to the gods.

'How can a man become a god?' 'By doing something a man cannot do.' Alexander had done a great many things as he expanded the empire and outdid his father. In the process, the warrior king fell victim to megalomania, and then to a belief in his own divinity. After his death, many of the Hellenistic rulers assumed divine status and exploited ruler cult for their own political ends. So too did the Roman emperors. Both of those worlds were entirely different from that of Alexander, and the attitude to divinity was different. Or, as time continued, was it?

15

Alexander: The Great

How does Alexander's belief in his own godhead affect his reputation of being great? How did he come by that title, and does he deserve it today? Should his greatness be measured only in the military sphere? At the end of his reign, was he 'his own greatest achievement'?[1]

Chapter 1 traced some of the reasons why and how the Alexander legend grew over time. If we try to stick to the historical Alexander, and consider him as the 'package' of king, what impression of his greatness do we then get?[2]

Exactly when Alexander was dubbed great is unknown. The first attested reference to Alexander as great is in a Roman comedy of the first century, showing that the epithet was common knowledge by then.[3] The Romans, who measured success by the number of body bags used, took to Alexander with gusto. It may well have been Ptolemy who first referred to him as great, as part of his attempt to consolidate his position in Egypt (see Chapter 13). If it was not him, then it must have been one of Alexander's successors, for they associated themselves closely with Alexander and his image. For example, they wore his combination of *kausia* (the wide-brimmed hat) and diadem, and minted his image on their coins (see Plates 20 and 21).

It is in the military sphere that the greatness of Alexander, if not proved, is demonstrably shown.[4] In the accounts of the battles of Granicus, Issus, Gaugamela and Hydaspes, Alexander's use of terrain, his strategy, its execution and his very boldness were astonishing. Philip had left him the best army in the world; it never once let Alexander down, or he it, in battle. He was always to be found in the thick of fighting, setting the ultimate example. The same is true of his sieges, whether they were short or long. His use of siege engines was exemplary, and set new standards. He was almost always eerily accurate in what the enemy would do in battle, and knew exactly how to 'read' an opponent's battle line, strategy, even his mind. That sort of thing cannot be learnt, but is instinct that few of his time (and later) possessed.

He was also very generous to his men. He rewarded them with high pay, bonuses, remission of taxes in certain cases, cancellation of soldiers' debts and various signs of royal favour. The men wanted to win battles, but they also wanted regular pay and booty. Alexander ensured both, and in return they fought ferociously for him.

At the same time, there are occasions when we can query Alexander's generalship and even his victories. After the Battle of Issus in 333, Alexander allowed Darius to escape while he pressed on to secure the Levant and Egypt (see Chapter 6). He was more interested in going to Egypt, and the Oracle of Zeus Ammon. He even went to the oracle not for any state reason but because of his *pothos*, his personal longing. In the meantime, Darius was able to regroup and eventually bring Alexander to battle again at Gaugamela in 331 (see Chapter 8).

Alexander's victories over his Persian and Indian foes that have so long excited the imagination were embellished by court historiography. A case in point is the Battle of Issus, where Darius threw victory away at that battle and then fled. Alexander was lucky, but this does not come in the 'official' account we have of the battle, probably since he told Callisthenes what to write about it. Similarly embellished is the great battle against Porus at the Hydaspes river in 326 (see Chapter 11). There is no question that Alexander's strategy in lulling the enemy into a false sense of security was brilliant, and his river crossing against such odds was superhuman. However, the battle was over before it began. Porus was outnumbered and outclassed, and he and his army never stood a chance. The commemorative coinage that Alexander struck to mark his defeat of Porus had a propaganda purpose, however, to exaggerate that defeat.[5]

In the case of his sieges, we again have that mixture of brilliance in execution but questionable motives. The siege of Tyre in 332 lasted several months, cost the king a fortune in money and manpower and yet achieved little (see Chapter 6). Control of Tyre was essential, but Alexander could simply have left a garrison on the mainland opposite the island town to keep it in check. He prosecuted the siege for personal reasons once the Tyrians defied him. The same is true of his siege of Aornus in 326 (see Chapter 11). Many of the Assaceni had taken refuge there, and Alexander needed to take the place to secure his communications route from Asia to India through the Cophen Valley. Once he heard that Heracles was supposed to have failed in taking take the rock, he seized the chance to outdo his divine ancestor. *Pothos* matched the strategic need. He was lucky that the people surrendered so quickly, but what if they had not?

Then we have the two army mutinies at the Hyphasis river in 326 (see Chapter 11) and at Opis in 324 (see Chapter 12). The term 'mutiny' for the army's resistance to Alexander has been queried. For example, Bosworth has this to say on the Opis incident: 'This protest can hardly be dignified with the term mutiny that is universally applied to it. The troops confined themselves to verbal complaints, but they were contumacious and wounding.'[6] In the case of both mutinies, it is important to focus not on what the men did or said after they stood fast, but at the fact that the army as a whole refused to carry out Alexander's orders. True, no one was put forward to replace Alexander (or rather, we do not hear of anyone), but the men rebelled against the king and commander. Refusal to obey the orders of a superior in this manner is mutiny. The army had been well rewarded by Alexander, and had marched wherever he directed, but eventually enough was enough. The mutinies showed a vote of no confidence in Alexander as a military commander and as a king, and that was not a great thing.

There are other factors that could be mentioned. For example, the terrible march across the Gedrosian Desert that was a major logistic and strategic blunder (see Chapter 11). Yet Alexander was eager to travel that route because Dionysus had taken it, and both Semiramis and Cyrus the Great had failed in their attempts. Another example is Alexander's many demands for reinforcements from Antipater, the result of the huge numbers of casualties from his campaigns. These seem to have depleted the manpower reserves that Antipater had at his disposal, thereby putting him under additional pressure.[7] When Agis III took his war to Greece in 331, Antipater's forces were not at full strength. Diodorus (18.12.2) says that he was short of 'citizen soldiers' (Macedonians), and that he had just sent 6,500 Macedonians to Alexander. Antipater defeated Agis (see Chapter 8). However, he was hard-pressed during the initial stages of the Lamian War in 323 before Leonnatus and Craterus reached him with reinforcements from Asia (see Chapter 13).

Alexander as the dashing, inspiring, and successful general was certainly true. At the same time, he had limitations in the military sphere that need to be taken into account as they impact on his generalship overall. The mutinies are clearly the most important here. But did he learn from them? Alexander does not seem to have known anything but conquest. He could not sit still. One contemporary says bluntly that in his plan to invade Arabia in 323 he 'was insatiably ambitious of ever acquiring fresh territory'.[8] He had no intention of returning to Pella, and those with him would have been wondering if this would ever happen. Had he lived, would their concern and his constant activity have led to another Hyphasis situation?

Alexander opened up trade with Asia and within Asia. This is certainly true, and his stimulation of the economy throughout his empire is a tribute to him. For example, at Begram (Alexandria in Caucaso), north of Kabul, have been found glass from Alexandria, lacquer work from China, Hindu ivory figurines from India, and Buddhas wearing Greek dress. All of this, and more, may be tracked back to Alexander and his stimulation of trade and trade routes. Greece thrived, and so too would his empire.

In Greece, Athens especially prospered. The politician Lycurgus, by careful manipulation of the tax system and especially income from trade, rescued the city from the economic distress that had affected it in past years.[9] He was able to introduce legislation that included a new building programme (it was at this time that the Theatre of Dionysus by the Acropolis was built; it is still there today) aimed at fortifying and beautifying the city. He also ordered an official edition be made of the plays of the three great fifth-century tragedians Aeschylus, Sophocles and Euripides, and bronze statues of them were cast. This was all in keeping with a new, grand, phase of Athenian history after the darkness of recent decades. Lycurgus died in 324, an old and sick man. However, just before he died he was tried by the Athenians for corruption and, so the story goes, he had to be carried into court on his deathbed.[10]

Greece in time came to accept the Macedonian hegemony. Philip II had enforced the Common Peace of 337 through the medium of the League of Corinth (see Chapter 2). The Greeks had revolted on his death, but Alexander had reimposed it (see Chapter 4). We would expect that the Greeks, given their belief in freedom, would have tried to get rid of Macedonian control at every opportunity. This was not the case (Agis III's war does not really count, for Sparta was not a member of the League and very few states supported him). Perhaps the lesson of Thebes' destruction in 335 had been learned. On the other hand, the Greeks were finding life under Macedonian control not that onerous. Alexander was allowing them the right to make their own domestic decisions, and he was generally responsive to their needs, particularly the Athenians. Given the warfare that plagued the Greek states throughout their history, its passivity under Alexander (and Antipater) is one of his achievements.

The reaction to Alexander's Exiles Decree supports this argument. The decree clearly flouted the individual autonomy of the states, but instead of warfare the Greek states sent embassies to the king (see Chapter 13). In Athens, Harpalus's arrival with his force and money afforded the Athenians a real chance to spearhead a revolt against Macedon, all the more understandable given the decree. However, Demosthenes persuaded them against this militant course (see Chapters 12 and 13). There is no doubt that the Greeks were dismayed and worried over the Exiles Decree, but dismay was very different from rebellion.

However, in 323 Greece did revolt from Macedonian rule in the Lamian War. That was because Alexander had died and left behind no strong successor (see Chapter 13). This was a signal failing on his part. After Alexander ended the Greek revolt that broke out on the death of Philip II, Parmenion and Antipater apparently urged Alexander not to become actively involved in Asia until he had produced a son and heir.[11] He ignored them. His liaison with Barsine after the Battle of Issus produced a son, Heracles (see Chapter 6). Since they were unmarried, Heracles was not a legitimate heir. Alexander did marry Roxane in 327 (see Chapter 10), but she was still pregnant with their child when Alexander died in 323. Unlike his father, he failed to grasp the advantages of political marriages to consolidate and maintain power. The chaos and bloodshed that followed Alexander's death as his empire disintegrated was the result of his not providing an uncontested heir. Seeing to an heir was one of his most important duties of a king, and Alexander failed completely. The dynasty established by his father was no more.

The empire also faced other problems from Alexander's mismanagement of it. It was impossible for one man to administer it effectively because of its sheer size. The Great King knew that, and so did Alexander. He needed satraps to oversee the various regions of the empire, so he was right to use the Persian satrapal system as the basis of his imperial administration. He decided to use locals as satraps as before. However, a change to the existing system was that the satraps exercised only civil power. Macedonians controlled the army and the treasury of the various satrapies to ensure the loyalty of the native satraps.

In terms of financial administration, he continued with the previous system whereby the satraps levied taxes, deducted from them what they needed for the maintainance of their regions, and sent the rest to the Great King. The major Persian capitals continued to be the imperial 'banks', Babylon, Susa, Ecbatana and Persepolis. At Ecbatana alone Alexander had access to 180,000 talents. Where Alexander encountered people who did not have a monetary economy (such as the Uxians: see Chapter 8), he arranged for a tribute in animals or goods. However, he did create a single treasurer responsible for the oversight of all the imperial finances, who was headquartered at Babylon. From 330, this was Harpalus.

In an effort to help administration at more local levels, as well as to ensure Macedonian rule in the vast territory, he founded numerous cities. According to one source, he founded over 70, but this is exaggeration.[12] Some (for example Ai Khanoum) were cities in the true sense of the word, with trading connections, theatres, gymnasia and all the attributes to be expected in a city. Others were simply garrison posts, for the most part peopled by veterans. However, all contained a force of armed men that could be deployed if need be. The population was also a mixed one, Greeks and natives, which Alexander hoped would form a bond between conquerors and conquered that would be a deterrent against revolt. Administratively, the cities would be the link between their own areas and the satrap.

In the end, what Alexander did turned out to be not enough. His strategy of making former opponents in battle (such as Mazaeus, Phraterphernes and Satibarzanes) satraps was dangerous. They may have been under the thumb of the Macedonians in charge of the army and treasury, but it was not enough. Satibarzanes' revolt proved that (see Chapter 9), as did the king's Dissolution Decree to counter the apparently worrying power of all the satraps (see Chapter 12). Some 14 of his 23 satraps were seen by the king as a source of danger. While Alexander was away campaigning in Central Asia and India, they flagrantly abused their authority. Alexander also misjudged the native peoples who would live under his adapted Persian satrapal system. As he moved across Afghanistan and into Pakistan, he thought that defeated in battle meant conquered. The revolts of Bactria and Sogdiana as well as India proved him wrong (see Chapters 10 and 11).

Finally, on occasion he misjudged his own people. When Cleander and his force of 6,000 arrived in Carmania, the king executed him and another commander, Sitalces, for official misconduct in Media – as well as 600 of their soldiers for misconduct on the march to Alexander (see Chapter 12). Perhaps also he underestimated the resentment towards his integration of foreigners into the army. For example, he ordered local youths in Lydia, Lycia, Syria, Egypt and the north-east satrapies to be trained in Macedonian customs and tactics. The 30,000 *Epigonoi* from the north-east satrapies were not welcomed with open arms when, fully trained, they joined him at Susa in 324, and the king only ended the Opis mutiny in the same year by playing on the racial hatred between Greeks and natives (see Chapter 12).

Alexander did not devote much time to imperial administration. Then again, what could he do? He had an empire that was vast in size and had in it a multitude of people with different languages, customs and religions. Greece was passive under the Common Peace of the League of Corinth, but Greece was a fraction of the size of the Persian empire, and everyone spoke the same language and had the same customs. A Common Peace in Asia was unthinkable and unworkable. What Alexander aimed to do in his new kingdom of Asia was to rule as an autocratic king while allowing the satrapies some degree of autonomy. In return he expected their loyalty. He might have achieved his aim of ruling autocratically, but he never united the empire under him. His downfall though was not recognising this. Defeated in battle was the same as conquered to him, hence he followed a policy of constant expansion.

That raises the questions of where would Alexander stop, and why did he not do so after he defeated Darius. The king adhered to the panhellenic mandate of the League of Corinth (see Chapter 2) for only the first few years of the invasion before switching to a personal motive. He certainly did what he set out to do, namely to destroy the Persian empire as revenge for what the Greeks had suffered at the hands of Persia in the fifth century. However, as time continued, he showed an unwillingness to return home but rather insisted on exploring new lands. We can attribute this thirst for adventure to his *pothos* or personal longing.

At the same time, the longer he stayed on campaign, the more places he would conquer, and the more extensive his self-deification. Hence, the longer he stayed on campaign, the more he would outstrip Philip's exploits (see Chapter 3). His aim became not to establish a Macedonian empire in Asia but a kingdom of Asia. That would probably also mean a change of capital from Pella to probably Babylon. This was a far cry from Philip's intention in 336. There was nothing panhellenic about Alexander's new goal, and he had no legal right to pursuit it, not that that mattered to him.

However, it did matter to the people, those with him and those in Macedonia. He was using his own people for his own *pothos* now. His orientalism as manifested in his style of dress, his use of luxury items, his attempt to introduce *proskynesis* at the court, his use of foreigners in his army and administration (never mind that this was purely pragmatic: see Chapter 8), and especially his divine pretensions led to real resentment. Gone was the traditional warrior king: in his place was something akin to a sultan.

The reaction of the army at the Hyphasis and at Opis has already been noted. For the senior staff, dissatisfaction and criticism of the king were fatal. Philotas, Parmenion and Callisthenes were killed by manufactured conspiracy, the result of Alexander's paranoia and anger. Cleitus died by Alexander's own hand for similar reasons, exacerbated by excessive alcohol. It is hardly surprising that the contemporary source Ephippus says of Alexander that 'all the bystanders were silent, or spoke only words of good omen, out of fear. For he was a very violent man, with no regard for human life'.[13] A reign of terror thus existed at the royal court.

What must the people back in Macedonia have thought when they heard what Alexander was doing? At least until his death in 327 Callisthenes (as part of his duties as court historian) had sent back regular reports to Greece of Alexander's exploits. Whether someone else sent reports back after Callisthenes's demise is unknown, but given the number of men travelling between Asia and Greece the people on the mainland would have been kept informed of events.

Would the people back home really believe the reason that Alexander gave for the executions of Philotas and Parmenion? How would they have reacted to the circumstances of Cleitus's death? What would have been their reaction to the news that Alexander wanted to be worshipped by all his subjects? What *must* they have thought when they expected their king to return on completing his mission, only to see him move further east, killing his own men in paranoid or drunken (or both) frenzies, moving away from the traditions that his father had fought to uphold, ignoring the long-term administration of his empire, and giving no thought to a son and heir? They did not properly know him as a king anyway since he ruled at home for only two years before he left.

Bewilderment can only have changed to dissatisfaction with Alexander as an ideal Macedonian king. Evidence of this is seen in the Macedonian coinage, for the people continued to keep the same iconography on their coins as in the days of Philip. That is significant, given the propaganda value of coins. They did not want to proclaim the king's victories to all and sundry. Alexander himself minted all the coins that commemorated his victories at his mint in Babylon.

Moreover, Arrian says (7.8.1, 12.1–2) that Alexander was generous with pay and bounties to soldiers in order to encourage those at home to join him in Asia. If his people had supported his plans for further conquest there would have been no need for this measure. What we are dealing with here are bribes since those at home did not want to follow Alexander's *pothos*, and normal pay could not persuade them.

The adverse reaction of the army towards Alexander is further reinforced by the decision on the part of the Macedonian Army Assembly at Babylon after his death to abandon his future plans (see Chapter 13). They did so for reasons other than that Philip IV Arrhidaeus or Perdiccas were incapable of executing them, as for example Nicholas Hammond would say,[14] but because the plans represented all that the people had come to hate in Alexander. It is a far cry from their attitude to Philip.

Mention has been made several times throughout this book of Alexander's drunken behaviour and the Macedonians' drinking parties in which men died in an attempt to drink the most. The Macedonians were ferocious drinkers, who drank their wine neat rather than mixed it with water as the Greeks did. They were not alcoholics in our sense of the word, but they 'never understood how to drink in moderation, but rather drank copiously at the start of their feasts. Hence they were drunk while the first courses were still being served, and could not enjoy their food'.[15]

Alexander drank no less than the others, 'so that after the drinking binge he would sleep continuously for two days and two nights'.[16]

Sleeping uninterruptedly for two days and nights shows that serious drinking had been done. Alexander could claim some divine sanction for his drinking, as Dionysus was the god of wine. However, his alcohol consumption rose dramatically as his reign progressed. We can understand why, given the pressure he was under. He was the king. More than that, the men expected him to know what to do and where he was going all the time in a hostile environment. They were far from home, they were constantly fighting and they had placed their loyalty and trust in him. When they finally could endure no more, they were not afraid to mutiny.

However, those with him at the time reacted adversely against his drinking habits:

'The things that are not good about Alexander: They say that on the fifth of the month Dius he drank at Eumaeus's, then on the sixth he slept from the drinking. As much of that day as he was fresh, when he got up, he did business with the officers about the next day's journey, saying that it would be early. And on the seventh he was a guest at Perdiccas's and drank again, and on the eighth he slept. On the fifteenth of the same month he also slept, and on the following day he did the things as he was used to after drinking. On the twenty-fourth he dined at Bagoas's, whose house was ten stades from the palace. Then on the twenty-eighth he was at rest. Accordingly, one of two conclusions must be true, either that Alexander hurt himself badly by drinking so many days in the month or that those who wrote these things lie.'[17]

Alexander was not a victim to alcoholic abuse in the sense that it became the pattern to his life and ruled his actions.[18] However, he drank a lot and if the above account is true, he would often spend a day or two recovering. Alcohol was often the cause of serious miscalculations. It also shows more than recklessness given his position as king and the leader of the army for the most part in hostile territory. Clear thinking was necessary, for unclouded decisions had to be made. Reason had to be foremost in the leader's mind, and emotion needed to be kept at a distance for the good of the entire army.

Cleitus's murder is hardly an example of a king able to put reason over emotion (see Chapter 10). His excessive drinking that night muddled his thoughts and allowed rage and emotional turmoil to boil over to an uncontrollable level. The effect of Alexander's drinking habits on his army is ultimately unknown but alcoholic stupor and drink-induced murders are not endearing qualities in any man, and even less in a king and commander.

We have come quite a way from our dashing, heroic king. What, though, of the image of him as the philosophical idealist, trying to unite his people in one common race? That truly would make him great. Once again, though, the reality does not reflect the appearance when the legend is uncovered. Alexander had no such policy to unite the different peoples of his empire.[19] Perhaps, even, the implications of his acts did not fully occur to him. Plutarch, writing in a much later period, thought that he had founded new cities, for example, as a means of spreading Greek civilisation in 'barbarian' lands. That is not the case, for military considerations came first and culture second (see above).

The mixed population, Greeks and natives, might well form a bond, but not one intended to be the brotherhood of man. The same is true of the foreign youths who were trained in Macedonian customs and tactics. They might well learn to speak Greek and to like Euripides, but they were trained to join the Macedonian army and to fight. Alexander turned to foreigners, for example Iranian mounted archers, because his army needed them, and they had an expertise that his own men did not.

He also needed locals in his administration because of their linguistic expertise and integrating foreigners into his administration and army was part of a policy to ensure the smooth running of the empire and to keep the army at full strength. The attempt to introduce *proskynesis*, the mass marriage at Susa and the prayer for harmony between the races after the banquet at Opis, were all 'one-off' events, and had nothing to do with any unity of mankind.

Alexander might well have found administering his empire daunting, but he would not even have dreamed about the impossible task of bringing everyone together in a common harmony.

There is no denying that Alexander was influential, and throughout the following centuries he continued to be influential as history gave us Alexander the Great. We can read and study about him with the benefit of our hindsight, but he has not affected *us* as much as the peoples he conquered. Moreover, he did not affect them only in his own time. He continues to do so today, as is seen in the popular tales and folklore of the regions that he conquered or through which he travelled. One has only to read the recent fascinating account by Michael Wood (*In the Footsteps of Alexander*), for example, to see how and why Alexander is remembered today. Native writers told of his exploits from the mediaeval period onwards. Firdowsi, from Tus in eastern Iran, included Alexander in his *Shahnama* ('Book of Kings'), which was completed in AD 1010. Tale tellers perform it today (see Plate 22).

The portrayal is often not good. The Zoroastrians in Iran are the descendants of the Persians of Alexander's time. They still practise the religion that was founded by Zoroaster in about 1500 BC. Michael Wood travelled to Yazd in the Great Salt Desert to meet them. When he asked about Alexander one told him:

'He may be the Great to the Greeks and to you Europeans, but we call him a devil. This is because he burned down our temples, killed our priests; he forcibly made our children marry Greeks to make them lose their identity; he destroyed our most precious holy book, our Bible, the *Avesta* .... So, why should we call him the Great? To us he is a devil. For this reason we call him Iskander Gujaste. Alexander the Accursed.'[20]

The reference to Alexander's marrying their children to Greeks is to the mass marriage at Susa (see Chapter 12).

Since Alexander affected these people the most, would it be better for us to start calling him Alexander the Accursed?

16

Philip's Ghost

We can and must praise Philip II for what he did. He turned Macedonia from a backwater into an imperial power, one in which the people had a keen sense of nationalistic pride. He centralised the monarchy and so gave the state a unity that it had never felt before. He developed its mining, agriculture and trade, so that the people thrived. The economy boomed, and Macedonian coinage quickly became the strongest in Europe. He revolutionised its army, and created the premier fighting force that allowed Alexander to achieve what he did. He established a dynasty that allowed his son to succeed without any threats from invaders or pretenders. His policy combined diplomacy and military prowess. At the end of his reign, Macedonia, with Greece and the peoples to its north, west and east under its control, was already looking to Persia for its next imperial venture.

Philip was really the king behind Alexander, for the latter could not have achieved what he did without his father's great accomplishments. Alexander's reign, the empire he forged and the world he left behind, would have been utterly different. He may have been known in history as simply Alexander III of Macedonia. It is significant that Diodorus Siculus calls Philip 'the greatest of the kings in Europe' (16.95.1), yet he does say that Alexander achieved greater deeds than any king.

How different was Alexander's legacy from that of Philip. When Alexander died, the Macedonian empire was vast, and looked to grow larger as the invasion of Arabia was underway. Yet in Macedonia itself, nationalistic pride was probably at its lowest. Alexander had improved the economy of his state, and had encouraged trade and commerce in his empire by breaking down previously existing frontiers. Yet his death signalled the collapse of the dynasty. For over two decades, his successors – his generals and Eumenes, his secretary – would battle for power. Most would die in the process, as the empire became the scene of bloody warfare, and the Macedonian throne a symbolic bone of contention. When it was over, Macedonia was a shadow of its former self, and the empire as a single unit had ceased to exist. In its place were the Hellenistic king-doms, but that of Macedonia played a significantly weaker role than, say, Egypt or Syria.

Yet, we must not forget that Alexander was the most powerful individual of his time. For sheer distance covered, places subdued, battle strategy and breadth of vision he deserves praise. His plans for further conquest were well under way, ultimately ending with his establishment of a king-dom of Asia, perhaps with its capital at Babylon. Nor must we forget that his campaign was not a purely offensive and destructive one. He took with him a team of scientists and recorders that gathered, at his request, all sorts of information on the topography, geography, flora and fauna of the regions to which he went. His stimulation of trade and expansion of Greek civilisation were continued in the Hellenistic period. So too was his style of ruling. Without him, the Hellenistic kings could not have accomplished what they did, at least in those crucial few generations after his death as they worked to establish their power. And the Hellenistic period was a brilliant age in world history.

Where, then, did Alexander go wrong? The answer lies in Philip's ghost. Alexander strove to emulate his father in all matters and prove himself a worthy heir. This is not a novel argument in Alexander studies, but it is one that I think needs to be considered to a far greater extent than it has been. Alexander's desire and then the personal need to outstrip his father, regardless of the cost to the empire, however, replaced emulation. Here, his nature as a human being pushed his duty as a king into the background. Military conquest was one way, but simple conquest was not enough: Alexander had to outdo Philip in other areas. Deification while alive was the most obvious way. Everything else – his motives and actions – became subordinated to his drive towards self-deification. From that came his eventual and genuine total belief in his own divinity. Therein lies Alexander's real failing: his attempt to excel Philip at all costs that went out of control and fed his belief that he was a god on earth.

At Opis in 324 Alexander gave a passionate speech to his mutinous army in which he praised his father's achievements. He followed this, significantly, with a long harangue that Philip's deeds and services were small compared to his own (Arrian 7.9.2–10.7). This is not inconsistent with his attitude to Philip because it seems hard to believe that Alexander did not exhort his men with tales of Macedonia's greatness thanks to Philip and himself. Moreover, he was the one speaking of Philip, and hence in control of the situation. However, his true attitude to his father was revealed in his earlier, irrational murder of Cleitus in 328 for praising Philip above him.

Philip remained in spirit with Alexander throughout his reign. It must have been psychologically hard for Alexander, though, to measure up to and excel Philip in every action he performed, good or bad. Divinity was the escape. However, in the process, Alexander lost the most important thing a king needed: the loyalty of his own people. By the time he died, he had faced two army mutinies, numerous conspiracies against his life, and the discontent of the people in Macedonia. Almost everything that Philip had fought for lay in ruins.

Does Alexander deserve to be called 'Great' or should we side with the Persians that he is Alexander the Accursed? He was, after all, responsible for the deaths of tens of thousands of his own men and for the unnecessary wholesale slaughter of native peoples. How 'great' is a king who prefers constant warfare over consolidating conquered territories? Or who, through his own recklessness, often endangered his own life and the lives of his men? Or who drank too much and could not control a violent temper that on occasion led him to murder? And who towards the end of his life believed he was a god?

These are questions posed by our standards of today, but we can ask them of Alexander because he himself invites us to do so. His legend began in his own lifetime, at his own doing. He was responsible for the exaggerated reports of his battles, and for the stories that made him out to be great. He wanted posterity to know about him in this way, and posterity took him up throughout the centuries. The same posterity that can add to him can also question him, and even take away from him.

Alexander allowed himself to be haunted by his father. He was after all only a man, and he had a lot of baggage to carry, especially from the last days of his father. Psychologically, the warrior king fell victim to megalomania given his spectacular successes and the need to succeed, and then to a belief in his personal divinity. His mortality, however, was proved at Babylon on 10 June 323. How difficult his life must have been as he tried to reconcile Alexander the man and the god in his own mind. We can only try to understand how he must have thought and what he must have thought. The mental stress and the paranoia that he developed from it, especially from the conspiracies directed against him, go some way to explaining his behaviour, and the way he dealt with critics.

At the same time, despite all this negativity and criticism, one cannot help but admire Alexander. Perhaps the real source of his greatness lies not in his military achievements or indeed in anything he did, but in his complexity as a human being. He comprises within himself both the good and the evil that characterise most human beings, but on a scale a hundred times larger than life.

There is no consensus of opinion on Alexander. There never can be, and perhaps there ought not to be. Ultimately, does it even really matter? The fascination with him and his longevity through the centuries and in popular folklore show the impact he had. This impact was not only on his own state in his own time but was also on most of the known world. That is perhaps the true mark of his greatness: the facts that, unlike so many figures in history, he has endured, and that he is as fresh today as when he lived.

Alexander the Great or Alexander the Accursed: how do you like your Alexander?

Notes

1 Introduction: Uncovering the Legend

1. Plutarch, *Alexander* 64.9. See Chapter 1 for the background to this question.

2 Alexander's Inheritance

1. See G.T. Griffith, 'The Macedonian Background', *Greece and Rome* 12 (1965): 125–39, J.R. Hamilton, 'Alexander's Early Life', *Greece and Rome* 12 (1965): 117–24, and more on the influence of Philip, Ian Worthington, 'Alexander, Philip, and the Macedonian Background', in J. Roisman (ed.), *Brill's Companion to Alexander the Great* (Leiden, 2003), 69–98.

2. See, for example, E. Badian, 'Greeks and Macedonians', in B. Barr-Sharrar and E.N. Borza (eds), *Macedonia and Greece in Late Classical and Early Hellenistic Times* (Washington DC, 1982), 33–51, E.N. Borza, *In the Shadow of Olympus: The Emergence of Macedon* (Princeton, 1990), 77–97 and 'Greeks and Macedonians in the Age of Alexander. The Source Traditions', in W.R. Wallace and E.M. Harris (eds), *Transitions to Empire. Essays in Honor of E. Badian* (Norman, OK, 1996), 122–39.

3. See Herodotus, *Histories* 5.22.

4. On the geography and natural resources, see E.N. Borza, 'The Natural Resources of Early Macedonia', in W.L. Adams and E.N. Borza (eds), *Philip II, Alexander the Great, and the Macedonian Heritage* (Lanham, MD, 1982), 1–20, Borza, *In the Shadow of Olympus*, 25–57, and J.R. Ellis, *Philip II and Macedonian Imperialism* (London, 1976), 28–34.

5. On Alexander's death, Ptolemy of Alorus became regent of Perdiccas until 365. On these kings, see, for example, Ellis, *Philip II and Macedonian Imperialism*, 40–4, N.G.L. Hammond and G.T. Griffith, *A History of Macedonia* 2 (Oxford, 1979), 137–50 and 167–88, Borza, *In the Shadow of Olympus*, 161–97.

6. On Philip's reign in detail, see Ellis, *Philip II and Macedonian Imperialism*, G.L. Cawkwell, *Philip of Macedon* (London, 1976), Hammond and Griffith, *A History of Macedonia* 2, 203–698, N.G.L. Hammond, *Philip of Macedon* (London, 1994), I. Worthington, *Philip II, The King behind Alexander the Great* (forthcoming).

7. On Philip's diplomacy, see now T.T.B. Ryder, 'The Diplomatic Skills of Philip II,' in Ian Worthington (ed.), *Ventures Into Greek History: Essays in Honour of N.G.L. Hammond* (Oxford, 1994), 228–57.

8. See further, N.G.L. Hammond, *The Macedonian State* (Oxford, 1989), 21–4, 62–70, 166–70.

9. On the army reforms, see further, Hammond and Griffith, *A History of Macedonia* 2, 405–49.

10. On this period, see John Buckler, *The Theban Hegemony* (Cambridge, MA, 1980).

11. On women in the reign of Philip, see E. Carney, *Women and Monarchy in Macedonia* (Norman, OK, 2000), 51–81.

12. On Demosthenes, see the essays in Ian Worthington (ed.), *Demosthenes: Statesman and Orator* (London and New York, 2000).

13. By 'Macedon' I mean the state (the political entity) as opposed to 'Macedonia' (the geographical area).

14. See further, C. Roebuck, 'The Settlement of Philip II with the Greek States in 338 BC', *Classical Philology* 43 (1948): 73–92, Hammond and Griffith, *A History of Macedonia* 2, 623–46.

15. Diodorus Siculus 16.60.4–5.

16. P.A. Brunt, 'The Aims of Alexander', *Greece & Rome* 12 (1965): 205–15, argues that Alexander simply took over the invasion plan from Philip. E.A. Fredricksmeyer, 'On the Final Aims of Philip II', in W. L. Adams and E. N. Borza (eds), *Philip II, Alexander the Great, and the Macedonian Heritage* (Lanham, MD, 1982), 85–98, argues that Philip had more ambitious plans, which included an absolute monarchy and his own deification. If so, then Alexander's inheritance was not a simple panhellenic invasion of Persia.

17. See further, H. Montgomery, 'The Economic Revolution of Philip II – Myth or Reality?', *Symbolae Osloenses* 60 (1985): 37–47, N.G.L. Hammond, 'Philip's Innovations in the Macedonian Economy', *Symbolae Osloenses* 70 (1995): 22–9.

18. Diodorus Siculus 16.8.6–8.

19. Theopompus, *FGrH* 115 F 224; cf. Diodorus Siculus 16.53.3.

20. Onesicritus, *FGrH* 134 F 2 = Plutarch, *Alexander* 15.2.

21. See further, E. Badian, 'The Death of Philip II', *Phoenix* 17 (1963): 244–50, J. Rufus Fears, 'Pausanias, the Assassin of Philip II', *Athenaeum* 53 (1975): 111–35, and J.R. Ellis, 'The Assassination of Philip II', in H.J. Dell (ed.), *Ancient Macedonian Studies in Honour of C.F. Edson* (Institute for Balkan Studies, Thessaloniki, 1981), 99–137.

22. Diodorus Siculus 16.95.1.

3 Alexander's Boyhood

1. See A.D. Tronson, 'Satyrus the Peripatetic and the Marriages of Philip II', *Journal of Hellenic Studies* 104 (1984): 116–26.

2. Hegesias, *FGrH* 142 F 3 = Plutarch, *Alexander* 3.5–9.

3. See Plutarch, *Alexander* 2 for the following stories in full.

4. See, for example, M. Bieber, 'The Portraits of Alexander', *Greece and Rome* 12 (1965), 183–188 and A. Stewart, 'Alexander in Greek and Roman Art', in J. Roisman (ed.), *Brill's Companion to Alexander the Great* (Leiden, 2003), 31–66.

5. Ephippus, *FGrH* 126 F 5 = Athenaeus 12.537e.

6. Onesicritus, *FGrH* 134 F 38 = Plutarch, *Alexander* 8.2, with T.S. Brown, 'Alexander's Book Order (Plut. *Alex.* 8)', *Historia* 16 (1967): 359–68.

7. Exactly what Aristotle taught Alexander is unknown, but see J.R. Hamilton, *Plutarch, Alexander: A Commentary* (Oxford, 1969), 17–19.

8. Plutarch, *Alexander* 9.1.

9. Plutarch, *Alexander* 9.2–3.

10. In a speech of 330 called *On The Crown*, at Section 67.

11. See further, E. Carney, 'Women in Alexander's Court', in J. Roisman (ed.), *Brill's Companion to Alexander the Great* (Leiden, 2003), 227–52.

12. Plutarch, *Alexander* 5.7.

13. Arrian 3.6.5.

14. For more on this, see the arguments of E. Fredricksmeyer, 'Alexander and Philip: Emulation and Resentment', *Classical Journal* 85 (1990): 300–15.

15. *Anonymous History of Alexander, FGrH* 151 F 10.

4 King at Last

1. Arrian 1.25.2, Plutarch, *Moralia* 327c.

2. On the time-frame, see J. R. Ellis, 'The First Months of Alexander's Reign', in B. Barr-Sharrar and E.N. Borza (eds), *Macedonia and Greece in Late Classical and Early Hellenistic Times* (Washington DC, 1982), 69–73.

3. See M. Andronikos, *Vergina: The Royal Tombs* (Athens, 1984), 'Some Reflections on the Macedonian Tombs', *Annual of the British School at Athens* 82 (1987): 1–16, and 'The Finds from the Royal Tombs at Vergina', *Proceedings of the British Academy* 65 (1979): 355–67.

4. J.H. Musgrave, R.A.H Neave and A.J.N.W. Prag, 'The Skull from Tomb II at Vergina: King Philip II of Macedon', *Journal of Hellenic Studies* 104 (1984): 60–78.

5. N.G.L. Hammond, 'Philip's Tomb in Historical Context', *Greek, Roman & Byzantine Studies* 19 (1978): 331–50.

6. For example, P.W. Lehman, 'The So-called Tomb of Philip II: A Different

Interpretation', *American Journal of Archaeology* 84 (1980): 527–31 and 'The So-called Tomb of Philip II: An Addendum', *American Journal of Archaeology* 86 (1982): 437–42 and E.N. Borza, 'The Royal Macedonian Tombs and the Paraphernalia of Alexander', *Phoenix* 41 (1987): 105–21.

7. See most recently, Olga Palagia, 'Hephaestion's Pyre and the Royal Hunt of Alexander', in A.B. Bosworth and E.J. Baynham (eds), *Alexander the Great in Fact and Fiction* (Oxford, 2000), 167–206.

8. P.A. Brunt, 'The Aims of Alexander', *Greece & Rome* 12 (1965): 205–15, argues that Alexander's invasion was merely his inheritance from Philip. E.A. Fredricksmeyer, 'On the Final Aims of Philip II', in W.L. Adams and E.N. Borza (eds), *Philip II, Alexander the Great, and the Macedonian Heritage* (Lanham, MD, 1982), 85–98 and 'Alexander the Great and the Kingship of Asia', in A.B. Bosworth and E.J. Baynham (eds), *Alexander the Great in Fact and Fiction* (Oxford, 2000), 136–66, argues that Philip wanted to establish an absolute monarchy and his own deification. If true, then Alexander's inheritance and invasion were, therefore, not for purely panhellenic reasons, but personal ones.

9. On the revolt and Alexander's actions, see Ian Worthington, 'Alexander's Destruction of Thebes', in W. Heckel and L. Tritle (eds) *Crossroads of History. The Age of Alexander* (Claremont, CA, 2003), pp. 65–86.

10. Arrian 1.7.5.

11. Diodorus Siculus 17.14.4, Plutarch, *Alexander* 11.12.

12. Hegesias, *FGrH* 142 F 12.

13. Aristobulus, *FGrH* 139 F 2b = Plutarch, *Moralia* 259d–260d.

14. Aristobulus, *FGrH* 139 F 3 = Plutarch, *Demosthenes* 23.4–6.

5 The Very Gates of Asia

1. In his speech *Against Ctesiphon*, delivered in 330, at Section 164.

2. See further, Ian Worthington, 'Demosthenes' (In)activity during the Reign of Alexander the Great', in Ian Worthington (ed.), *Demosthenes: Statesman and Orator* (London and New York, 2000), 90–113.

3. On Antipater (including his role in the aftermath of Alexander's death), see further, E. Baynham, 'Antipater, Manager of Kings', in Ian Worthington (ed.), *Ventures into Greek History: Essays in Honour of N.G. L. Hammond* (Oxford, 1994), 331–56.

4. Onesicritus, *FGrH* 134 F 2 = Plutarch, *Alexander* 15.2, *Moralia* 327d.

5. See further, P. Green, *Alexander of Macedon* (Harmondsworth, 1974), 155–6.

6. See D. Engels, *Alexander the Great and the Logistics of the Macedonian Army* (Berkeley and Los Angeles, 1978), 146–7 (Table 4).

7. See on his army generally, R.D. Milns, 'The Army of Alexander the Great', in

E. Badian (ed.), *Alexandre le Grand, Image et Réalité*, Fondation Hardt, *Entretiens* 22 (Geneva, 1976), 87–136.

8. Plutarch, *Alexander* 16.

9. A.M. Devine, 'A Pawn-Sacrifice at the Battle of the Granicus: The Origins of a Favorite Stratagem of Alexander the Great', *Ancient World* 18 (1988): 3–20.

10. N.G.L. Hammond, 'The Battle of the Granicus River', *Journal of Hellenic Studies* 100 (1980): 73–88.

11. Aristobulus, *FGrH* 139 F 5 = Plutarch, *Alexander* 16.15.

12. Plutarch, *Alexander* 16.

13. Not all saw his action as rash, for Diodorus Siculus (17.23.1) cryptically refers to 'those who say that Alexander's strategic conception was sound when he dismissed his fleet'.

14. Callisthenes, *FGrH* 124 F 31.

15. Aristobulus, *FGrH* 139 F 7a = Arrian 2.3.

16. Cf. E.A. Fredricksmeyer, 'Alexander, Midas, and the oracle at Gordium', *Classical Philology* 56 (1961) 160–8.

17. Cf. A.B. Bosworth, *Conquest and Empire, The Reign of Alexander the Great* (Cambridge, 1988), 53.

6   A Bridge of Corpses

1. *Anonymous History of Alexander, FGrH* 148 F 44.

2. A.M. Devine, 'The Strategies of Alexander the Great and Darius III in the Issus Campaign (333 BC)', *Ancient World* 12 (1985): 25–38 and 'Grand Tactics at the Battle of Issus', *Ancient World* 12 (1985): 39–59.

3. Chares, *FGrH* 125 F 6 = Plutarch, *Moralia* 341c.

4. See further, A. Cohen, *The Alexander Mosaic. Stories of Victory and Defeat* (Cambridge, 1997).

5. Ptolemy, *FGrH* 138 F 6 = Arrian 2.11.8.

6. On Darius see now E. Badian, 'Darius III', *Harvard Studies in Classical Philology* 100 (2000): 241–68.

7. Aristobulus, *FGrH* 139 F 11 = Plutarch, *Alexander* 21.7–9.

8. Ptolemy *FGrH* 138 F 7 = Arrian 2.12.3–6.

9. See further, P. Romane, 'Alexander's Siege of Tyre', *Ancient World* 16 (1987), 79–90.

10. Chares, *FGrH* 125 F 7 = Plutarch, *Alexander* 24.5–9.

11. See further, P. Romane, 'Alexander's Siege of Gaza', *Ancient World* 18 (1988): 21–30.

12. Hegesias, *FGrH* 142, fragment from an untitled work (no. 5).

7 Son of Ra, Son of Zeus

1. S Burstein, 'Pharaoh Alexander: A Scholarly Myth', *Ancient Society* 22 (1991): 139–45.

2. Aristobulus, *FGrH* 139 FF 13–15 = Arrian 3.3–4.

3. See A.B. Bosworth, 'Alexander and Ammon', in K. Kinzl (ed.), *Greece and the Ancient Mediterranean in History and Prehistory* (Berlin, 1977), 51–75 and D. Kienast, 'Alexander, Zeus, and Ammon', in W. Will and J. Heinrichs (eds), *Zu Alexander d. Gr., Festschrift G. Wirth* (Amsterdam, 1988), 309–34. See further, Chapter 14.

4. Aristobulus, *FGrH* 139 FF 13–15 = Arrian 3.3–4.

5. Callisthenes, *FGrH* 124 F 14a = Strabo 17.1.43.

6. Aristobulus, *FGrH* 139 FF 13–15 = Arrian 3.3–4.

7. Callisthenes, *FGrH* 124 F 14b = Plutarch, *Alexander* 27.3–4.

8. Ptolemy, *FGrH* 138 F 8 = Arrian 3.3.5.

9. Aristobulus, *FGrH* 139 FF 13–15 = Arrian 3.3.

10. M. Wood, *In the Footsteps of Alexander the Great* (Berkeley and Los Angeles, 1997), 75.

11. Callisthenes, *FGrH* 124 F 14a = Strabo 17.1.43.

12. Ptolemy, *FGrH* 138 F 9 = Arrian 3.4.5.

13. *Anonymous History of Alexander, FGrH* 151 F 11.

8 Lord of Asia

1. A.J. Sachs and H. Hunger, *Astronomical Diaries and Related Texts from Babylonia 1* (Vienna, 1988).

2. Callisthenes, *FGrH* 124 F 36 = Plutarch, *Alexander* 33.1.

3. See further, A.M. Devine, 'Grand Tactics at Gaugamela', *Phoenix* 29 (1975): 374–85 and 'The Battle of Gaugamela: A Tactical and Source-Critical Study', *Ancient World* 13 (1986): 87–115.

4. Callisthenes, *FGrH* 124 F 37 = Plutarch, *Alexander* 33.9–11.

5. See further, E. Badian, 'The Administration of the Empire', *Greece and Rome* 12 (1965): 166–82 and W.E. Higgins, 'Aspects of Alexander's Imperial Administration: Some Modern Methods and Views Reviewed', *Athenaeum* 58 (1980): 29–52.

6. Chares, *FGrH* F 2 = Athenaeus 12.514e–f.

7. See in detail, E. Badian, 'Agis III: Revisions and Reflections', in Ian Worthington (ed.), *Ventures Into Greek History. Essays in Honour of N.G.L. Hammond* (Oxford, 1994), 258–92.

8. Diodorus Siculus 17.70.

9. On the destruction see, for example, E.N. Borza, 'Fire from Heaven: Alexander at Persepolis', *Classical Philology* 67 (1972): 233–45 and N.G.L.

Hammond, 'The Archaeological and Literary Evidence for the Burning of the Persepolis Palace', *Classical Quarterly* 42 (1992): 358–64.

9 Conquest and Conspiracy

1. Onesicritus, *FGrH* 134 F 5 = Strabo 11.11.3.
2. See in more detail on Alexander's campaigns, F.L. Holt, *Alexander the Great and Bactria* (Leiden, 1988); cf. his *Thundering Zeus: The Making of Hellenistic Bactria* (Berkeley and Los Angeles, 1999).
3. On this organ by now, see R.A. Lock, 'The Macedonian Army Assembly in the Time of Alexander the Great', *Classical Philology* 72 (1977): 91–107.
4. Ptolemy, *FGrH* 138 F 13 = Arrian 3.26.
5. Much ink has been spilled on the so-called conspiracy of Philotas. See for example, E. Badian, 'The Death of Parmenio', *Transactions of the American Philological Association* 91 (1960): 324–38, W. Heckel, 'The Conspiracy against Philotas', *Phoenix* 31 (1977): 9–21, W.Z. Rubinsohn, 'The "Philotas Affair" – A Reconsideration', *Ancient Macedonia* 2 (Institute for Balkan Studies, Thessaloniki, 1977): 409–20. See too Badian's discussion of the conspiracies against Alexander: 'Conspiracies', in A.B. Bosworth and E.J. Baynham (eds), *Alexander the Great in Fact and Fiction* (Oxford, 2000), 50–95.
6. Ptolemy, *FGrH* 138 F 13 = Arrian 3.26.
7. Ptolemy, *FGrH* 138 F 14 = Arrian 3.29.6–30.5.

10 Bactria and Sogdiana

1. The chronology of these months of Alexander's campaign is controversial; I follow A.B. Bosworth, 'A Missing Year in the History of Alexander the Great', *Journal of Hellenic Studies* 101 (1981): 17–39.
2. See E. Carney, 'The Death of Clitus', *Greek, Roman, and Byzantine Studies* 22 (1981): 149–60.
3. Curtius 8.4.27; cf. A.B. Bosworth 'Alexander and the Iranians', *Journal of Hellenic Studies* 100 (1980): 10–11.
4. Chares, *FGrH* 125 F 14b = Arrian 4.12.3–5.
5. Aristobulus, *FGrH* 139 F 30 = Arrian 4.13.5.
6. See E. Badian's discussion of the conspiracies against Alexander: 'Conspiracies', in A.B. Bosworth and E.J. Baynham (eds), *Alexander the Great in Fact and Fiction* (Oxford, 2000), 50–95.
7. Ptolemy, *FGrH* 138 F 17 = Arrian 4.14.3.
8. See further, E.N. Borza, 'Anaxagoras and Callisthenes: Academic Intrigue at

Alexander's Court', in H.J. Dell (ed.), *Ancient Macedonian Studies in Honour of C.F. Edson* (Institute for Balkan Studies, Thessaloniki, 1981), 73–86.

9. Nearchus, *FGrH* 133 F 11 = Arrian, *Indica* 6–17.

11 India

1. On Alexander's Indian campaign, see in detail A.B. Bosworth, *Alexander and the East* (Oxford, 1996); cf. A.B. Bosworth, 'The Indian Campaigns, 327–325 BC' in J. Roisman (ed.), *Brill's Companion to Alexander the Great* (Leiden, 2003), 59–168. See too A.K. Narain, 'Alexander and India', *Greece and Rome* 12 (1965): 155–65 and A.B. Bosworth, 'The Indian Satrapies under Alexander the Great', *Antichthon* 17 (1983): 37–46; cf. E. Badian, 'The Administration of the Empire', *Greece and Rome* 12 (1965): 166–82.

2. Aristobulus, *FGrH* 139 F 35 = Strabo 15.1.17–19.

3. Archelaus, *FGrH* 123 F 1 = Solinus 52.18–23.

4. Nearchus, *FGrH* 133 F 11 = Arrian, *Indica* 16–17.

5. See further, Richard Stoneman, 'Who are the Brahmans?', *Classical Quarterly* 44 (1994): 500–10 and A.B. Bosworth, 'Calanus and the Brahman Opposition', in W. Will (ed.), *Alexander der Grosse: Eine Welteroberung und ihr Hintergrund* (Bonn, 1998), 173–203.

6. Aristobulus, *FGrH* 139 F 42 = Strabo 15.62.

7. Archelaus *FGrH* 123 F 7 = Plutarch, *Moralia* 1 5.

8. See further, A.M. Devine, 'The Battle of Hydaspes; A Tactical and Source-Critical Study', *Ancient World* 16 (1987): 91–113.

9. Onesicritus, *FGrH* 134 F 19 = Plutarch, *Alexander* 60.1, 5–7.

10. Chares, *FGrH* 125 F 18 = Aulus Gellius, *Attic Nights* 5.2.1–5.

11. See further, Bosworth, *Alexander and the East*, 6–8.

12. An alternative view is put forward by P.O. Spann, 'Alexander at the Beas: Fox in a Lion's Skin', in Frances B. Titchener and Richard F. Moorton Jr. (eds), *The Eye Expanded. Life and the Arts in Greco-Roman Antiquity* (Berkeley, 1999), 62–74. Spann argues that Alexander himself orchestrated the mutiny in order to save face because he did not wish to go further into India. I find this view hard to accept given Alexander's plans.

13. Although note E. Carney, 'Macedonians and Mutiny: Discipline and Indiscipline in the Army of Philip and Alexander', *Classical Philology* 91 (1996): 19–44.

14. On Alexander's involvement in Coenus' death, see Ian Worthington, 'Alexander the Great and the "Interests of Historical Accuracy": A Reply', *Ancient History Bulletin* 13.4 (1999): 136–40; *contra* F.L. Holt, 'The Death of Coenus', *Ancient History Bulletin* 14.1–2 (2000): 49–55.

15. Ptolemy, *FGrH* 138 F 25 = Arrian 6.10.1.

16. Aristobulus, *FGrH* 139 F 46 = Plutarch, *Moralia* 341c.

17. Nearchus, *FGrH* 133 F 23 = Strabo 15.66–67.

18. Note also that Michael Wood had a tough time too, and this with food, water and modern transport: *In the Footsteps of Alexander the Great* (Berkeley and Los Angeles, 1997), 214–15.

19. Aristobulus, *FGrH* 139 F 49a = Arrian 6.24.

20. Aristobulus, *FGrH* 139 F 49a = Arrian 6.24.

12 'We'll Say Goodbye in Babylon'

1. Cleitarchus, *FGrH* 137 F 30 = Athenaeus 13.586c–d.

2. Onesicritus, *FGrH* 134 F 18 = Aelian, *Varra Historia* 17.6.

3. There is no translation of this in the Penguin Classics series, but there is a translation by P.A. Brunt in the second volume of the Loeb Classical Library edition of Arrian (Cambridge, MA and London, 1983).

4. Onesicritus, *FGrH* 134 F 18 = Lucian, *De mort. Peregr.* 25.

5. Nearchus, *FGrH* 133 F 4 = Arrian 7.3.6.

6. Chares, *FGrH* 125 F 19a = Athenaeus 10.437a–b.

7. See E. Bickerman, 'La lettre d'Alexandre le Grand aux bannis Grecs', *Revue des Études Anciennes* 42 (1940): 25–35 and E. Badian, 'Harpalus', *Journal of Hellenic Studies* 81 (1961): 25–31, for example.

8. Diodorus Siculus 18.8.4, from Hieronymus of Cardia.

9. At 17.111.1.

10. Chares, *FGrH* 125 F 4 = Athenaeus 12.538b–539a.

11. E. Badian, 'Alexander the Great and the Unity of Mankind', *Historia* 7 (1958): 425–44 and A.B. Bosworth, 'Alexander and the Iranians', *Journal of Hellenic Studies* 100 (1980): 1–21.

12. Aristobulus, *FGrH* 139 F 55 = Arrian 7.19.3–6.

13. Arrian 7.11.9.

14. In a speech of 323 by Hyperides, *Against Demosthenes*, at Section 31.

15. Plutarch, *Moralia* 219e.

16. Ephippus, *FGrH* 126 F 5 = Athenaeus 12.538b.

17. Plutarch, *Alexander* 72.4.

13 Death and Disorder

1. Aristobulus, *FGrH* 139 F 54 = Arrian 7.16.1.

2. Aristobulus, *FGrH* 139 F 58 = Arrian 7.24.1–3.

3. Aristobulus, *FGrH* 139 F 55 = Arrian 7.22.

4. Aristus, *FGrH* 143 F 2 = Arrian 7.15.5.

5. Plutarch, *Moralia* 219e.

6. See further, G.L. Cawkwell, 'The Deification of Alexander the Great: A Note', in Ian Worthington (ed.), *Ventures into Greek History: Essays in Honour of N.G. L. Hammond* (Oxford, 1994), 293–306 and E. Badian, 'Alexander the Great between Two Thrones and Heaven: Variations on an Old Theme', in A. Small (ed.), *Subject and Ruler: The Cult of the Ruling Power in Classical Antiquity* (Ann Arbor, 1996), 11–26.

7. Cf. N.G.L. Hammond, *The Genius of Alexander the Great* (London, 1997), 195.

8. See further, E. Badian, 'Harpalus', *Journal of Hellenic Studies* 81 (1961): 16–25, and in detail, Ian Worthington, *A Historical Commentary on Dinarchus. Rhetoric and Conspiracy in Later Fourth-Century Athens* (Ann Arbor, 1992), 41–77.

9. There were ten, but we have only those by Dinarchus and by Hyperides: translated in Ian Worthington, *Greek Orators 2, Dinarchus and Hyperides* (Warminster, 1999).

10. M.N. Tod, *Greek Historical Inscriptions 2* (Oxford, 1948), no. 202. There is a translation in P.E. Harding, *From the End of the Peloponnesian War to the Battle of Ipsus* (Cambridge, 1985), no. 122, pp. 150–2.

11. Nicoboule, *FGrH* 127 F 1 = Athenaeus 12.434c.

12. *FGrH* 117 F 3b = Plutarch, *Alexander* 76–77.1; cf. Arrian 7.25.1–26.3.

13. See, for example, A.B. Bosworth, 'The Death of Alexander the Great: Rumour and Propaganda', *Classical Quarterly* 21 (1971): 112–136.

14. See further A.B. Bosworth, 'Ptolemy and the Will of Alexander', in A.B. Bosworth and E.J. Baynham (eds), *Alexander the Great in Fact and Fiction* (Oxford, 2000), 207–41, arguing that Ptolemy forged the will in probably 309/8 to help his own political ambitions and to consolidate his power in the struggles with the other generals.

15. Ptolemy, *FGrH* 138 F 30 = Arrian 7.26.3.

14 Man and God

1. Plutarch, *Alexander* 64.9.

2. Ephippus, *FGrH* 126 F 5 = Athenaeus 12.537e.

3. See too L. Edmunds, 'The Religiosity of Alexander', *Greek, Roman, and Byzantine Studies* 12 (1971): 363–91.

4. See further, E.A. Fredricksmeyer, 'Divine Honors for Philip II', *Transactions of the American Philological Association* 109 (1979): 39–61 and 'On the Background of the Ruler Cult', in H.J. Dell (ed.), *Ancient Macedonian Studies in Honour of C.F. Edson* (Thessaloniki, 1981), 145–56.

5. Cf. E. Badian, 'The Deification of Alexander the Great', in H.J. Dell (ed.), *Ancient Macedonian Studies in Honour of C.F. Edson* (Thessaloniki, 1981), 41.

6. E.A. Fredricksmeyer, 'Alexander's Religion and Divinity', in J. Roisman (ed.),

Brill's Companion to Alexander the Great (Leiden, 2003), 253–78, argues that it was not surprising that Alexander thought himself to be a god given his background, divine ancestry and visit to Siwah.

7. Aristobulus, *FGrH* 139 FF 13–15 = Arrian 3.3–4.

8. For the episode, see now G.L. Cawkwell, 'The Deification of Alexander the Great: A Note', in Ian Worthington (ed.), *Ventures into Greek History: Essays in Honour of N.G.L. Hammond* (Oxford, 1994), 293–306 and E. Badian, 'Alexander the Great between Two Thrones and Heaven: Variations on an Old Theme', in A. Small (ed.), *Subject and Ruler: The Cult of the Ruling Power in Classical Antiquity* (Ann Arbor, 1996), 11–26.

9. In Hyperides's speech *Against Demosthenes* at Section 31.

10. Aristobulus, *FGrH* 139 F 55 = Arrian 7.20.1.

15 Alexander: The Great

1. C.B. Welles, 'Alexander's Historical Achievement', *Greece and Rome* 12 (1965): 216–28 – the quote is from p. 228.

2. On Alexander's greatness see further, Ian Worthington, 'How "Great" was Alexander?', *Ancient History Bulletin* 13.2 (1999): 39–55, replied to by F.L. Holt, 'Alexander the Great Today: In the Interests of Historical Accuracy?', *Ancient History Bulletin* 13.3 (1999): 111–17. A large part of this chapter is adapted from my article, but I think this is necessary, given the image of Alexander that I present in this biography.

3. *Tranio*: Alexander the Great and Agathocles, so I've heard say, were the two foremost champion wonder-workers of the world. Why shouldn't I be a third; aren't I a famous and wonderful worker? (Plautus, *The Ghost Story*, 775–8).

4. See, for example, Major General J.F.C. Fuller, *The Generalship of Alexander the Great* (New Brunswick, 1960), A.R. Burn, 'The Generalship of Alexander', *Greece and Rome* 12 (1965): 140–54, A.M. Devine, 'Alexander the Great', in J. Hackett (ed.), *Warfare in the Ancient World* (New York, 1989), 104–29 and B. Strauss, 'Alexander: The Military Campaign', in J. Roisman (ed.), *Brill's Companion to Alexander the Great* (Leiden, 2003), 133–58.

5. On this, see in detail A.B. Bosworth, *Alexander and the East* (Oxford, 1996), 6–21.

6. A.B. Bosworth, *Conquest and Empire: The Reign of Alexander the Great* (Cambridge, 1988), 160. See also E. Carney, 'Macedonians and Mutiny: Discipline and Indiscipline in the Army of Philip and Alexander', *Classical Philology* 91 (1996): 19–44.

7. See further, A.B. Bosworth, 'Alexander the Great and the Decline of Macedon', *Journal of Hellenic Studies* 106 (1986): 1–12.

8. Aristobulus, *FGrH* 139 F 55 = Arrian 7.19.3–6.

9. See further, F.W. Mitchel, 'Athens in the Age of Alexander', *Greece and Rome* 12 (1965): 189–204 and 'Lykourgan Athens: 338–322', *Semple Lectures* 2 (Cincinnati, 1970).

10. Plutarch, *Moralia* 842e.

11. Diodorus Siculus 17.16.2.

12. Plutarch, *Moralia* 328e. See now P.M. Fraser, *Cities of Alexander the Great* (Oxford, 1996), who suggests that apart from Alexandria in Egypt Alexander founded only eight cities.

13. Ephippus, *FGrH* 126 F 5 = Athenaeus 12.537e.

14. N.G.L. Hammond and F.W. Walbank, *A History of Macedonia* 3 (Oxford, 1988), 105.

15. Ephippus, *FGrH* 126 F 1 = Athenaeus 3.120c–d.

16. *Ephemerides*, *FGrH* 117 F 2b = Athenaeus 10.434b.

17. *Ephemerides*, *FGrH* 117 F 2a = Aelian, *Varra Historia* 3.23.

18. See in expanded form, J.M. O'Brien, *Alexander the Great: The Invisible Enemy* (London, 1992).

19. See E. Badian, 'Alexander the Great and the Unity of Mankind', *Historia* 7 (1958): 425–44 and A.B. Bosworth, 'Alexander and the Iranians', *Journal of Hellenic Studies* 100 (1980): 1–21.

20. Michael Wood, *In the Footsteps of Alexander* (Berkeley and Los Angeles, 1997), 117.

Bibliographic Essay

Ancient sources

Some mention of the ancient source material on Alexander and of its problems has already been made in Chapter 1.

Only a small number of inscriptions, numismatic evidence and occasional comments in some of the Greek orators in Athens actually date from Alexander's reign. It is not until the late first century BC that we get the first connected narrative history of Alexander's reign by Diodorus Siculus, who worked in Rome during the period 30 to 8 BC. He wrote a *Universal History* in 40 books that started with the earliest, mythical times of Greece and went down to 54 BC. Only 15 of these books survive in any sort of entirety. Alexander's reign is in Book 17 and the first few sections of Book 18. A precise date is hard to fix for Quintus Curtius Rufus, but sometime in the mid to later first century AD seems the most likely. His *History of Alexander* was written in Latin in ten books, and almost all of it has survived. Arrian's *Anabasis of Alexander* was written in seven books, in the second century AD, and all have survived. Plutarch wrote a number of biographies of prominent Greeks and Romans, including Alexander, in the second century AD. Finally, Justin's history is an *epitome* of an earlier work by Pompeius Trogus (now lost), which he copied in either the second or the third century AD.

At first sight it appears puzzling why our histories of Alexander were written so much later – centuries later – than his reign. The answer is that accounts written in Alexander's time and in the generation or so after him have not survived in their entirety. The 'Alexander industry' began in his own lifetime with the account of the contemporary Callisthenes of Olynthus, and after Alexander's death its pace picked up considerably. Callisthenes was the official court historian. His account of the reign went down to at least 330 and perhaps a little further. He was executed in 327, but it is unknown if Alexander sanctioned a replacement.

Dozens of histories of his reign were written, but these 'primary' sources (those written in and around Alexander's time) were perhaps consigned to oblivion by the 'secondary' sources (Diodorus, Curtius, Pompeius Trogus, Plutarch and Arrian), who used them in their own accounts. Perhaps some of the primary sources treated only aspects of Alexander's reign rather than its entirety. For example, Anaxarchus of Lampsacus may only have written about the reign down to the Battle of Issus, and Ptolemy of Lagus seems only to have begun his account with the siege of Thebes in 335. Nearchus of Crete seems only to have recorded his great voyage along the Makran Coast, while Aristobulus of Cassandria seems particularly interested in geography, fauna and flora, as was Amyntas. Perhaps some focused more on Alexander as a man and explored the scandalous side of his life, such as Cleitarchus of Alexandria or Chares of Mytilene, for example. The answer is unknown.

Two other sources need to be mentioned. One is a combination of the primary and of the secondary: the *Alexander Romance*. It is possible that Callisthenes began it, but more likely is that it was written in the third century, and then rewritten and expanded over the following centuries. Its very name reveals its problem as what it contains is mostly unhistorical. However, as a stirring 'novel' of Alexander's reign and his time-travelling exploits it cannot be bettered.

The other source is Plutarch's treatise *On The Fortune or The Virtue of Alexander* of the second century AD. It is not meant to be a historical study or evaluation of Alexander, but one that explored the interface of a warrior king and an intellectual and idealist. Alexander in it is depicted as a man of action who set out to impose Greek civilisation on the peoples he conquered. Too much importance has been attached to it, however, as a proper treatment of Alexander.

We know of many of the primary works because the secondary authors quote parts of them, or at least refer to them. Over 400 quotations in fact. Some are extensive, others short, but all allow us to build a picture of sorts of the primary works. For example, some of the primary authors show a bias in favour of, and others against, Alexander. Aristobulus, for example, and especially Callisthenes wrote of Alexander in a most favourable light. Callisthenes may even have embellished his account to fit the image that the king was creating of himself; for example, the Pamphylian Sea performing obeisance before Alexander. That means we need to treat Callisthenes with some caution because of his potential bias. On the other hand, his execution in 327 may have been a turning point in the criticism of Alexander. He was Aristotle's nephew, and those sympathetic to his philosophy and shocked by his death might have been influenced to write critically of Alexander.

Ptolemy and Nearchus also accompanied Alexander on his campaigns. Ptolemy gives a very straightforward and sterile account of the reign, with the emphasis on the military side, as we would expect from a soldier. It is likely to be accurate because of the military attention to details, especially in the battles. Then again, Ptolemy wrote his account after Alexander's death in 323 and after he had seized Egypt. The lure of elevating his own exploits, especially over his fellow generals with whom he was then embroiled in warfare, must have been very strong. Human nature being what it is, we should expect him to magnify his role and actions. Indeed, there are times when one primary author will say that Ptolemy has got something wrong or is not to be trusted. Nearchus may well have embellished his great voyage to make what was already a magnificent achievement even greater – the 'me element' is very strong in it. Against that, we must set his very careful descriptions of the topography of the places he sailed past and of the people he encountered. What, though, of all the other primary authors? The answer is frustrating.

The source problem is becoming obvious. Since we do not have the primary works in full, we do not know what each author actually dealt with or their degree of accuracy. That of course means we do not know whether the secondary sources have properly followed or interpreted the earlier material, and hence how accurate are their accounts of the reign. Generally, though, we can attach greater importance to a secondary author who quotes his sources and uses what we decide are more reliable primary sources. That is why Arrian's account is accepted as the most reliable.

For one thing, Arrian's narrative is unromantic and factual, and it shows little bias. More importantly, he names his sources and gives some idea of his methodology for using one account over another. He used Ptolemy the most because Ptolemy was present with Alexander, and the same goes for his use of Aristobulus and of Nearchus, the latter not only for his voyage but also for what he knew about the march through the Gedrosian Desert. It is his critical and balanced approach that sets Arrian apart from the rest.

Diodorus, on the other hand, does not name his sources consistently. He seems to make use of Cleitarchus, who does have an interest in the seamier side of life at court and elsewhere. Then again, this should not stop us dismissing Cleitarchus, who was supposed to have written an account of the whole reign in at least 12 books. Indeed, Diodorus gives us a generally factual account. The downside is that it is marred by chronological and geographical inaccuracies. Curtius's account also has its problems. It is rhetorical and contains a number of speeches that are likely fabricated in order to create a sense of dramatic immediacy to his narrative. Plutarch's biography is not history and so needs to be read with caution as a historical source. His life of Alexander gives a narrative of sorts, but he is more interested, as we would expect, in Alexander the man and with gossip and moral issues. Finally Justin has been condemned for 'bad copying', errors and telescoping of events. Pompeius Trogus's earlier account is lost, so we have no way of making an informed decision on Justin's worth. However, more recent work, especially by Waldemar Heckel (see below), has elevated Justin's value somewhat as a source for Alexander (and for his father Philip II for that matter). All of the sources are well discussed by E. Baynham, 'The Ancient Evidence for Alexander the Great', in J. Roisman (ed.), *Brill's Companion to Alexander the Great* (Leiden, 2003), 3–29. Her analogy of the Alexander sources with a kaleidoscope – turn it one way and there is one pattern, turn it another and there is a different one – is very appropriate.

Reading

Translations (often many, especially of Plutarch) exist of all of the above ancient sources. The following are the most accessible.

Arrian, *The Campaigns of Alexander*, translated by A. de Sélincourt, Penguin Classics (Harmondsworth, 1971).

Diodorus Siculus, Book 17, translated by C. Bradford Welles, Diodorus Siculus, Loeb Classical Library Vol. 8 (Cambridge, MA and London, 1963).

Plutarch, *The Age of Alexander*, translated by Ian Scott-Kilvert, Penguin Classics (Harmondsworth, 1973).

Plutarch, *On The Fortune or The Virtue of Alexander*, translated by F.C. Babbitt, Plutarch's *Moralia*, Loeb Classical Library Vol. 4 (Cambridge, MA and London, 1936).

Quintus Curtius Rufus, *The History of Alexander*, translated by John Yardley, Penguin Classics (Harmondsworth, 1984).

John Yardley and Waldemar Heckel, *Justin. Epitome of the Philippic History of Pompeius Trogus, Books 11–12: Alexander the Great* (Oxford, 1997).

The Greek Alexander Romance, translated by Richard Stoneman, Penguin Classics (Harmondsworth, 1991).

Legends of Alexander the Great, translated by Richard Stoneman, Everyman Library (London, 1994).

The fragments of the primary sources were collected together by F. Jacoby, in his *Die Fragmente der griechischen Historiker* (*The Fragments of the Greek Historians*), which has their Greek texts and Jacoby's commentary in German. The Alexander historians are in Volumes IIB, nos 117–53 (Berlin, 1927) and IIIB, nos 742–3 (Berlin, 1930), and the German commentary is in IID (Berlin, 1927), pp. 403–542. They are translated by C.A. Robinson, *The History of Alexander the Great* 1 (Providence, 1953), and about a third are reprinted in Ian Worthington, *Alexander the Great: A Reader* (London and New York, 2003). Their problem is comprehensively discussed by Lionel Pearson, *The Lost Histories of Alexander the Great* (New York, 1960).

The contemporary inscriptions are collected in M.N. Tod, *Greek Historical Inscriptions* 2 (Oxford, 1948), nos 183–203 and L. Moretti, *Inscrizioni Storiche Ellenistiche* (Florence, 1967 and 1976). Many are translated (with notes) by P.E. Harding, *From the End of the Peloponnesian War to the Battle of Ipsus* (Cambridge, 1985). There is a Greek text and translation as well as a very full discussion of the epigraphical evidence relating to Alexander's dealing with the Greeks in A.J. Heisserer, *Alexander the Great and the Greeks* (Norman, 1980).

Modern works

The modern bibliography on Alexander and on his times is vast, and shows no sign of abating. I cannot talk about every book that has been published, so I restrict my comments to a few. In the process, I want to show that as the output of works on Alexander increased, so too did the way he was presented by modern scholars.

Two terrific books that help to introduce Alexander and have lavish photographs of the areas through which he marched and the towns and peoples that he encountered are Robin Lane Fox, *The Search for Alexander* (Boston and Toronto, 1980) and Michael Wood, *In the Footsteps of Alexander* (Berkeley and Los Angeles, 1997). Lane Fox's book is the more detailed by far. Both men have done what few Alexander scholars have (myself included): they have walked the routes taken by Alexander. It is only when looking at their photographs of the rugged yet beautiful terrain and inhospitable topography that we realise how truly remarkable were Alexander's successes.

There are two books that also serve as a very good introduction to Alexander and to specific aspects of his reign (including the sources, his aims, unity of mankind and deification). These are J. Roisman, *Alexander the Great: Ancient and Modern Perspectives* (Lexington, MA, 1995) and Ian Worthington, *Alexander the Great: A Reader* (London, 2003). Roisman gives translated extracts of the secondary sources, but (the publisher's decision) edits the modern scholars' works and omits their notes, which causes confusion. Worthington gives a selection of translated inscriptions and primary sources, together with some modern scholars' works that give different interpretations of the same topic. This shows something of the controversy that surrounds Alexander: that there is no single approach to him, and that there can be substantial disagreement.

The German historian J.G. Droysen was the first to work seriously on Alexander. He began in 1833 with a biography and in 1842 with a book on Alexander's successors. The turning point came when he produced what was a history of that whole period, his *Geschichte Hellenismus* (Gotha, 1877). His Alexander was a unifier of the peoples in his empire and a promoter of Hellenism, who had the backing of the gods, and so could do no wrong.

Another German scholar, H. Berve, also did groundbreaking work, but not by writing a biography. He compiled a prosopography of everyone who was named in an Alexander source, and for each one he gave all of the ancient sources and, importantly, a critical analysis of them. So was born his two-volume *Das Alexanderreich auf prospopographischer Grundlage* (Munich, 1926), which remains indispensable today. For those without German, Waldemar Heckel has performed an immense service with his *The Marshals of Alexander's Empire* (London, 1992). Although not as wide in scope as Berve, since it deals with Alexander's military and senior administrative personnel, it continues the tradition of tough source analysis and incorporates publications since Berve.

Not everyone lets the sources do the talking, however. In post-Second World War Britain Sir William Tarn built on Droysen's Alexander in his two-volume *Alexander the Great* (Cambridge, 1948). Tarn was a member of the British upper class who saw only the gentleman in the Macedonian king because of his class. His Alexander was the one of the *On The Fortune or The Virtue of Alexander*, a philosophical idealist who made it his policy to unite his peoples together in a unity of mankind. In the process Tarn tried to argue away all the bad sides of Alexander that the sources give, especially his excessive drinking. His historical methodology is thus severely flawed, but Tarn's biography is a major achievement, and everyone needs to read it. Tarn also wrote other books on Hellenistic civilisation, on warfare, even on the Greeks in Bactria and India. His achievement is all the more remarkable since he was by profession a lawyer, and wrote on ancient history as an 'amateur'.

In 1949 another German scholar, F. Schachermeyr, influenced by Nazi ideology and the course of the Second World War, gave us an Alexander as different from Tarn as one could get. In *Alexander der Grosse, Ingenium und Macht* (Vienna, 1949), Alexander is a ruthless, ambitious imperialist who over the course of his conquests changed from king to despot. He set himself up at the centre of a new World Order. Alexander, then, encapsulates everything that is wrong and evil in a leader.

The biggest attack on how 'great' was Alexander, and the dawn of a new era in Alexander scholarship, came in 1958 with Ernst Badian's article 'Alexander the Great and the Unity of Mankind', *Historia* 7 (1958): 425–44. Badian was also influenced by the Nazis' rise to power, but he took a less extreme or emotional stance than Schachermeyr. Guided properly by the ancient sources, Badian's Alexander was an imperialist, who had no ideas of a brotherhood of man. He saw him as a young man whom Philip's senior general thought they could control when he became king. As Alexander established himself, he got rid of the old guard, but in the process Asia turned his mind from Macedon. His orientalism distanced himself from his men and state, so he found out that, despite his great power, it was lonely at the top. The scenario is brilliantly laid out in his 'Alexander the Great and the Loneliness of Power', in E. Badian, *Studies in Greek and Roman History* (Oxford, 1964), 192–205.

A very different Alexander is presented in Robin Lane Fox's *Alexander the Great* (London, 1973), written, as he says 'self-indulgently'. His Alexander is a Homeric hero who conquered on a vast scale and whose actions and desires reveal a fair amount of idealism.

In Peter Green's *Alexander of Macedon* (Harmondsworth, 1974), we have a combination of the ruthless and self-absorbed Alexander with the Homeric hero type. There are plenty of good stories, many scandalous, about Alexander in this book, and it is a great read. However, Green often seems to accept stories at face value, and hence motives are ascribed to Alexander and insights made about him that are doubtful.

The best scholarly biography of Alexander is that of A.B. Bosworth, *Conquest and Empire, the Reign of Alexander the Great* (Cambridge, 1988). Bosworth is now the most influential scholar working on Alexander and, like Badian, his work has revolutionised Alexander studies. His biography is a tough read, with a lot of dense narrative and copious notes, but the reward of reading it is great (no pun intended). Anchored firmly on a critical analysis of the ancient sources, Bosworth gives us both the good and bad sides of Alexander. He followed it some years later with a critical account of Alexander's Indian campaigns in his *Alexander and the East* (Oxford, 1996).

Also critical of Alexander is J.M. O'Brien, *Alexander the Great: The Invisible Enemy* (London, 1992), which presents the drunken Alexander. Dionysus was the god of wine, and Alexander modelled himself on that god. For O'Brien, Alexander's actions were all due to his excessive drinking, and the pattern to his reign is alcohol and more alcohol. O'Brien's thesis has been criticised, not least for his use of the sources. While the Macedonians did drink a lot, it is important to note that at the end of his reign Alexander's mind was not muddled and pickled by the amount of alcohol he drank. He was lucid enough to plan the invasion of Arabia down to the last detail, for example.

There are still those who excuse the downside of Alexander's reign in order to portray him in a rosy light. Here N.G.L. Hammond, who until his death a few years ago was the 'grand old man' of Greek history, springs to mind. Hammond's numerous books on the history and institutions of Greece and of Macedon, including his three-volume *History of Macedonia*, are outstanding. He also wrote two biographies of Alexander: *Alexander the Great: King, Commander and Statesman* (Bristol, 1989) and *The Genius of Alexander the Great* (London, 1997). The first is by far the better and the title of the second speaks volumes.

Some collections of articles by different scholars that deal with different aspects of Alexander's reign are in A.B. Bosworth and E.J. Baynham (eds), *Alexander the Great in Fact and Fiction* (Oxford, 2000), G.T. Griffith (ed.), *Alexander the Great: The Main Problems* (Cambridge, 1966), and most recently J. Roisman (ed.), *Brill's Companion to Alexander the Great* (Leiden, 2003). The last in particular covers all aspects of Alexander's reign, including the cultural background and Alexander's legacy.

Reading

The following list gives some more biographies of Alexander as well as books that deal with topics affecting him in English. For further bibliography, including works other than in English, consult the very full bibliographies in, for example, O'Brien (good only to 1992) and the collections edited by Bosworth and Baynham and by Roisman.

E. Carney, *Women and Monarchy in Macedonia* (Norman, OK, 2000).
D. Engels, *Alexander the Great and the Logistics of the Macedonian Army* (Berkeley and Los Angeles: 1978)
P.M. Fraser, *Cities of Alexander the Great* (Oxford, 1996).
Major General J.F.C. Fuller, *The Generalship of Alexander the Great* (New Brunswick, 1960).
J.R. Hamilton, *Alexander the Great* (London, 1973).
N.G.L. Hammond, *The Macedonian State* (Oxford, 1989).
— *The Miracle that was Macedonia* (New York, 1991).
— and F.W. Walbank, *A History of Macedonia*, Vol. 3 (Oxford, 1988).
F.L. Holt, *Alexander the Great and Bactria* (Leiden, 1985).

R.D. Milns, *Alexander the Great* (London, 1968).

A. Stewart, *Faces of Power. Alexander's Image and Hellenistic Politics* (Berkeley and Los Angeles, 1993).

R. Stoneman, *Alexander the Great* (Lancaster, 1997).

U. Wilcken, *Alexander the Great*, translated by G.C. Richards (New York, 1967).

Source studies

E. Baynham, *The Unique History of Quintus Curtius Rufus* (Ann Arbor, 1998).

A.B. Bosworth, *From Arrian to Alexander* (Oxford, 1988).

T. Duff, *Plutarch's Lives* (Oxford, 1999).

N.G.L. Hammond, *Three Historians of Alexander the Great* (Cambridge, 1983) (Diodorus, Curtius and Justin).

— *Sources for Alexander the Great* (Cambridge, 1993) (Arrian and Plutarch's *Alexander*).

K. Sacks, *Diodorus Siculus and the First Century* (Princeton, 1990).

Index